What's Wrong with My Hormones?

by Gillian Ford

PMS AND MENOPAUSE EDUCATOR

The text of this book is composed in Centaur MT.
Printed by J & M Printing, Rocklin, California.
Cover artwork by Alphonse Mucha, 19th century Art Nouveau artist.
Typography by Gillian Ford.

Library of Congress Cataloging-in-Publication Data
Ford, Gillian
    What's Wrong with My Hormones?—revised edition
    ISBN   1-883619-11-4

This book is available from Desmond Ford Publications for $15.95.
Add 7.25% sales tax (within California only), and $2.50 postage and
handling. Send order to: Desmond Ford Publications, 7955 Bullard
Drive, Newcastle, CA 95658, or phone (916) 888-7677.

Contents

Millions of women in the United States suffer with symptoms that are hormonally caused or related.

Some have PMS (premenstrual syndrome); others have depression after pregnancy; others experience perimenopausal symptoms.

Sometimes there is an associated low-thyroid condition. At other times, the hormonal problem is linked with endometriosis, polycystic ovaries, ovarian cysts, fibroids, or even a pituitary tumor.

For some women, these conditions are only temporary, occurring perhaps after pregnancy or at menopause. The symptoms may be severe at the time, but they are relatively short-lived, and the imbalance often corrects itself.

But other women have a genetic tendency towards hormonal problems, seen in the family history and beginning around puberty. For these women, every hormonal event in life—menstruation (or even missing periods), going on or off the birth control pill, pregnancy, having a tubal ligation, a hysterectomy, or menopause—has the possibility of fueling a major crisis.

Women's symptoms vary and can be both physical and emotional. Many women become angry, depressed, and irritable. Some women experience panic attacks. Others have headaches, migraines, epilepsy, respiratory problems (including asthma), allergies, or skin problems (such as eczema and acne).

Frequently physicians fail to recognize a hormonal connection and only treat isolated symptoms. If it's depression, give her Prozac; if it's migraines, give her Fiorinal; if it's panic attacks, give her Xanax. For skin problems, give cortisone cream or antibiotics. However, hormonal problems often don't respond to treatment for isolated symptoms.

The main hormones involved are estrogen, progesterone, and thyroid, each of which affect the function of many cells in the female body. The pattern and type of symptom experienced vary with each hormone, though many symptoms are common. Since the glands—the pituitary, the ovary, the thyroid, the adrenals—all function as a team, each affects the other.

Women with more severe problems may not respond to life-style changes alone and may need temporary or long-term hormone replacement. This is not always easy to obtain because medical research has tended to underrate the tremendous impact hormones have on the way women feel.

Many times the treatment for these problems is relatively safe and simple, but finding a physician who is knowledgeable about these areas—in a way that produces practical results—is not easy. It is not uncommon for women to trail from specialist to specialist, even at university centers, with no recognition or treatment.

Many physicians don't recognize the difference between natural and synthetic and animal hormones. Commonly prescribed hormones—for example, the many types of birth control pills containing synthetic estrogen and progestin, conjugated animal estrogens, and medroxyprogesterone (a synthetic progestin)—frequently cause adverse reactions in susceptible women. This is because the hormone receptors in the human body do not always recognize these nonhuman hormones.

Many women who experience side effects while taking hormones, as typically prescribed, don't know that there are better hormones available. The major reason natural hormones are not more easily available is that the patent ran out on them years ago, and major drug companies are reluctant to spend the exhorbitant amount it would cost to get FDA approval. [Estrace and Estraderm are an exception—they are a good match for human estradiol.]

A number of compounding pharmacies make natural progesterone and other natural hormones [see p. 244]. The FDA would like to stop them doing this, and so the availability of natural progesterone is precarious.

Gillian's book makes a unique contribution by relating different hormonal problems to each other. She outline each problem, discussing its unique symptoms and patterns. One-third of the book is about solutions—hormonal and otherwise.

This book will be especially appreciated by women with severe hormonal problems. It is a gold mine of practical information—especially for women who have sought in vain for help and found none.

Acknowledgements

I would like to thank Marian Fritz, Katie Lynch, and Sandra Reeves for their invaluable help with my manuscript and for their wonderful friendship and support.

I would also like to thank the doctors I have worked with, beginning with Dr. Myrtle Caton, a board-certified internist, who took an interest in my own problems, and came with me to hear Dr. Katherina Dalton speak in 1982 in San Francisco. This meeting inspired her to specialize in treating PMS and postpartum depression. She sent me to PMS Action in Wisconsin that same year, and, together, we set out to help women with hormonal problems.

I have also particularly appreciated working with Drs. Mike Jones, Byron and Neva Lake, and Phil Weaver. I have worked with many other physicians, but I owe the ones I have mentioned a special debt. They have helped so many of my clients, and my clients love them for it. It takes a special kind of person with a lot of courage to risk the approbation of their peers in treating patients with hormonal problems.

A special thanks to my husband, Dr. Desmond Ford, who has been so consistently supportive of my venture to help women. An evangelist and teacher, he believes that mine is a real ministry—helping women with problems that cruelly attack them physically, emotionally, and spiritually.

Another special thanks to Dr. Katharina Dalton. Every book written about PMS builds on her work. Now in her 70s, she still cheerfully travels the world defending women with PMS in court and in mental institutions, giving seminars, and taking part in research studies. Though her work is still not given the recognition it deserves in the U.S., thousands, maybe millions of grateful women are in her debt.

Thanks also to Judith Bardwick, an American psychologist who wrote a classic book in 1970, *The Psychology of Women*, which certainly saved my life. She was twenty years ahead of her time in pointing out the beneficial effects of estrogen on the mind. She also risked the approbation of her peers and met a great deal of opposition in taking her stand.

And thanks to all those who are out there working to improve women's hormonal health.

Last, thanks to all the women I have counseled over the past ten years. It's been a mutual help. I helped them, and they gave me their experiences to build up mine. It's been a pleasure.

★ ★ ★

For information on how to reach Gillian Ford for a consultation or to purchase *What's Wrong with My Hormones?*, please contact PMS Relief, Inc., 11710 Education Street, Auburn, California 95602, (916) 888-7677.

For information on how to secure Gillian Ford as a speaker for an event, for an organization, or for a personal appearance, please call or write TalkPro, (contact: Karen McElhatton), 1306 Montgomery Street, #1, San Francisco, California 94133, (415) 434-9191.

For physician referrals, listed below are some resources that may be helpful in your area:

Denise Mark, M.D., is an internist in San Francisco, California, who specializes in women's health. Her phone number is (415) 566-1000.

Kathryn Morris, M.D., is a family physician in Santa Cruz, California, who specializes in hormone balancing. She does phone consultations. Her number is (408) 464-7777.

Ramon Scruggs, M.D., practises alternative medicine and uses hormonal therapy. His number is (714) 646-1252.

Elizabeth Lee Vliet, M.D., is a board-certified psychiatrist with a background in internal medicine. She practices in Tucson, Arizona and does phone consultations. Her number is (602) 577-1097.

Philip Warner, M.D., is an OB/Gyn. in Los Gatos, California. He specializes in implanting estrogen pellets and uses natural progesterone. His phone is (408) 379-8640.

Rick Wilkinson, M.D., is a family physician in Yakima, Washington, who specializes in multiple chemical sensitivies and allergies, and also uses hormonal therapy. His number is (509) 453-5507.

About the Author

Gillian Ford is a women's health advocate who empowers women with the tools they most need—education and current research findings—to convey their PMS and menopause symptoms to their physicians. Her book, *What's Wrong with My Hormones?*, provides insightful and practical information on the important role hormones play for most women in maintaining optimal health. She highlights physician's case studies that connect PMS, menopause, postpartum depression, low thyroid, and endometriosis by their common symptoms, and shows key relationships that form a complete picture of a woman's life.

Ford recognized a real need for advocacy when it became apparent that many women could not articulate typical PMS and menopause symptoms such as depression, exhaustion, irritability, and physical pain to their doctors. Her own experience with intense PMS in her 20s, followed by early menopause at age 37, initially inspired Ford to seek information that would educate and allow her to communicate her needs clearly to her doctor. Through reading and making contact with established women's health professionals, she learned of the potential benefit of hormones in sustaining physical and emotional well-being.

Ford's commitment to research and self-education launched a formal course of study and networking among physicians. In 1982 she was sponsored by internist Dr. Myrtle Caton to receive training at

PMS Action. Since then, she has devoted her career to hearing and documenting women's stories.

Encouraged by physicians who applaud her efforts, Ford spends hours in private consultation with women from all over the United States, and even fields international calls to help women make sense of the often severe effects brought on by significant life changes. Her confidential two-hour consultations include recording an extensive family history, providing a physician referral, a written summary of the interview, educational literature, and ongoing support. Women leave the consultation armed with solid information and a great understanding about the changes they undergo, now able to ask their doctors intelligent, direct questions that hopefully lead to treatment.

Gillian Ford has a B.A. in education. She consults with women who have hormonal problems in her office in Auburn, California. She also does phone consults. She is not a physician, nor does she prescribe treatment; however, she creates a solid partnership between patients and doctors in the quest for practical solutions to hormonal issues through research, education, and patient participation.

Introduction

T he hormones that are necessary to create life—estrogen, progesterone, thyroid, and testosterone—are also necessary to maintain optimum life in the host. This is why when women's estrogen levels drop (estrogen being the most important hormone for women), they have increased heart disease, crumbling of the skeletal structure, and, potentially, similar degeneration in every part of their body.

The same principle also applies to the emotional life. Estrogen, in particular, acts in women as a mood elevator, and is responsible for a feeling of well-being and joyfulness. Natural progesterone (so-called to distinguish it from progestins) and thyroid also contribute to emotional health. When one or more of these hormones recede (this can happen when women are quite young), women may feel awful, and experience all sorts of physical and emotional symptoms. Too often, the wonderful properties of these hormones are overlooked and ignored, and such women may spend years trudging from doctor to doctor to find help for what could often be simply helped with the right hormonal replacement therapy.

This book is written especially for women with hormonal problems. Other authors have written on premenstrual syndrome, menopause, postpartum depression, low thyroid problems, and endometriosis, treating them as isolated disorders; but these different problems are often found together. Besides describing these problems individually, the book shows their relationship to each other, and offers an abundance of practical information on treatment, including the use of hormones.

I decided to write this book because of my own experience with severe PMS and hypothyroidism in my twenties, my entry into premature menopause at age 37, and the experience I have had over the past ten years as a PMS/menopause counselor. I have included many case histories in the book to help women identify their own problems. They are all true, though the names have been changed.

It is extremely difficult for most women to find help for their hormonal problems. My own experience in trying to get help is not uncommon. Over a period of twenty years, I lived in England, Australia, New Zealand, and the United States, and sought help every place I went. I saw numerous physicians, including six psychiatrists who told me I was either depressive or manic-depressive. I took most of the antidepressants available at the time, with no relief. I knew instinctively that my problems were related to my menstrual cycle because they started at ovulation and ended when I began my period, month after month. But nobody believed I had a hormonal problem, nor did they believe in PMS. They thought I was manic-depressive—but lithium and other psychotropic drugs didn't help, whereas hormones helped me dramatically. I had to read myself to health, and, fortunately, there were a few good books around to help me on my way, and kind physicians who cooperated with me.

A book called *The Pill on Trial,* written by Paul Vaughan, a medical journalist and published in 1970, shed the first ray of light when it described the role of progestins in the pill in causing depression. I also read *The Menstrual Cycle,* a book on premenstrual syndrome by Dr. Katherina Dalton, and *The Psychology of Women,* a book on women's sexuality, by Dr. Judith Bardwick. Dr. Bardwick's book was not about PMS, but it contained a chapter on women's physiology which explained how the menstrual cycle worked and the role of the birth control pill in producing depression. She showed, using research evidence, that a woman's mood is universally at its highest just before ovulation when the estrogen is high, and lowest premenstrually when both estrogen and progesterone are low.

Armed with that book, at age 29, I headed for my local physician in Australia and begged him for estrogen. He probably didn't believe my problem was hormonal; but out of a merciful heart, he agreed to give me a prescription for estrogen. I literally recovered overnight, to the amazement of myself, my doctor, and my husband. It was as though mentally I walked out of a dark tunnel into the light of day. I blossomed physically as well—my hair had been dank, I had bad acne, and severe menstrual cramps—and these also disappeared. Afterwards, in subsequent years, doctors repeatedly tried to take me off estrogen because they were afraid of cancer, though there has never been any evidence that I had it.

I learned back then, and repeatedly over the following twenty years, the amazing impact of estrogen on the mind. Its antidepressant action on the hypothalamus and central nervous system via the estrogen receptors, and its catalyst action, in association with other psychotropic drugs, is presently being studied. Researchers are finding that estrogen increases the endorphins, and the seratonin and dopamine levels, and decreases MAOs, functioning much as an antidepressant would. It helps memory, recall, verbal coordination, and mood. I knew all that by experience by the time I was 29.[1]

Other hormones also affect the mind. Lacking enough thyroid or natural progesterone can also cause depression. The pill is more likely to cause depression, as can Provera, because synthetic progestins do not match the chemistry of the body's natural progesterone, and may actually deplete progesterone levels in the body. Women with a predisposition to hormonal problems may be worsened by using these synthetic substances. This information on synthetic progestins has been known for at least twenty years, but its importance has been overlooked. So a woman who goes on the pill or is given Provera at menopause and complains of depression often isn't heard—even though many doctors admit women frequently complain and refuse to take progestins because of the emotional problems these medications give them.

Physicians often give the impression that the only really important issues around menopause are the obvious physical ones. They pore over breasts and reproductive organs, cardiac vessels and bones, as with some cadaver—not seeing the person behind the body, who may be struggling to stay sane, her life fast unraveling. The emotional problems— depression, irritability, anger, anxiety, and paranoia—suffered by some women with severe hormonal problems are passed off as unimportant. For other women, it's their treatment-resistant skin problems, their horrendous hormonal migraines, or their seizures that are overlooked. Neurologists, psychologists, dermatologists, and other specialists often completely overlook the hormonal cause or connection.

In my case my main symptom was suicidal depression, and it was very serious. My life, my personality, my sanity, my reason for living were at ransom, and finding help was like digging for gold. Like many women, I feel angry that it was so difficult to find help **when the information is already known,** and the only options I had were antidepressants and tranquilizers, which didn't help. Because of the tortuous path I trod trying to find help, I began helping other women in 1982. I found there are many women with hormonal problems who still have as much difficulty getting help as I did twenty years ago. The beneficial effects of the right hormones—particularly estrogen, progesterone, and thyroid—on a woman's emotional and physical well-being are still highly underestimated. The effect of these hormones is ubiquitous—that is, as widespread as the cells they affect. Because these three hormones are basic ingredients in the cell production of enzymes and the production of energy, deficiencies can effect the whole body, though symptoms vary from woman to woman, both in type and severity.

To put this in perspective, it is important to keep in mind that many women don't have hormonal problems. They have no trouble with their periods or pregnancies; they can take the birth control pill for ten or twenty years without effect, have tubal ligations, hysterectomies, and go through menopause with no problems. But, at the other end of the scale there is a large subset—millions of women with severe, incapacitating hormonal problems who are finding it difficult to get any practical help.

This book is for them.

Footnotes

I. Vliet, E.L., M.D., "New Perspectives on the Relationship of Hormone Changes to Depression and Anxiety in the Menopause," presentation at the North American Menopause Society meeting, September 1992. Dr. Vliet is a clinical assistant professor at Eastern Virginia Medical School, Norfolk, VA. "Estrogen and Memory in Postmenopausal Women," Sherwin, Barbara, B., Ph.D., McGill University, Montreal, Canada. "Estrogens Regulate Brain Structure and Chemistry," Bruce S. McEwen, Ph.D., Laboratory of Neuroendocrinology, New York.

WHAT GOES WRONG?

Section One:
What Goes Wrong?

CHAPTER I

What's Wrong With My Hormones?

A woman who feels emotionally or physically sick often senses that her symptoms are connected with her menstrual cycle, and they began at a time of hormonal change. She may visit her doctor hoping to have her suspicions confirmed. Instead, the idea that her symptoms have a hormonal cause is more likely to be dismissed or ridiculed.

If the doctor tests her, the results may be normal, and he or she will assume, "There's nothing wrong with your hormones." But the woman knows there's a hormonal link. She may have premenstrual syndrome, or be experiencing side effects from the birth control pill. Her problems may have started with a pregnancy, or after a tubal ligation, at menopause, or after her uterus or ovaries were removed. She knows the way she feels is not normal, but it's difficult to argue with a doctor who depends heavily on medical tests for diagnosis.

Hormonal problems are frequently difficult to discern because they present themselves so differently, with symptoms varying dramatically in type and intensity. This is because the endocrine system affects the body at so many different levels, from the brain to the individual cells. Because the hormonal system is complex and intimately linked to so many different body functions, women may experience any of hundreds of symptoms.

Case Histories

The following examples illustrate typical cases of women with different hormonal problems:

Betty, 28, comes from a family in which all the women have cyclical symptoms that recur before each period. Her PMS began about puberty and seems to worsen year by year. Instead of acknowledging her PMS, physicians have told her that she is suffering from depression. Betty has been on six or seven antidepressants, including lithium, but they have failed to relieve her symptoms. Her psychiatrist has suggested shock therapy; her OB/Gyn has suggested taking Lupron to put her in chemical menopause or removal of the uterus and ovaries to put her in actual menopause. Betty thinks it all sounds very drastic, and she's very frustrated and discouraged.

Heather, 26, has terrible menstrual cramps and PMS. Her doctor thinks she may have endometriosis and wants to put her on the birth control pill. Heather is reluctant to do this since she's been on the pill before, and it made her mood swings worse. She talked to a woman whose PMS disappeared when she went on danocrine, though it returned when the treatment was finished. Another woman was helped by laser surgery; but, after two or three years, the pain and depression returned. Heather doesn't want a hysterectomy, but she's wondering how she can cope with endometriosis and PMS for the next twenty years.

Lila feels as though she's going through menopause, even though she's only 38. The symptoms began after she had surgery on one of her ovaries. Her periods are becoming scanty and irregular, and she's getting mood swings, hot flashes, depression, insomnia, occasional night sweats, and anxiety attacks. Her doctor says she is not menopausal, and won't be until she's about 50. Lila wonders why she must endure such symptoms for ten or fifteen years before her doctor will agree to help her.

Linda, 39, began having seizures after she had toxemia in pregnancy. When she delivered her children, she had massive seizures and was put in intensive care for several days. She takes medication for seizures, which keeps them mainly under control. But, just before her periods, she still starts to shake, a preliminary warning of an imminent seizure.

Louise, 31, never had any hormonal problems until six or seven years after she had a tubal ligation. "I used to think women used PMS as an excuse and that it didn't really exist. Now my husband has told me to get help for my PMS or he'll divorce me." Before Louise had the tubal ligation, her surgeon assured her that there were no side effects. Louise recalls, "His nurse told me otherwise, but I still believed him. I would never have had my tubes tied if I had known I would develop these problems."

Anna, 41, began having terrible migraines after being treated with hormones for bleeding irregularities. "I had a series of six intramuscular shots of medroxyprogesterone, and started having migraines on the medication. Now I've stopped it, but the headaches have not gone away." Anna is taking several headache medications prescribed by her neurologist. The medications stop the nausea, but she still has a continual headache and takes ten Advil daily.

Mitzi, 28, first began to have panic attacks the day she came home from the hospital after having a tubal ligation. Within a short time, she could not leave her home, because even visiting the supermarket brought on an anxiety attack. Now, particularly before her period, she often wakes up in a sweat, terribly afraid, her heart pounding. Sometimes she feels as though she is dying. The doctor says the anxiety is a reaction to stress, and he has put her on Xanax and sent her to a counselor. But Mitzi knows the problem is hormonal and began after her tubal ligation.

Laura is only ten years old. Her mother has PMS, and Laura is already having one week a month when she is weepy, cranky, and hard to get along with, even though she hasn't started her periods yet. Laura's mother called the PMS clinic where she was treated to find out if it's possible for a girl that young to have PMS before she begins her periods. She learned that girls can get PMS one or two years before puberty, and that some preteen and early teenage girls run away, are addicted to drugs or alcohol, and become behavior problems, just because of PMS.

Rosa is 24. There is a strong history of thyroid disorders, stroke, and diabetes among her female relatives. Rosa's thyroid tests have always shown normal or low-normal, even though she has many low thyroid symptoms—fatigue, hair falling out, sensitivity to cold, dry skin, eczema, and respiratory infections. Her periods are heavy and irregular, and she has PMS, but her physician will not give her thyroid because her tests show normal.

Gail is 32. She has a responsible job, but her PMS is interfering with the quality of her work and she worries about being fired. At home, Gail drinks too much and, before her period, she can't take alcohol at all. Her husband is an alcoholic and, premenstrually, they get into fist fights. She has put her fist through the wall several times, and she once yanked out a fluorescent light and threw it at him.

Kathy is 30 and has postpartum depression, which began about three months after the birth of her second child. She felt exhausted, disoriented, and alienated, and she was secretly afraid that she might harm her baby. Her doctor put her on the birth control pill, which didn't help her depression, and he now wants to put her on an antidepressant. This would require her to stop nursing which she does not want to do. Her sister also suffered from postpartum psychosis after two pregnancies and had to be hospitalized.

Betsy, 32, came from a very dysfunctional family and never had a normal childhood. Her mother behaved very erratically and made Betsy, from the age of three, responsible for running the house and raising her brothers. Because her mother had PMS and was nonfunctional and frequently absent from home, Betsy had no supervision or protection. Consequently, neighborhood boys took advantage of her sexually from early childhood to puberty. Like her mother, Betsy also has PMS. Unlike her mother, she is doing a wonderful job of trying to raise her own children, but she has never resolved her dreadful childhood. "I find I can manage my feelings about it quite well most of the time, but just before my period I go to pieces."

Kay's mother was a cheerful, optimistic woman until about 50, when she went into a deep depression at menopause, even though she was taking estrogen and progestin at the time. She was so depressed that she shot herself in the head, a terrible shock to the family. Ever since, Kay has worried that she would go through the same type of menopause. At age 43, Kay started feeling extremely fatigued. She cried easily, had low self-esteem, and mild depression. She began spotting before her periods and within a few months, she started having hot flashes. When she went on a different type of estrogen and progesterone than her mother had taken, she felt better within a few days. She needed far less sleep, and her energy and mood lifted dramatically. When she later tried the type of treatment that her mother had taken, her symptoms came back, and she finally understood why her mother had become so desperate.

Diana, 33, has a very strong family history of thyroid disorders but her tests are normal. Her symptoms include severe allergies and respiratory infections, difficulty becoming pregnant, and difficulty maintaining the pregnancy. She has had several miscarriages. The only time she became pregnant and carried the baby to term was when she had previously been put on thyroid by a doctor who suspected this was her problem. Later she moved, and her new physician tested her thyroid and, finding it "normal," made her go off the medication. Immediately, her allergies and other symptoms returned.

Alice, 34, had a hysterectomy but retained her ovaries. Nevertheless, she is going through premature menopause. The particular combination of estrogen and progestin that her physician put her on did not help her depression, so she stopped taking the medication. This caused her to go into an even deeper depression. She kept running away from home, had long crying jags, and tried to commit suicide. She now has found that a combination of estrogen, thyroid, progesterone, and an antidepressant have brought her to normalcy. Stopping any one of them throws her into a whirlpool. She needs each one to maintain her equilibrium.

Dorothy, 19, is extremely aggressive and feels suicidal premenstrually. She is overweight, has a male pattern of body hair, and has irregular periods. Her doctor says she has polycystic ovaries. Not all women with polycystic ovaries have PMS, but some have it severely, possibly because of the high levels of testosterone this condition causes. Another doctor found that Dorothy had a swollen pituitary which was, at least, indirectly connected with the polycystic ovaries. He put her on bromocriptine, a drug which reduces inflammation of the pituitary or helps shrink pituitary tumors. He prescribed smaller than usual doses, because higher doses made her very sick. Her PMS disappeared.

Donna, 37, has always had PMS as does her mother and her daughter, her sister, and niece. After a tubal ligation, Donna became increasingly depressed and suicidal. No one suspected the extent of her depression, but it had been a long time since anyone had seen her smile. She began looking for ways to commit suicide. Fortunately a caring and discerning friend who had similar problems recognized Donna's condition, and told her how to get help. "I hate to think how close I came to ending my life," she says. "My life has been completely different these last ten years since I've been treated with natural progesterone."

Marian had breast cancer at age 41. The cancer contained estrogen receptors, and she was given Tamoxifen to strip the fat cells in the breast of estrogen. Now, Marian is suffering from extreme hot flashes and other estrogen-deficiency symptoms, but her OB/Gyn is reluctant to prescribe estrogen fearing it will encourage a return of the cancer. The internist said that Marian, now 43, has the vaginal tissue of a woman about 55. She feels damned if she takes estrogen and damned if she doesn't. She wishes she knew what to do.

All these case histories deal with obvious endocrine problems, some genetic, some triggered by a hormonal event, such as the pill, pregnancy, or a tubal ligation. Such women frequently suspect their problems are hormonal, and they often say, "There's something wrong with my hormones," and ask for hormonal help. But so often, when they ask about it, their physician acts as though hormonal problems don't exist or aren't important.

"This has nothing to do with your hormones." "Your hormones are normal." "You're too young." "You're working too hard." "You're under too much stress." "This is just part of being a woman." "You have to put up with this." "There's nothing we can do." "When you have a baby it will go away." "We'll put you on the birth control pill." "I'll give you some Xanax," "I think you ought to see a psychiatrist." Often there's a patronizing pat on the head, and the intimation that the problem is of no consequence, and the woman is neurotic.

Are these comments an exaggeration, or is it really difficult to find help for these problems? The women I see frequently tell me they have gone from one doctor to another with little practical help. Why is this so? The next chapter will discuss some of the reasons.

CHAPTER 2

Why Is It So Hard to Find Help?

*W*omen with hormonal problems, particularly those who experience depression and fatigue as a result, often find it very difficult to find a physician who will affirm and treat their problems sympathetically. Of course, this is not always true. There are doctors who are very sympathetic and treat hormonal problems successfully. Others are sympathetic but often don't know what to do.

Few Doctors Believe in Hormonal Problems

Generally, it is not easy to find a doctor who really believes that women can have extremely severe symptoms just because their hormones are out of balance. Comparatively few doctors recognize PMS as a legitimate physiological disorder, and they offer only limited options for treatment. In England, 25 percent of general physicians follow Dr. Katherina Dalton's suggestions for treating PMS, and natural progesterone suppositories and injections are available through the National Health Service. Here in the United States, a concerted effort has been made to discredit her work, despite the fact that thousands of women attest to the efficacy of progesterone.

I do not believe that natural progesterone is the answer for all women with PMS. I am one who did not respond to it. Nevertheless, I have seen many, many women who do very well on it long-term, and I believe women should have the right to try it.

It is easier to find help for menopausal problems than for PMS. Researchers agree that menopause is a real problem, and that estrogen deficiency in the later years of life can be devastating to physical health. Their concern is more with the physical results of hormone depletion— osteoporosis and heart disease. They aren't always sympathetic with the emotional problems that some women endure.

Treatment Not Uniform

Nevertheless, there does not seem to be any uniformity in treatment at menopause or after hysterectomy, partly because some physicians still worry about the risk of cancer for women taking estrogen. Some doctors will only give small doses of estrogen after removing a woman's ovaries, even if the woman still has obvious symptoms. Another doctor might give four times the amount the first doctor gave. So doses are not always uniform, and, if a woman does not respond to the usual brand and dose, the physician may not offer her other choices.

Usually, these days, most doctors will automatically give women some estrogen after having their ovaries removed. But if she has only her uterus removed, many doctors don't seem to take into account that she may have estrogen depletion symptoms immediately, or a few years down the line. Many still believe the old adage that if a woman only has part of one ovary, she will have enough estrogen to get her through menopause. This is not really true, despite the fact that some women seem to be fine after this surgery. When a woman loses the uterus, part of the ovarian-uterine artery which goes through the uterus is removed. She also loses the hormones which the uterus produces (prostaglandins, and possibly even estrogen, since some researchers think that the uterus may make a little). The ovaries may subsequently shrink as a result of less blood flow and less hormones coming from the pituitary.

It is not uncommon to see a young woman in her late twenties and early thirties, who has had her uterus removed and is experiencing migraines, joint pains, sweating, or depression. Often her doctors shake their heads and don't know what's wrong with her. One young woman I know, whose uterus was removed at age 28, lost 10 percent of her bone mass within a year! Of course, this is not a typical result, but these and other menopausal symptoms are not uncommon in such young hysterectomized women, even if they retain their ovaries.

Premature Menopause Is Fairly Common

When we use the words premature menopause, we refer not only to women who cease having periods earlier than normal, but also to those who still have periods yet experience a decline of estrogen before their time. Such women have a very difficult time finding sympathetic treatment. "You are too young to be going through menopause," is the usual comment. Their hormone levels may appear normal, but they are experiencing typical physical and emotional symptoms of menopause.

When the topic of menopause is discussed, very often fifty- to sixty-year-old women are the focus. Since 7 to 10 percent of women go through premature menopause in their thirties, according to Dr. Winnifred Cutler, physicians should not tell women that they won't go through menopause until they are about fifty. There are too many exceptions. Women often start experiencing gradual ovarian failure and consequent estrogen decline in their mid-thirties.

A minister's wife I saw, recently, started having night sweats at age thirty-four. Her doctor said that if she wasn't so young, he would have thought she was going through menopause. He put her on a series of psychotropic drugs which worsened her condition and changed her into a couch potato. When I saw her, her next option was shock therapy. The doctor's first thought was best. Her mother had gone through menopause at thirty-seven, and since this is often a congenital pattern, it was no surprise that my client was having hot flashes. After I saw her, she had a severe reaction to her antidepressant and was hospitalized. Taking her off the medication and treating her hormonally for menopause transformed her within a few weeks. I see so many similar cases of misdiagnosis with hormonal problems that I know this type of incident is common.

Postpartum Sufferers Not Recognized

Even less attention has been paid to women with postpartum depression, and it has not had the attention in the U.S. that it has in Europe. Typical treatment in the United States is with antidepressants, not hormones. Dr. Alexander Hamilton of San Francisco believes that PPD is a polyendocrine disorder, occurring because of the dramatic decline of estrogen and progesterone within a few days of delivery, making the pituitary gland sluggish and, in some cases, leading to lowered cortisol and thyroid levels as well. He believes this problem should not be treated as a typical clinical depression, since it is obviously hormonally triggered. This is not to say that these women never benefit from antidepressants, but they are more likely to need hormones for this type of depression.

The Caring Versus the Callous

Because I am not a doctor or a biochemist, I can only use the information doctors and biochemists generate, and I am grateful for it. I don't know as much as they do about how the body functions or about disease in general. But I do know what hormonal problems are like, and how it feels to have them. The criticisms I make of doctors are not an attack on their intelligence or undeniable skill. I am pointing out an area where there is frequently a gap in diagnosis and treatment, and one in which they have little training and sometimes little sympathy.

Medicine has, in general, been very slow to focus on women's problems. The research is sometimes confusing with large information gaps in the literature. And the treatments are frequently not FDA-approved. Doctors who treat women for PMS and premenopause often step ahead of their colleagues and receive their disapproval for using "unconventional measures." They read up on the subject after they leave medical school, because hormonal problems are barely discussed there. Such physicians are to be commended, because they take a risk treating these women's problems.

Through the years, I have worked with many caring physicians, and I am extremely grateful for the support they give women. I have met many idealistic physicians who enter medicine with the aim of alleviating suffering. They really listen to their patients and try to help them.

Having given accolades to the best of physicians, let me say that, because physicians are scientists, largely dependent on medical research, they sometimes tend to treat their patients as scientific experiments, and don't really listen to them. I hear frequent complaints from women that their doctors don't listen to them. Because physicians are in charge of the prescription pad, they are part of the reason why women find it difficult to get help for hormonal problems.

Is It Difficult to Get Help?

Is it really an exaggeration that women find getting help difficult? Yesterday, a woman going through menopause called me on the phone.

She had had a hysterectomy some time ago and then started having menopausal symptoms. She was trying to get some answers about the need for estrogen, and what the side effects would be. She had called the education department of every hospital in the Sacramento area, contacted physicians' offices and numerous women's organizations. She said she couldn't believe there was no organization dispensing the kind of information she needed and added, correctly, that there must be thousands of women in their 50's going through these problems. Why, she asked, aren't there women's groups everywhere dealing with this problem?

I have frequently asked myself the same question. It continually amazes me that the whole area of women's hormonal problems is so neglected when: I. demographically, the population of older women increases year by year; 2. These hormonal problems are so common; 3. There is sufficient information available to make diagnosis and treatment possible for most cases; 4. The treatments are relatively safe and the results are usually spectacular.

What prejudices are operating to make it so difficult for women to recognize and get help for hormonal problems? The answers are multiple and complex and not just restricted to the attitude of the physician. Here are some reasons:

Women's Attitudes
• Everyone tends to go by her own experience. We need to remember that a large group of women don't have hormonal problems, and they are as much in the dark about menstrual problems as men are. They can be most unsympathetic. How often I see a woman who had no problems until she had a tubal ligation. She used to think PMS was just an excuse. Now that she has PMS, she's changed her mind! If women haven't experienced hormonal problems themselves, they don't believe in them. If they have mild problems, they believe a little bit. When women have very severe symptoms, hardly anyone believes them.
• Among the women who don't have extreme hormonal problems are those who resent the largely male profession telling them they need hormones after menopause to be "nice" and "good-looking" till they die. Some women are violently opposed to hormone therapy, and this is fine. But it's a shame if they oppose hormonal replacement therapy for all

women because some women are dying emotionally and spiritually inside for lack of it.

• Many women feel that PMS or menopause can be used as an argument to limit women who are trying to excel in their careers, competing against men for high-level jobs. Other women who wouldn't classify themselves as hard-nosed feminists resent the word PMS because it's one more argument men can use to downgrade women. Isn't PMS a large part of the evidence men use to label women fickle, changeable, moody, and incompetent? I can understand why these women are upset and their observations are correct, but denying the existence of PMS and menopause won't make the problems go away.

• Women are extremely sensitive about their hormones, perhaps because of the association with their feminity and sexuality, their very being. They seem to treat this area of their lives as something apart from the rest of their body. While they willingly take other medications for depression or panic disorders or diabetes or other chronic problems, they may reject hormone therapy because they don't want to feel they are being controlled by their hormones.

• When you ask women how their grandmothers and mothers went through menopause, you find this was a topic many never openly addressed. Times are changing. Some women with problems are willing to talk openly about them, but the old taboos fade slowly, and many women are still reluctant to discuss these subjects. When women become unreasonable, irritable, and angry, they are embarrassed by their behavior and practice denial by pretending the behavior never happened. It's not always pretense. They really have forgotten how badly they behaved. Sometimes, of course, they don't care.

• Women with severe hormonal problems are extremely vulnerable. They usually have very low self-esteem, and it is difficult for them to speak up for themselves and insist on being heard by their doctor (particularly in a situation with a male gynecologist while the woman is naked on the examination table). Women are often unable to communicate effectively what they are going through, since mental confusion and inability to think clearly are common hormonal symptoms. Their minds become confused and their thinking incoherent, and so these women appear to have a psychological rather than hormonal disorder.

• Women often forget that medicine is big business, and they are paying the bill. They treat their physicians like gods and are afraid to differ with them. They don't assert themselves and demand better treatment.

• Women today prefer to treat their hormonal problems by natural methods. This may be perfectly appropriate for some women, and, as a thirty-year vegetarian who believes in a healthy life-style, I'm all for it, but there are many women whose quality of life will be greatly reduced if they don't take hormones.

• Women often don't like the idea of taking hormones. Hormones have had bad press, and as soon as the word "hormone" is mentioned, many women simultaneously think "cancer." Recent studies, however, support the idea that women are less likely to get cancer if they are on hormones rather than off them.

• Many postmenopausal women think going on estrogen is optional rather than important, and they often only take it for a short time while the hot flashes are bad. They don't understand the effects of lack of estrogen in old age or know that once they go off estrogen, it will soon be as though they've never been on it. They don't know that current research supports long-term low-dose estrogen and progesterone therapy for most women.

• Another problem with women after menopause, whose periods have stopped, is that they don't wish to keep having periods by inducing them hormonally each month. They often don't know there are ways to take hormones which makes it unnecessary to have a period (at least most of the time).

• Also, women don't like the effects of the progestin part of hormone replacement therapy because it makes them irritable and depressed. They often stop taking estrogen for this reason.

Men's Attitudes

• Men often find the topics of menstruation and menopause repulsive—a sexual turnoff—so, they talk about these subjects as a joke in a way that degrades women. Consequently, women tend to avoid discussing their problems in any real depth with their partners, and understanding breaks down. The personality changes resulting from PMS and menopause are a large, often unrecognized, factor in many divorces. Typically, women with hormonal problems become irrationally angry, and often there is a seed of validity in their anger, but the whole thing is blown out of proportion. The woman is at the time convinced she is right. The man is perplexed and bewildered, and likely to accuse the woman of being crazy, which leads to verbal and, sometimes, physical fights. When this occurs over a period of time, marriages break down.

Lack of Research, the FDA, and Insurance Companies

• Insurance companies often won't pay for doctor's visits where the diagnosis is PMS or menopausal problems. This is because of lack of conclusive research and lack of FDA approval for hormonal treatments. There is no incentive for doctors to accept patients when they know insurance companies won't reimburse. There is no incentive to open PMS and Menopause clinics, because doctors know they can't make them pay. Indeed, most PMS clinics have a very short life span for this reason.

• For sexist, political, and economic reasons, and a wish to avoid dealing with fluctuations of their monthly chemical changes and pregnancy, women have been dreadfully discriminated against in medical studies. In the past, men and male rats have been almost exclusively used in studies, even in studies of equal impact to both sexes—for example, heart disease. Women are physiologically quite different from men, and it is devastating to women's health if both sexes are viewed as one generic type. When women are a few years through menopause, their incidence of death from strokes and heart disease rises dramatically and reaches the same level as men. Their capillaries are finer than men's, and death occurs more often with the first heart attack in women. Despite this, millions of dollars have been spent on research in heart disease on men, but very little, if any, on women. The subjects of menopause, osteoporosis, PMS, premenopause, and the effects of tubal ligations and hysterectomies have been thinly researched, resulting in huge gaps in the information. There is, however, enough information already gathered to help women with hormonal problems, though finding it is not always easy.

• There is, I think, a downside in the way researchers face this problem, though probably this attitude is unavoidable. In trying to be exact about the causes of PMS and the way it manifests itself, the plight of the individual living with these symptoms ceases to be important. One researcher participating in a panel on PMS mentioned that, in some ways, there has been no real progress in defining PMS in fifty years. What happens to the women with these problems in the meantime while the researchers search for definitions? Because of the uncertainty on the part of researchers, many doctors are likewise hesitant to treat, because they want to understand exactly what goes wrong before they will try to find solutions for the problem. Because no one can say with certainty what goes wrong with PMS, do we as sufferers have to wait another fifty years to get treatment?

• Doctors are often hesitant to treat because the research, particularly on PMS, but also on using natural progesterone for menopause instead of progestins like Provera or Norlutate, is skimpy.

• Fueling this conservative response is the fact that the FDA has not given approval for the use of natural progesterone for PMS or its use after menopause with estrogen. Because of this, doctors are reluctant to prescribe progesterone. Women should realize, however, that Provera is not FDA-approved for use after menopause either. Neither are such drugs as Prozac, Xanax and Lithium, all of which are widely prescribed for PMS.

• FDA approval has to do with advertising. In other words, a drug cannot be **advertised** for a particular disorder unless it has FDA approval for **that** disorder. Lack of FDA approval, therefore, does not mean that a doctor cannot prescribe progesterone. A physician can prescribe a certain drug if it is considered typical medical practice by the local state board in the area where he practices.

• The FDA lumbers along like some hypothyroid monster when it comes to approval for hormones. Perhaps this is due to the shadow of such drugs as stilbestrol, which caused so many problems in the past. Approval for Provera has been sought ten times during the past fourteen years, the last time two years ago. Each of the ten-member board that met at that time voted for approval for Provera. But two years later, the decision is still shelved (not that I am for Provera, but it illustrates a point). The FDA is also working on approving estradiol pellets, which have been approved and used in Europe for a long time. The studies required in the U.S. have been submitted, but it will take a few years for approval to come.

• The FDA seems to speed up when it comes to patrolling and controlling the supplement industry to make it impossible eventually for you buy supplements except on prescription. It is also hounding those pharmacists who compound hormones such as natural progesterone. If the FDA has its way, soon you will not be able to obtain natural progesterone for PMS. It is not produced for prescription by any large drug companies at present, and your only source is individual pharmacies who compound it. The FDA is trying to classify such compounding pharmacists as manufacturers, and also trying to stop them from sending progesterone over state borders. If they are successful, progesterone will soon be unavailable to women in need. The FDA and medical boards are also making things very difficult for practitioners who practice nontraditional medicine—the ones most likely to try hormonal therapy. While there has to be control to stop quackery, it is often those who are doing the most good who are closed down.

• The FDA has said that progesterone is a relatively safe drug. But researchers in the United States have not been able to duplicate Dr. Katherina Dalton's studies in England, which demonstrated success in treating PMS with natural progesterone. Without the confirmation of its own studies, the FDA will not give its approval for the use of natural progesterone for PMS. Approximately eight to ten studies have been done using progesterone treatment for PMS, concluding that progesterone works no better than placebo. These studies have all been criticized as inadequate for one or more of the following reasons:

1. The PMS patients were not properly screened for these studies, and, therefore, some participants did not have genuine PMS.

2. The progesterone was not given in sufficiently high doses. Dr. Dalton says 400 mg. is the normal dose in suppository form. The studies used no more than 200 mg. suppositories.

3. The patients did not take the progesterone often enough. When patients took it in the morning and not again until evening, their symptoms came back midday. This is because progesterone has a short half-life and only covers symptoms for five to six hours. The return of symptoms was seen as an indication that progesterone was ineffectual, but, had the progesterone been given at noon and, possibly, again at night, the symptoms most likely would have been controlled.

4. There may have been a problem with poor absorption. Suppositories are made from different types of medium, some better than others. Some pharmacists believe that using oral capsules of micronized natural progesterone in oil would produce better results.

Doctors' Attitudes

- The subject of hormonal problems, specifically depression is not taught at medical school, and, according to an acquaintance who works at a medical school, the curriculum is taught by the butterfly method where attention alights gently on each subject and quickly flies to the next.

- Women with the hormonal problems dealt with in this book tend to fall between the cracks of the medical specialties. Family physicians are more likely to be helpful because their specialty is more general.

- The training for the OB/Gyn specialty centers on surgery and delivering babies. Training about the hormonal disorders I have described is not given in any detail. It is still fairly common practice to perform a hysterectomy and oophorectomy on women with severe PMS. It's done on the basis that if women don't ovulate, they won't have PMS. I don't believe this is true because I have seen women who don't ovulate who do have the symptoms of PMS, if not the strict pattern. Also, hysterectomy or treatment with Lupron can produce PMS in someone who doesn't already have it.

- Endocrinologists are the specialists who should treat these hormonal disorders, but they seem to deal with obvious thyroid, pituitary, adrenal, pancreatic problems, and endocrine cancers, leaving the ovarian problems to the OB/Gyns. I have seen a lot of women who have been to endocrinologists, and find they don't address these problems either.

- Women who have severe hormonal problems are frequently sent to the specialist who deals with mood problems—the psychiatrist. And their approach to treatment is to give psychotropic drugs and, occasionally, shock therapy—rather drastic forms of treatment which often result in severe side effects and treatment failure.

- Doctors, being scientists, often unwittingly treat women impersonally like a scientific experiment. They sometimes give the impression they are interested in the workings of the machine but not the person. I am very grateful for the fine physicians I have met, but, all the same, I talk to women every day who are very dissatisfied with the arrogant attitude of their doctors and the poor medical care they have received. To understand this point, every physician should read the book *The Doctor*, by Dr. Edward E. Rosenbaum.

- Doctors tend to underestimate or treat as superficial the hormonal problems that women experience. They are used to life-and-death drama in the delivery room and the surgery. These other problems seem so inconsequential by comparison. But if these doctors could really get inside the mind and find out what it really feels like to want to put your fist through the wall or worse—your husband or child, they might think differently.

• There is a popular TV doctor who takes the position that PMS doesn't exist and that menopause is not a disorder and shouldn't be treated. Of course menstruation and menopause are part of the natural order and are not problems in themselves, but malfunction of the reproductive organs happens, as with any other system in the body.

• Doctors may acknowledge that PMS is a real problem, but controversy still exists about treatment. Some will suggest that women work on their diet (eliminate sugar, salt, and caffeine; take magnesium, vitamin B6, primrose oil, and certain herbs) and exercise. But, generally, women with problems that do not respond to these simple changes have limited options for treatment apart from the pill, Prozac, and other even more drastic alternatives.

• When doctors do feel free to prescribe hormones, they often use the birth control pill, which can cause depression in women who are predisposed to it. Synthetic progestins do not work the same as natural progesterone does in the cell's progesterone receptors, and, by occupying the space that natural progesterone should use, they lower the body's levels of natural progesterone, often causing depression.

• There is a realistic fear of malpractice. Going into medicine these days is no sinecure. There has been increasing litigation, and the cost of malpractice insurance, especially for OB/Gyns, has escalated dramatically. As a result, many OB/Gyns have stopped delivering babies, and have become very conservative about treatment and are forced to practice defensive medicine, using only approved prescriptions and procedures.

• Since the endocrine system and the cell function is so complex and relatively little understood, doctors should try not to worsen symptoms by doing anything that would interfere with the delicate balance of the endocrine system, including prescribing the pill, other synthetic progestins, and Lupron, or performing surgical procedures, such as tubal sterilization, hysterectomy, and oophorectomy.

Rather, they might try the simplest natural hormones first—a small amount of oral estradiol taken daily with enough natural progesterone cyclically to make the necessary changes in the uterus and relieve symptoms. If doctors would try this simple combination, with its great physical and emotional benefits and relative lack of side effects on their patients suffering from moderate PMS and premenopause, I believe they would be convinced. The minimum treatment that works is all that many women need to take.

Summary

You can see that there is little recognition of these problems and relatively little research. The attitude of the FDA and insurance companies is unhelpful, and the hands of physicians are consequently tied even if they want to treat these problems, which many don't. This is why it is frequently difficult for women to find help for their hormonal problems. In fact, many women are powerless to get help because the odds are stacked against them one way or another.

The present situation in medicine that makes it so hard to get help will not change until women are able to convince other women and their doctors that their problems are real. Women will have to demand treatment, realizing that their body belongs to **them,** not to their doctor. The physician must realize who pays the bills and take a few classes in PR.

When I go to see my OB/Gyn, Dr. Jones, I find his attitude so refreshing. As he examines me, he explains what he's doing and why. If there's a problem, he tells me what it is, what he knows about it and how it can be helped. He gives me options and lets me make educated choices. And, at the end, when I'm about to leave, he always says, "And is there anything else I can do to help you today?" I always leave his office in a wonderful frame of mind.

Not only is Dr. Jones well-informed on hormonal problems, he knows how to treat his patients with dignity, respect, and kindness. He treats us as though we have enough intelligence to take part in the decisions about our treatment. That is why women flock to him and are ecstatic about him as a physician and surgeon.

But his kind is rare. Many doctors are not like him. They should beware. There is a new generation of women coming who will not stand for the treatment given in the past—male-dominated, chauvinistic, unsympathetic, uninformed, and, as far as results are concerned—useless and sometimes dangerous.

CHAPTER 3

How Your Hormones Work— The Endocrine System

Mona, 40, had a family history full of hormonal problems. Her mother and sister both had menstrual disorders, thyroid problems, trouble with their pregnancies, and both, like Mona, ultimately had hysterectomies.

Mona was fairly healthy until puberty, but there her good luck ended. She had horrendous menstrual periods, during which she would bleed for ten days, stop for four, bleed again for ten days, and so on. The flow was extremely heavy, and her cramps were very severe. At age sixteen, a doctor put Mona on birth control pills to regulate her cycle and control the bleeding. She was later diagnosed as having polycystic ovaries and endometriosis, and she was told that her chances of becoming pregnant were very small.

Mona had a miscarriage before the age of twenty which left her with severe postpartum depression. She had difficulty conceiving again, so she took Clomid and became pregnant, but was dreadfully sick the whole nine months and was hospitalized because of vomiting and dehydration. The delivery was very difficult and, afterwards, she had milk fever. The penicillin treatment caused her to develop a violent reaction with a fever of 106° lasting ten days. She needed surgery on her breasts, which had to be pumped afterwards. The bleeding and the pain were unendurable, as was her depression.

The second child was unplanned, and this pregnancy was a similar nightmare. The delivery was, again, very difficult, with third degree tearing and a great deal of hemorrhaging.

Two years later, her uterus was removed because of heavy bleeding, and she was given a low dose of Ogen. After many visits to the emergency room for continually rupturing ovarian cysts, both ovaries were removed two years later. Her estrogen was doubled, but it did not help her symptoms, and the hormonal protocol was never adjusted to meet her needs.

After the hysterectomy, Mona's physical and emotional health deteriorated. She became more and more depressed and was, finally, admitted to a psychiatric ward. Over a period of three years, she was given almost every available antidepressant, including monoamine oxidase inhibitors, tricyclics, and Prozac. She became violent as a result of taking all this medication and, at one point, tried to commit suicide after being on Prozac. She was also treated with electric shock therapy, and when I saw her, she told me her doctor wanted to give her another course of twelve more shock treatments.

Mona's problem, it seemed to me, was basically hormonal; she needed an endocrinologist, not a psychiatrist.

The Endocrine System Is Complex

When one looks at the complexity of the endocrine system and the menstrual cycle, it is not really surprising that they can break down, just like any other part of the body. The surprising thing is that some physicians almost act as though the endocrine system doesn't exist.

Women's hormonal and immune systems are much more intricate than men's because of ovulation and pregnancy. Men may have their own hormonal cycles, but they do not have the dramatic rise and fall of hormones that women experience during their monthly cycle. Pregnancy creates the need for a stronger immune system since the fetus is a foreign object which normally would be rejected by the body. The complexity of the female immune system enables her to carry the baby to term.

Because of the complexity of the immune system, women have 90 to 95 percent of autoimmune system diseases, such as lupus and rheumatoid arthritis.

Likewise, women have many problems with menstruation because the cycle is so intricate. Problems often begin at puberty, and some women lose their health after a particular pregnancy.

The Menstrual Cycle Can Easily Go Wrong

The menstrual cycle is natural, but many women have been programmed to believe that menstrual problems are also natural. They have been told for generations that pain and discomfort are simply to be endured. The truth is that the endocrine system and menstrual cycle are very sensitive and can easily go wrong, just like any other part of the body. In some cases, the problem is not easily resolved.

The Brain As Team Manager

The hypothalamus and pituitary glands in the brain control the hormonal system like a sensitive conductor leading his orchestra or a team manager controlling his team. If the team manager sends out the wrong messages, the team will run around in confusion. If one of the players doesn't cooperate, he may ruin the performance of the other members of the team. So it is with the hypothalamus-pituitary axis, controlling a myriad of hormonal and immune system functions.

Rhythm and Synchronization

Dr. Dean Black makes the point that PMS is a "dynamical" disease,[1] characterized by abnormal body rhythms, rather than by a simple chemical deficiency that can be measured. Dr. Black says this may be why the results of many PMS research studies have been inconclusive and why the usual double-blind approach has not worked.

Black mentions that our body pulses with rhythm. Most major systems in the body have two distinct types of function that constantly switch back and forth with opposite effects. Dr. Black cites the brain, which has a right and left half, as an example. The left half notices things, the right gives them meaning, and the two sides switch back and forth.

The nervous system can be divided into the sympathetic and parasympathetic halves. One controls the world without; the other controls the world within. We repeatedly swing back and forth, between the outside and inside world.

The hormonal system also has two components—the catecholamines and the endorphins. In general, the catecholamines arouse us, the endorphins calm us. Again there is a constant swinging back and forth between the two.

Black also mentions the immune system with its aggressive immune cells and its suppresser cells.

There are two categories of body processes—the catabolic and the anabolic which alternate between breaking apart and combining, freeing energy and recovering it again.

The menstrual cycle is another example. Estrogen builds up the lining of the uterus, and progesterone breaks it down when pregnancy doesn't take place. Estrogen dilates the blood vessels; progesterone constricts them. Estrogen produces progesterone receptors and primes them to work. Progesterone switches off the estrogen receptors. This is constantly happening, back and forth and on and off.

To the rhythm principle, Dr. Black adds synchronization, a principle in physics which demonstrates that stronger rhythms can capture weaker rhythms and coordinate them. The hypothalamus synchronizes the many disparate rhythms in the body and makes them march to one tune in team formation.

When women have hormonal problems, the rhythm and the synchronization of their menstrual cycle are thrown out of gear. It's as if members of the same orchestra were playing discordant notes. Treating hormonal problems includes restoring the body rhythms.

How the Hormonal Team Works
The bloodstream functions as a transport system, carrying hormones to and from the brain, glands, and cells. It also carries nutrients to the cells and waste products from them.

The brain begins the endocrine processes by sending out a variety of releasing and stimulating hormones into the bloodstream. These travel to various glands—the thyroid, the ovaries, the adrenals, the pancreas, and the breast. (Some hormones such as calcitonin, insulin, epinephrine and norepinephrine are produced more indirectly under the influence of the pituitary.)

The glands, in turn, produce other hormones which travel to the cells. There they enter the cell receptors, combine with the DNA in the cell nucleus, and work to maintain the healthy function of each cell.

There are also individual feedback systems to the brain for each hormone, so the brain knows what is going on in the body and can adjust its own output of hormones.

Hypothalamus
puts out releasing hormones TRH, CRF, FSH-LHRH, etc.

Brain

Pituitary
produces prolactin and growth hormone. Sends out stimulating hormones FSH, LH, TSH, ACTH, etc.

Controls blood sugar indirectly

FSH
LH

TSH   ACTH

Ovaries   Thyroid   Adrenals   Pancreas

Estrogen
Progesterone
Androgens
Ovarian Thyroid   Thyroxine   Adrenalin   Insulin
                   Calcitonin   Cortisol   Glucagon
                                 Androgens

Hormone
Receptor

Cell

Feedback Loops
for each hormone go to the brain to notify the hypothalamus when it needs to start producing releasing hormones again.

DNA

Steroid Hormones
are the glue that holds the functions of the cell together and have a major part in the production of enzymes in the DNA.

Three Levels

To express it simply, you could say that there are three main working levels—the brain (hypothalamus and pituitary); the glands (thyroid, ovaries, adrenals, pancreas); and the cells.

How the Endocrine System Works—at the Brain Level

Recent studies have suggested that a disruption of certain neurotransmitters in the brain is responsible for PMS. Neurotransmitters are chemical messengers passed from one point to another in the brain by the firing of neurons. They are responsible for the process of thought. When they don't function properly, people may become depressed, psychotic, or schizophrenic. Doctors use antidepressants to change thinking by chemically altering the neurotransmitters in the brain.

Neurotransmitters, such as seratonin, dopamine, norepinephrine, and the endorphins, play a large part in controlling the hormonal system. And, at the same time, estrogen increases these neurotransmitters and improves memory and mood. The hormones and the neurotransmitters are intimately related, and this is important because it explains why many women with hormonal disorders have severe emotional problems and why some find improvement from antidepressants.

The Hypothalamus and Pituitary Glands

The hypothalamus is a tiny gland in the brain situated close to the pituitary. It acts like a radar station, catching and fielding all the outside impulses entering the brain. It has many functions, including overseeing the endocrine system.

The hypothalamus also controls the central nervous system, the immune system, and the sympathetic nervous system which controls all our unconscious acts—temperature, sex drive, hunger, thirst, sleep, and how the body handles stress. The hypothalamus works very closely with the pituitary gland located nearby.

The pituitary has its own specific functions. It produces growth hormone and prolactin. Prolactin is elevated during pregnancy, and controls lactation afterwards. One of the functions of prolactin is to inhibit the ovarian hormones, and it does this after pregnancy. Estrogen and progesterone levels plummet to almost zero after delivery which can cause a menopause-like postpartum depression in some women, who may have drying of the vagina, fatigue, hot flashes, low sex drive, headaches, and depression. This inhibiting function of prolactin can also affect the thyroid, causing either a temporary or permanent condition of low thyroid after pregnancy.

Prolactin is also present during the menstrual cycle, and elevated levels of prolactin can inhibit progesterone levels. One of the theories about the cause of PMS is that women have too high a level of prolactin, though tests do not support this thesis. Still, high prolactin levels may be one cause of PMS. Women who have inappropriate leakage from the breast (galactorrhea) may have high prolactin levels, and sometimes this is due to a tumor, usually benign, in the pituitary.

The pituitary is also a major producer of the endorphins, neurotransmitters which help women have that "great to be alive" feeling. Researchers have found that women with PMS have only 25 percent of the endorphin levels that normal women have premenstrually. Women going through menopause also have lower levels of endorphins. Taking estrogen and natural progesterone raises the endorphin levels.

A More Detailed Look

The hypothalamus puts out **releasing** hormones (including TRH for the thyroid, CRF for the adrenals, and FSH-LH-RH for the ovaries). These are chemical messengers that go to the pituitary gland and cause it, in turn, to produce **stimulating** hormones (including TSH for the thyroid, ACTH for the adrenals, and FSH and LH for the ovaries). These stimulating hormones then travel to the glands (particularly, the thyroid, adrenals, ovaries, and pancreas).

Any time one of these glands doesn't function properly, it tends to throw out the production by the other glands, because they are all closely related and their functions are interdependent.

How the Thyroid Functions

The hypothalamus puts out a hormone called TRH (thyroid releasing hormone), which travels to the pituitary which, in turn, sends out TSH (thyroid stimulating hormone).

TSH goes through the bloodstream to the thyroid, where several types of thyroid hormones (thyroxine) are produced. Two main kinds are tetraiodothyronine T4 and triiodothyronine T3. The thyroid also indirectly produces calcitonin, a hormone that regulates the calcium in the bones. [The parathyroid also produces calcitonin.]

The various hormones produced in the thyroid, enter the bloodstream and make their way to the cells where they are responsible for many varied functions. For instance, the thyroid controls your body's heat and metabolism. When the thyroid is low, you tend to feel the cold excessively. Your bodily functions, movement, coordination, and speech slow down, and you may feel exhausted.

The body also has a thyroid feedback system to the brain. When you are cold and your blood levels of thyroxine are low, the feedback system notifies the hypothalamus to send out more TRH and start the process again. When blood levels of thyroxine are high, the hypothalamus switches off the production of TRH.

How the Adrenal Gland Functions

The hypothalamus sends CRF to the pituitary which triggers the pituitary to produce ACTH, (adrenocorticotropin hormone). The adrenals produce several different kinds of hormones—adrenaline; glucocorticoids, including cortisol (hydrocortisone); mineralocorticoids, including aldosterone; and androgens, including dehydroisoandrosterone or dehydroepiandrosterone, and androstenedione (which are converted to testosterone and dihydrotestosterone).

Adrenaline is the fight and flight hormone that helps you control stress. Cortisol is the hormone that helps control infections and allergies. Aldosterone helps regulate fluids and electrolyte balance. Androgens, including testosterone and DHEAS, are 'male' hormones which women also produce, just as men have low levels of female hormones. Men have twenty to forty times the amount of androgens as women. Androgens break down in the fat cells into estrone, a weak estrogen. Women who are overweight, particularly with fat deposited around the middle (android obesity) have higher levels of androgens. As a consequence, they have higher levels of unbound estrogens.

The adrenal gland has many necessary functions, and without its hormones, the body cannot handle stress and dies.

How the Ovaries Function

The hypothalamus puts out FSH-LH-RH (follicle stimulating hormone and luteinizing hormone releasing hormone), which travels to the pituitary, which, in turn, produces FSH and LH.

Traveling through the bloodstream at different times of the month, FSH and LH produce estrogen and progesterone—the two main female hormones in the ovaries. The FSH causes the production of estrogen in the first half of the cycle. LH causes ovulation and the production of progesterone and lower levels of estrogen during the second half of the cycle.

Estrogen has many functions in the female body. Estrogen stimulates the breast tissue. It also builds up the lining of the uterus ready to house a pregnancy each month. Without estrogen, skin, hair, bones, muscles, mucous membranes, the vascular system, in fact, just about everything in the body, begins to dry and deteriorate.

Progesterone supplements and balances the effects of estrogen in the breasts and uterus. Like estrogen, its function is ubiquitous and its influence on the body is very calming and sometimes depressive. The ovaries also produce androgens and a type of ovarian thyroid.

After menopause, the ovaries still produce hormones, though the quantities and types change.

How the Glands Interrelate—The Team Effect

All the glands controlled by the pituitary not only have an individual function, they also strongly influence each other and function as a team. The ovaries produce a type of ovarian thyroid, and the thyroid sends a releasing hormone to the hypothalamus that starts the whole menstrual cycle rolling. Women with thyroid problems frequently have menstrual problems as a result. The thyroid also exerts control over the adrenals.

In the adrenals, androgens break down into weak forms of estrogen and progesterone, and, so, the adrenals function as backup sex organs supporting the ovaries. They have a particularly important role after menopause when the ovaries shut down their major production of estrogen. After menopause, women are supplied with estrogen through the breakdown of androgens, produced by both the adrenals and ovaries. If a woman loses one or both ovaries, her estrogen levels are obviously affected. Many women function well after menopause until they experience a shock or trauma such as a car accident or the death of a close family member, which may bring on adrenal exhaustion.

You can easily see the team effect. When one gland doesn't work properly, the others may be affected to one degree or another.

More Than One Problem

Many women have polyendocrine disorders, in which more than one gland is affected, and more than one hormone may be low or malfunctioning. When one hormone is low, there is a tendency for all to become low in sympathy. It is not surprising that hormonal problems can become complicated. For example, women with PMS, postpartum, or menopausal difficulties, have a high incidence of known thyroid problems, often with a strong family history. Thyroid, estrogen, and progesterone are closely related in function—opposing, augmenting, and balancing each other.

Blood Sugar Levels Are Affected

The pituitary produces growth hormone, and one of its functions is to produce glucogon in the pancreas. Insulin is also produced in the pancreas under the indirect control of the pituitary. Glucagon and insulin control the blood sugar and this is why blood sugar levels are affected when thyroid and sex hormones don't work properly. This is true with PMS. Progesterone and gamma globulin (which carries the blood sugar) share one of the receptor sites in the cells. When progesterone levels are low, blood sugar levels tend to be low because one of the functions of progesterone is to metabolize sugar. During pregnancy, when progesterone levels are very high, some women develop gestational diabetes, a high blood sugar condition which may be temporary, or may herald the onset of permanent diabetes.

Dr. Katherina Dalton states that treatment for low blood sugar for women with PMS is essential. These women need to eat more frequently, premenstrually, because of the erratic fluctuation of their blood sugar levels. Tests may not show any problem, but in effect women are functionally hypoglycemic. When blood sugar levels drop below a certain level, it can cause shock, and adrenaline is quickly produced to counteract this. Since blood sugar drops much more quickly premenstrually, adrenaline spurts out sooner. When this occurs, women may often find they have headaches, become suddenly irritable and tired, or have angry, violent episodes, especially when they haven't eaten for a long time.

Once the blood sugar drops, it can take a week to rise to normal levels again. Though it may seem a minor point, following a hypoglycemic diet, and eating some complex carbohydrates every three to four hours can result in significant improvement. Hormonal therapy alone, without such a diet, may be a treatment failure, and both treatments may be necessary for success.

There is also a known connection between alterations in blood sugar in women with low thyroid problems—at each extreme—both hypoglycemia and diabetes. Dr. Nathan Becker has said that 75 percent of female diabetics are also low thyroid.

Also, at menopause, when estrogen is low, women are subject to unpredictable fluctuations in blood sugar.

The message is, when the hormones malfunction, changes in blood sugar are inevitable, and attention to diet is extremely important.

Down at the Cellular Level

The target organs—the thyroid, adrenals, and ovaries—produce hormones, and the hormones enter the bloodstream, heading for the cells.

There are trillions of cells in the body. Biologists group them according to their similarities, and there are approximately three hundred different types. Each cell functions as a team member, little factories keeping the whole body working at peak performance.

Inside the cells are tiny, very specific receptors for each hormone. Hormone molecules are unable to directly enter the cell nucleus, but they can combine with their specific cell receptors, enabling them to pass into the cell nucleus.

Hormone receptors, such as the one for progesterone, are more prevalent in the cells of certain organs, such as the limbic area of the brain which controls the emotions, the breasts, the uterus, the lungs, the skin, and the liver. When the endocrine system doesn't work properly, hormonal levels can change. Deprived of their particular hormone molecules, receptors decline in number. Everywhere that these cell receptors are missing or nonfunctional, symptoms are likely to occur. So, wherever cell receptors are lacking or malfunctioning, symptoms of a hormone deficiency will occur.

Individuals with hormonal problems may have widely different symptoms, affecting many different parts of the body. This is because the hypothalamus controls so many different body systems and, at the cell level, there is such a widespread dispersal of cell receptors.

The Gate Theory

If the body were dependent on nerve impulses to control the function of every cell, it would need many more nerves and use more energy than it presently has. Controlling the cells by hormones is a much more efficient and economical process.

Cells are like little factories. They contain enzymes, made of protein molecules which take raw material (organic molecules coming into the cell), and make it usable within the cell or prepare it for export to other needy cells.

To protect the cell, there are protein "gates" protruding from both sides of the cell wall. These "gates" have several functions. They release waste products from the cell and help keep in nutrients. They also act as sentries, blocking or allowing any invasive substance that tries to enter the cell.

There are exceptions that bypass the gate or sentry, however. The main steroidal hormones—estrogen and progesterone in women, testosterone in men, and thyroid in both sexes—have "open season" tickets. They can go in and out of the cell wall at will and can enter all 300 types of cells. They do not have to pass through the "gates."

According to Dr. Norman Farb's unpublished manuscript on the gate theory:

> Steroids (sex hormones) have a peculiar capability. They do not need a gate in the cell wall to allow them to enter the cell. Once inside the cell, they connect with their receptor, pass through the nuclear pores and reach the site of the nucleus that contains the genes (the DNA). The binding of the hormone with the gene somehow enables the cell to maintain itself, to repair and rebuild the gates on the cell wall and the enzymes. Without this maintenance, the cell deteriorates and ages, with effects on the entire organism.

The steroid hormones, therefore, largely control the health and well-being of the cell. When the steroid hormones are low, repair and rebuilding of the gates and production of important enzymes cannot take place, nitrogen is thrown out of balance, and the cell breaks down. Waste products accumulate; invaders have open access; nutrients leak out of the cell; the connective tissues are affected. Because hormones increase or decrease the rate of activity of the cell, a decrease in the number of receptors means that the cell will no longer function properly.

The Body's Switching Mechanism

When the estrogen levels drop, the estrogen receptors also diminish. Taking estrogen increases not only the blood levels, but increases the number of receptors, making estrogen more available to the cells.

Estrogen also increases the number of progesterone receptors and primes them to work, while progesterone tends to shut off the estrogen receptors. This switching back and forth between estrogen and progesterone is a strong argument for giving women **both hormones** for PMS and premenopause.

The Feedback System to the Brain

The body has many feedback systems which send information to the brain. And each hormone has a feedback system to the brain, able to notify the hypothalamus about what is happening hormonally in other parts of the body. If the feedback system indicates the body is low in certain hormones, the hypothalamus will switch on its production of releasing hormones, and the whole process is started again.

Antibodies

The immune system is programmed to destroy foreign proteins that it doesn't recognize. Hormones are made of protein and, sometimes, when your hormones drop significantly or fluctuate wildly, the immune system sensors lose their memory bank for these hormones. This may result in the production of antibodies and white blood cells, which can fight and destroy a person's own hormones.

This is particularly true of the thyroid—the most common endocrine gland that builds up antibodies—partly because the U.S. and Europe have soil that is low in iodine. Thyroiditis can result from this, and while the hormonal blood levels may appear normal, a high antibody count may show the problem. Women may have normal hormone levels, but the thyroid doesn't work in the cell because the thyroid antibodies destroy them at three levels—in the thyroid, in the bloodstream, and in the cell receptors.

What happens to the thyroid also happens to the ovaries and adrenals. And not only does your body sometimes fight the hormones it makes, it may also fight the hormones you take. So, sometimes, women taking estrogen, progesterone, or thyroid experience side effects, though they really need these medications.

Blood Tests Not Always Reliable

This means you can have enough hormone in the bloodstream, according to blood tests, but because of the action of antibodies, your hormones "don't work" at the cell level. Dr. Broda Barnes uses a helpful illustration of money in the bank to explain why blood tests may not always show up hormonal deficiencies. A man may have plenty of money in the bank (i.e., blood levels of hormones), but not be spending any money (i.e., at the cell level). It's not so much a matter of "Do you have enough of a certain hormone?" but rather, "Does the hormone work?"

Summary

Interference with the hormonal system at any level—from the hypothalamus to the pituitary, to the glands, to the cell, and the feedback system, can cause a woman to experience chemical changes and alterations in rhythm and synchronization, with resulting symptoms of hormonal distress. For some women, this is a genetic problem; for others it happens after certain hormonal events, such as pregnancy or the pill. This explains why there are many different causes for PMS and other problems. They can arise from genetic tendencies; the use of the birth control pill, and other hormones, such as Provera, Lupron and Clomid; hypothalamic or pituitary problems, including tumors, thyroid malfunction, especially hypothyroidism; pregnancy, miscarriage, abortion; anorexia and bulimia, amenorrhea; surgery such as tubal ligation, hysterectomy, ovarian cysts, polycystic ovaries, endometriosis, uterine fibroids. Stress and life-style also play their roles. Knowing how the endocrine system works at different levels enables women to understand how important the hormones are to health and well-being and why hormonal problems can create so many different symptoms.

Footnote

1. Dr. Dean Black, *PMS: When Bodies Lose Their Beat,* 1-800-333-4290.

CHAPTER 4

How Your Hormones Work—
the Menstrual Cycle

*A*fter looking at the bigger picture of how the endocrine system functions, we can now focus on how the menstrual cycle works. The menstrual cycle bridges the years in which a woman is in her prime. It is a process with a beginning, a decline, and an end.

The ovaries, from birth, contain the entire supply of a woman's eggs, and a pair of ovaries only lasts approximately fifty years at the most. Once they are depleted, reproduction is no longer possible, and estrogen declines sharply, leading to menopause and the end of menstruation.

Overview of a Woman's Reproductive Life
Even before a female baby is born, all the eggs or follicles she will ever have are present in her two ovaries. Figures vary tremendously, but some say there are up to billions of eggs present before birth. A baby may have from 500,000 to 5,000,000 eggs in her ovaries. These immediately begin to involute and die off, forming scar tissue, and by puberty, the numbers are down to 200,000 to 300,000. The follicles, stimulated by FSH, grow to maturity before ovulation; then the LH surge midcycle causes ovulation, after which one or two chosen eggs produce progesterone during the last half of the menstrual cycle. Estrogen is produced most of the month by FSH stimulation of special estrogen-producing cells in the ovary, but it is at its highest levels just before ovulation, and lowest before the period.

Every menstrual cycle, not one or two, but at least hundreds of eggs are used up. Only one or two eggs per cycle will fully mature; the rest die. Women go through menopause when the estrogen cells and the eggs in their ovaries gradually run out, abruptly causing the hormones to drop to a much lower level. After menopause, the ovaries still produce hormones—mainly androgens, and the adrenal gland acts as a backup.

Age of Menopause
The average age for women going naturally through menopause is about 51.4 years. But, possibly because of differences in the numbers of estrogen cells and eggs a woman is born with, some may stop their periods and go through menopause earlier than normal (about seven to ten percent in their thirties). Some women may stop their periods as early as twenty-eight or thirty; and it is often the case that their mother and grandmother did too. At the other end of the scale, some women still menstruate in their early sixties.

In previous ages, women had many more pregnancies with about fifty menstrual cycles over a lifetime. Women today have about 400 cycles, with ovulation taking place many more times. The number of eggs and estrogen cells used up is accelerated, and the pituitary and ovarian hormone levels begin to fluctuate earlier. Removal of one ovary reduces the factories to half and may lead to premenopausal symptoms. Removal of both ovaries puts women into instant menopause, and women with only part of an ovary or a fallopian tube removed may also start symptoms prematurely.

Some women have a gradual descent into menopause, experiencing subnormal hormonal levels at a relatively early age. This may cause chronic hormone deficiency symptoms, manifesting themselves as PMS and premenopause. These symptoms can last from as early as the thirties (for a few even younger) to the time a woman actually stops menstruating (averaging in the mid-forties or early fifties).

The Normal Menstrual Cycle—How It Works
The menstrual cycle occurs on an average of every 28 to 29 days, day one being the first day of flow. FSH (follicle stimulating hormone) is produced mainly during the first part of the menstrual cycle, towards the end of the period. Produced by the pituitary gland, FSH goes through the bloodstream to the ovaries and causes hundreds of eggs (or follicles) to

Different Hormonal Levels Throughout the Menstrual Cycle

ESTROGEN, PROGESTERONE

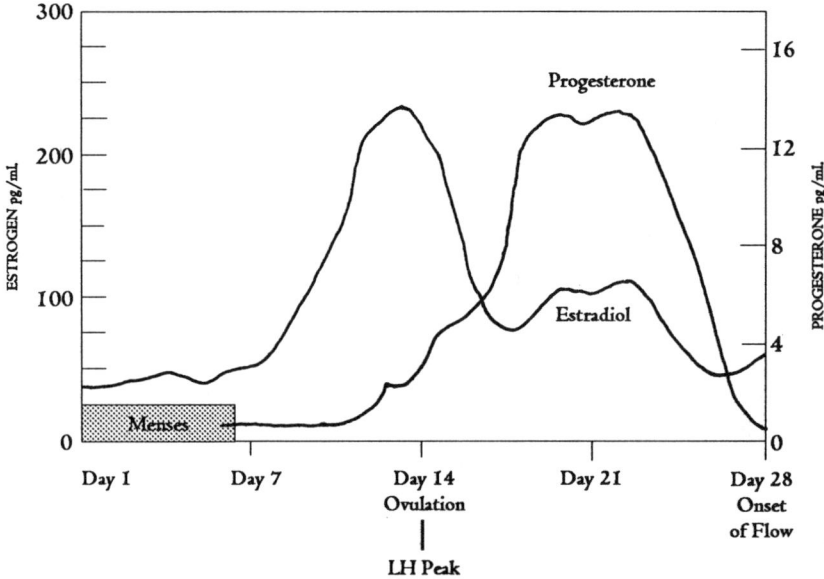

FOLLICLE STIMULATING AND LUTEINIZING HORMONES

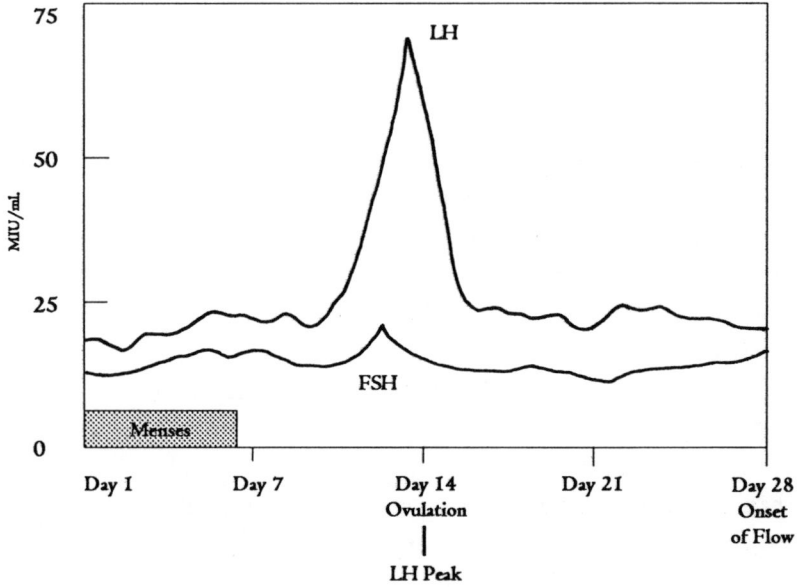

43

rise to the surface of the particular ovary selected to ovulate that cycle. FSH also stimulates estrogen cells that produce estrogen, so that estrogen levels soar to their highest just prior to ovulation and then suddenly drop.

The first part of the menstrual cycle up to ovulation is called the follicular phase, when estrogen is dominant. Progesterone, the second female hormone is almost absent at this time. During this phase, the endometrial lining in the uterus gradually builds up like a nest, preparing to receive and nourish the egg in the event that fertilization and pregnancy occur.

Meanwhile, in the ovary, just before mid-cycle, one or two eggs have developed to become the egg(s) of the month. The others die off, and the estrogen levels drop precipitously. As this happens, LH (luteinizing hormone) is released into the bloodstream by the pituitary in a mid-cycle surge which causes ovulation. The "egg of the month" is catapulted out of the ovary, into the waiting, undulating fallopian tube.

At the place on the ovary where the egg has been released, a yellow patch called the corpus luteum is formed. This patch produces a high level of progesterone, the second female hormone, during the second half of the cycle. Progesterone is low, or even absent during the first part of the menstrual cycle, but very high during the second half when women ovulate. Estrogen continues to be produced during the second half of the cycle.

When a woman is young, the second curve (postovulation) of estrogen is about as high as the first preovulatory curve. But, as women enter their thirties and forties, the tendency is for the first estrogen curve to rise and the second estrogen curve to drop. (However, in some women, the first curve can also begin to decrease.) Women with high preovulatory curves will have heavier bleeding because the estrogen overstimulates the endometrial lining. Conversely, women with lower preovulatory curves will have lighter bleeding. As some women approach menopause, they may have both tendencies, depending on which ovary is functioning that particular cycle.

The first half of the cycle is estrogen dominant because progesterone is absent. The second half of the cycle, after ovulation, is progesterone dominant. Estrogen is present, but progesterone levels are usually higher. When a woman does not become pregnant, her progesterone levels drop precipitously, and the lining of the uterus sloughs off causing her to menstruate, ending the cycle. Then the cycle begins all over again with the rise of FSH.

How Hormone Levels Change with Age

As the eggs or follicles are used up month by month, the hormone levels start to change. A gradual lessening of the ovaries' supply of eggs and estrogen cells causes the ovary to notify the pituitary to send more FSH. Higher levels of FSH overstimulate the few remaining eggs and estrogen cells. The high levels of estrogen produced cause greater thickening of the endometrial lining of the uterus, resulting in heavier periods.

Conversely, FSH may become lower, producing less estrogen in the ovaries and a thinner lining of the endometrium. This will cause periods to be lighter. Or women will have irregular spotting because a woman does not have enough estrogen to "hold" the endometrium intact, and the lining keeps continually sloughing off. Some women may get both extremes—heavy or light bleeding—occurring in alternate months.

Women may begin to notice symptoms of premenopause in the first half of the cycle, particularly between the fifth to eighth or tenth day of the cycle (the time when estrogen normally rises). The symptoms may be very subtle, and she may begin to feel a gradual emotional and physical decline with common symptoms such as low-grade depression, fatigue, low self-esteem, anxiety, insomnia, heart palpitations, muscle tightness in the neck, dizziness, or even hot flashes and drying of the vagina. Women suffering from depression or panic attacks at this time of life should ask themselves whether or not it might be hormonal.

Beginning in their mid-thirties, some women will not ovulate every month and will skip periods. When that happens, the corpus luteum may not form. Even if it does, it may not produce adequate levels of estrogen and progesterone in the second half of the cycle. During this time (the luteal phase), hormones will be low. This is why PMS, which occurs after ovulation, may begin or worsen around age 35.

Some Women Have Hormonal Problems Early in Life

There are all sorts of reasons why the hormonal cycle can stop working at its best. Some women have a hormonal system that doesn't function normally from early in life, and they are often subclinically low thyroid or have congenital PMS. Symptoms may begin around puberty or after a pregnancy, and tend to worsen as a woman ages.

PMS may begin after some hormonal event—being on the pill, going off the pill, being pregnant, or having a tubal ligation, hysterectomy, or surgery on the ovaries or tubes. Other women who have such physical problems as endometriosis, or polycystic ovaries, cysts on the ovaries, fibroid tumors, scarring of the ovaries/fallopian tubes as a result of an infection, etc., may have disruption of their hormones. So do some women who have anorexia, bulimia, or amenorrhea (having no periods). Some of the same triggers can bring on premature menopause with estrogen deficiency.

Because the hypothalamus also controls the immune system, women with hormonal problems frequently have allergies and respiratory problems, such as bronchitis or asthma.

Summary

It should come as no surprise that when the endocrine system and the menstrual cycle are out of synchrony, a large variety of symptoms are produced, and women feel both physically and emotionally sick, as a result.

Often, one gland rather than another—e.g. pituitary, thyroid, ovaries—is the main problem. When each different hormone malfunctions, certain patterns and symptoms are produced. And with a little help and information, many women can work out for themselves what is happening to them. We will enlarge on this in later chapters.

Section Two:
Hormonal Problems

CHAPTER 5

Premenstrual Syndrome

*E*very month before her period, Mary becomes depressed, irritable, and angry for no apparent reason. She screams at her children and finds fault with her husband. Things that wouldn't bother her most of the time become huge in her imagination, blown all out of proportion.

Initially, Mary thought she was just a moody, unstable person. The up-and-down moods among the females in her family had often been the topic of conversation. So, understandably, Mary blames her symptoms on her environment. She thinks her feelings and reactions are just learned behavior aggravated by daily stress. Underneath, she's convinced that if she exerted just a little more willpower, she could control her behavior.

But she's noticed these symptoms happen cyclically; that is, sometimes she has them and sometimes she doesn't. Her symptoms are intensifying now that she's reached thirty-five. Sometimes she thinks her period has something to do with the way she feels, though her symptoms seem to last two or three weeks out of the month. "I only have one good week a month," she complains. Her symptoms worsened with her last pregnancy, and after she had a tubal ligation, her problems seemed to become even more severe.

Her doctor says it's all in her mind, but Mary knows it's more than that. She has a week or so each month when her symptoms disappear and she feels normal and emotionally stable. Then, at ovulation, it's as though a switch is thrown, and she's back into symptoms. "It can't be my imagination," she insists. She's become very hard to live with, and every month she wants to run away. She has little self-worth, feels she is a failure, sometimes thinks she's going insane, and thinks she may be better off living alone.

Besides the emotional symptoms, Mary also has some physical problems. Her skin breaks out before each period. Her breasts swell, her head aches, and her joints are stiff. She has premenstrual hot flashes and occasional panic attacks too. [She's fortunate her physical symptoms aren't a lot worse—some PMS sufferers get migraines and even epileptic seizures.] But her emotional symptoms, like depression and anger, worry her more than the physical ones.

"It's the close relationships that are difficult," she confides. "I get so angry with my husband and the kids over nothing. I feel a complete loss of self-control. I can see afterwards that I've overreacted, and I keep reminding myself of this, but it never helps at the time."

Mary doesn't really want to kill herself, though she often thinks about doing it. She says she wouldn't mind being killed in an accident in order to end her life without the responsibility of doing it herself. "I sort of panic inside because I don't know how much more I can take of this," she says. "I sometimes think that if it gets just a little bit worse, I'll do myself some damage. It's very frightening and very hard to explain."

Her husband can't understand what's going on, and he's getting really fed up with it all. He says she's like two people—part of the month she's on top of the world (the girl he married); the other part, she's impossible.

"She cries a lot when she's not shouting," he says. "Sometimes I wonder how much longer I can stand it."

"He's so logical," says Mary, "and I'm often irrational. I can't get him to understand how I feel. But you can't blame him. I don't understand it either."

Mary's problems are probably hereditary, since her mother and sister also have mood swings. Mary's symptoms begin after ovulation and stop towards the end of her period. The week after her period, she feels fine. Mary has classic premenstrual syndrome.

Only a Mother Could Love Her

Only a woman who has severe premenstrual syndrome (or someone who has to live with her) really understands how traumatic this experience can be. Possibly 40 to 60 percent of menstruating women have some degree of PMS. Five to ten percent of them experience incapacitating problems. Their physical and emotional symptoms can interrupt family life and lead to problems at work, loss of jobs, divorce, child abuse, violence, alcoholism, drug abuse, depression, and even suicide.

Simply stated, such women have a variety of symptoms which appear like clockwork before their period each month and disappear after their period. Some women only have symptoms for a short time prior to menstruation. These symptoms disappear when the flow begins. Other women may be overwhelmed by symptoms beginning shortly before ovulation and lasting well into the flow causing these women to say they have only "one good week a month."

A woman may find she has one bad month, then one better month, alternately; or a worse month every third month. This is probably because ovulation tends to occur in alternate ovaries in consecutive cycles, although it sometimes occurs more than once in a row on one side. A woman may know which side the troublesome ovary is on, if she feels pain when she ovulates on that particular side.

The Definition of PMS

PMS is characterized by a clustering of symptoms in the premenstruum (before the period) and an absence of symptoms in the postmenstruum (after the period). The **timing** of the symptoms is more important than the **type** of symptoms. But there are **common** symptoms. The important factor in women with classic PMS is that these symptoms are cyclical.

What Are the Symptoms of PMS?

Irritability, lethargy, and depression are known as the PMS triad and are almost always present. Other emotional symptoms include feeling out of control, sporadic crying, uncontrollable rage, feelings of escape (wanting to run away), paranoia, sadness, anger, anxiety, phobias, worthlessness, and guilt.

There can be many physical symptoms, such as headaches and migraines, flu-like symptoms, recurrent yeast infections, food cravings, and, occasionally, epileptic seizures. Some women report eye problems like conjunctivitis, sties, visual disturbances, and tunnel vision; or skin problems, like acne, boils, herpes, hives; or respiratory problems, like hoarseness, asthma, tonsillitis. Dr. Katherina Dalton, a world expert on PMS, has identified about 150 symptoms of PMS. Nobody has them all. Some women have only emotional symptoms and no physical symptoms. Occasionally, a woman will just have migraines, but no emotional symptoms.

Some Common PMS Symptoms

Acne	Addiction	Aggression
Alcoholism	Allergies	Arthritis
Asthma	Backache	Bloating
Blurred vision	Boils	Bronchitis
Clumsiness	Colds	Colitis
Confusion	Conjunctivitis	Constipation
Crying jags	Depression	Dizziness
Epilepsy	Exhaustion	Eye problems
Fainting	Fatigue	Fear of crowds
Fibrocystic breasts	Flu-like symptoms	Food cravings
Forgetfulness	Headaches	Heart palpitations
Hemorrhoid flare-up	Herpes	Hives
Hot flashes	Hyperventilation	Increased sex drive
Insomnia	Irritability	Joint pain
Leg heaviness	Lethargy	Low blood sugar
Low self-esteem	Migraines	Mood swings
Muscle pain	Muscle weakness	Nausea
Nervousness	Numb extremities	Out of control
Panic Attacks	Paranoia	Physical violence
Rage	Recurrent colds	Recurrent infections
Rapid heartrate	Sinusitis	Sties
Suicidal tendencies	Tender breasts	Tension
Tonsillitis	Yeast infections	Weight changes

There Are Different Patterns

Notice below some common patterns of PMS symptoms (A, B, C, and D). Note that some women do not fit these classic pattern.

TYPICAL PATTERNS

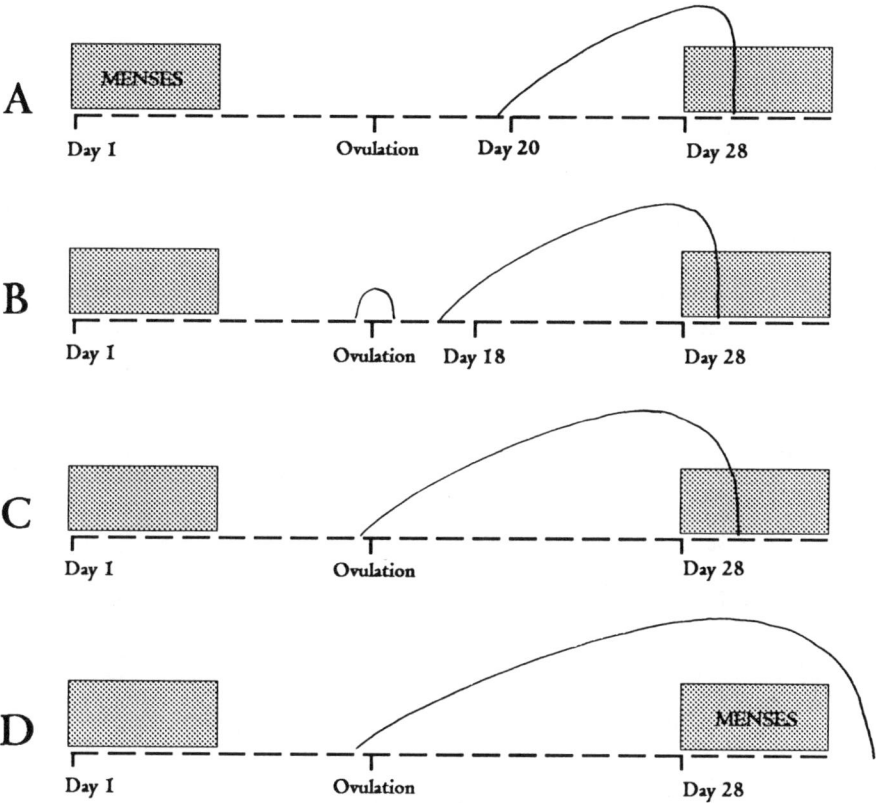

The Importance of Record Keeping

Filling in a Calendar

Many physicians ask patients to chart their symptoms for at least two months before beginning treatment for PMS. Keeping a calendar chart which records the timing of symptoms in relationship to your period will show a clear pattern if you have classic premenstrual syndrome. It is also helpful to fill in a day-by-day journal of your symptoms and feelings.

Day	Jan	Feb	Mar	Apr	May	Jun	Jul	Aug	Sep	Oct	Nov	Dec		Example	
1															
2															
3															
4															X
5															X
6															X
7														X	X
8														X	X
9														X	X
10													X	HX	HX
11													X	HX	HX
12													X	HX	HX
13													X	M	M
14													X	M	M
15													HX	M	M
16													HX	M	M
17													M	M	M
18													M		M
19													M		
20													M		
21													M		
22													M		
23															
24															
25															
26															
27															
28															
29															
30															
31															

Filling in the Chart—Use X for general symptoms; use appropriate initials for severe symptoms such as headaches (H), depression (D), seizures (S), etc. Write an M for menstruation or a P for period on the days you menstruate. See sample chart on right, where woman is having regular monthly cycles with 5 or 6 day periods. Chart can still be filled in with symptoms, even if menstruation is absent, as in prepubertal girls or postmenopausal women, who still have cyclical symptoms.

More Than PMS

Many women have symptoms which recur before each period and disappear after it, but there are those in an even more complicated predicament. They may have PMS combined with some other problem, such as postpartum depression following a recent pregnancy. Perhaps they are heading towards menopause and are experiencing estrogen-deficiency symptoms. Possibly they have a related adrenal or thyroid deficiency. Sometimes a chronic yeast infection or allergies make PMS worse. In these cases, the timing of the symptoms may vary from that in a clear case of PMS, and such women will not benefit as much when their PMS is treated alone. They need additional treatment to deal with their other health problems.

PMS Is Not Premenstrual Magnification

Contrast PMS with symptoms of chronic illness which may worsen premenstrually (premenstrual magnification). For instance, chronic migraines, chronic depression, chronic asthma, or chronic epilepsy may occur at any time and do not appear to be connected with menstruation. However, all chronic diseases tend to worsen around the time of menstruation. Sometimes these nonhormonal problems will not respond to hormonal therapy, but sometimes they do.

What Causes PMS?

Nobody really knows the exact cause of PMS, but there are many theories. No doubt, PMS is a multifactorial problem—not necessarily just one cause for one woman, but each woman may have multiple causes for her PMS.

Some believe that **poor nutrition** is a cause of PMS. They suggest that a **diet high in animal fat, high in calcium in proportion to magnesium,** and **lacking certain vitamins,** such as B-6, may cause or worsen PMS.

Some believe PMS is a hormonal problem, related to **low levels of progesterone.** Yet, there are women who do not ovulate and, therefore, do not produce any progesterone, and still do not get PMS. Other researchers believe that PMS is related to **low levels of estrogen.** Still others believe that the cause of PMS is related to **the ratio of estrogen and progesterone.** A useful definition is that PMS is a half-menopause. In some women, where the problem is cyclical, the progesterone is depleted. Other women may need some estrogen, especially as they age.

Others have postulated that PMS is a **thyroid disease.** It is true that women with thyroid problems, particularly low thyroid, often have PMS, and there does appear to be a link between the two conditions. But not everyone who has a thyroid problem has PMS, and not everyone who has PMS has a thyroid problem.

Those who promote primrose oil as a remedy for PMS say that women who have PMS have **high levels of prolactin,** the hormone which causes lactation after pregnancy and is also present during the menstrual cycle. One of prolactin's functions is to lower progesterone levels. This theory of high prolactin as the major cause of PMS does not hold, since many women with high prolactin levels do not have PMS, and many women with PMS have apparently normal levels of prolactin.

There is some evidence that women with PMS have **lower than normal levels of DHEA,** an adrenal hormone, which indicates that an adrenal gland dysfunction may sometimes be involved.

Women with PMS have some **disruption of the neurotransmitters** in the brain. Neurotransmitters are brain chemicals which send messages or impulses through the nervous system. Premenstrually, endorphin levels in women with PMS are only 25 percent of the levels of women who don't have PMS. Seratonin, another neurotransmitter in the brain, is also known to be low in women with PMS. One of the functions of neurotransmitters is to oversee and regulate hormonal function. Some researchers theorize that it is the disruption of these brain chemicals that throws the pituitary hormones out of synchrony.

There is no doubt that PMS often results **when the hypothalamus and pituitary become disturbed** for some reason. Because the pituitary produces hormones which go to a variety of target organs, several glands may be affected (e.g., ovaries, thyroid, adrenals).

Women with **polycystic ovaries** and **endometriosis** frequently also have PMS, and treatment for these specific conditions often helps the PMS.

Added to the problems, which appear to start primarily in the brain, are cases of PMS which seem directly triggered by surgery. For example, some women get PMS after having a tubal ligation, a hysterectomy, or surgery on the ovaries or fallopian tubes.

While the pituitary gland produces hormones in the ovary, there are also hormonal feedback systems to the brain from the ovaries. So you might say, the pituitary speaks to the ovary, but the ovary also speaks back to the brain. In the case of a tubal ligation or other abdominal surgery, the progesterone feedback system to the brain may possibly be interrupted in some way, triggering PMS.

Trillions of cells in the body contain specific hormone receptors. The sex hormones fit into their individual receptors, combine with the DNA in the cell nucleus, and help in the maintenance and functioning of the cells. Progesterone receptors are more prevalent in certain organs—the limbic area of the brain, the liver, the lungs, the breasts, the skin, and the uterus. Present research indicates that women with PMS may have less progesterone receptors than normal women.

This means that their cell function is affected, and may explain why blood tests for hormonal levels are often inadequate for diagnosis. It also helps explain why women with hormonal sensitivities do not do well on the contraceptive pill because of the pill's progestin content.

The pill frequently triggers or worsens PMS, as does the use of progestins such as Provera. Provera is frequently used for treating bleeding irregularities and amenorrhea (not having periods). It is also used as a progestational agent to prevent endometrial cancer at menopause, in combination with estrogen, usually Premarin. Provera can cause women to feel irritable and depressed and may compound PMS.

Others believe that some women who have PMS may have clamydia, a sexually-transmitted infection, or other infections. Some say that intestinal parasites can indirectly cause PMS. When the body produces antibodies to these parasites, the antibodies attack organs such as the ovaries and cause hormonal upsets. Others believe PMS is a candida or yeast-related disease, and others think women are allergic to their own hormones.

These are just a few of the current theories about the causes of PMS, which is, no doubt, a multifactorial problem.

PMS—the Progesterone Half-Menopause

A Los Angeles physician and his physician father spent a total of more than sixty years helping women with hormonal problems, and came to the conclusion that PMS is like a half-menopause. What they mean is that women have two main sex hormones circulating in their bodies—estrogen and progesterone. In some women, progesterone may be lower than it should be; in others, estrogen is depleted. And in still other women, both hormones are running low at the same time.

Progesterone is only produced by the ovaries in quantity after ovulation, so when it is low, a woman is likely to have symptoms of PMS, occurring only in the second half of the cycle. Women with symptoms of PMS that are severe enough to treat hormonally, often respond to natural progesterone therapy.

The Estrogen Half-Menopause

Other women may have a relative estrogen deficiency even during their menstruating years. Their symptoms are different from PMS (though many symptoms cross over) and the timing is different.

Estrogen-deficiency symptoms tend to be continual, but worsen premenstrually. These women may also feel awful about the fifth to the eighth day after the beginning of menstruation. A plausible theory is that estrogen should be rising as ovulation approaches, but levels are low. When estrogen is lower than normal at this time, women may have a cluster of symptoms such as insomnia, panic attacks, fatigue, vertigo, sweats, and muscle cramps in the neck, and severe headaches are common.

Even though women with PMS have cyclical problems, some women respond better to estrogen than they do to progesterone. Dr. John Studd of St. Thomas' Hospital in London has used over 10,000 estrogen pellets in treating female PMS patients, and has found this therapy very successful.

Not All Agree

It should be noted that some experts in treating PMS don't agree with the theory that PMS can also be related to estrogen deficiency. In the past, they have claimed that many women with PMS have excessive estrogen levels, and many claim that women can't be estrogen deficient if they still have periods. But other doctors believe a woman can cycle and have periods with lower levels of estrogen than normal.

Many physicians disagree with the suggestion that PMS is caused by a hormonal deficiency at all because women's hormonal blood tests often are normal.

Medical literature generally admits that PMS is a valid complaint, but suggests that progesterone works no better than a placebo, and says there is no known cure.

Don't Let Differences of Opinion Disturb You

- Some doctors believe women with PMS have high estrogen and low progesterone.
- Some doctors say the opposite—progesterone levels are high; estrogen levels low.
- Others believe either or both progesterone or estrogen may be low.
- The majority of physicians believe the problem is not a hormonal deficiency at all.

Don't be afraid of these differences of opinion. While the range of opinion among experts may be diverse and contrary, many women can still find a treatment that will help.

Practical Help for Women Is Available

Despite the differences of opinion on the cause of PMS and menopausal distress, the description of PMS as a progesterone deficiency or a half-menopause and estrogen deficiency as the other half-menopause is useful, even if simplistic. It serves as a useful explanation, and it makes a lot of sense. And, practically, treating women with a combination of estrogen and progesterone often works.

Many, many women with classic, severe PMS or postpartum depression **do** benefit from natural progesterone if given correctly, according to the protocol suggested by Dr. Katherina Dalton.

Some women, who do not fit the classic PMS patterns, may also benefit from taking estrogen for PMS. Others, with a low thyroid profile, may find adding a little thyroid medication makes a big difference to the way they feel.

What Activates PMS?

While the exact cause of PMS is still undetermined, there are known factors which can initiate or heighten symptoms.

Family history is a risk factor. Among susceptible women, it is common to find other family members with PMS—particularly on the maternal side. Each woman in the family will probably begin her own PMS pilgrimage at **puberty,** or even a couple of years earlier.

In such families, PMS is a lifetime battle, sometimes severe at onset, but other times starting mildly and worsening with age. When these especially susceptible women encounter any hormonal crisis— **taking or ceasing to use the pill, pregnancy, miscarriage, or abortion, having a tubal ligation or hysterectomy, having anorexia or bulimia, or amenorrhea (not having periods)**—their PMS may worsen. Menopause may be the end of PMS symptoms, but some women continue to have cyclical problems even long after they stop menstruating.

Some women who have never had a family history of PMS may also experience symptoms—after taking the pill, having a pregnancy, having a tubal ligation, or after a hysterectomy.

Sometimes stress or poor diet can trigger PMS, and it tends to begin or worsen as women age—particularly from age 35 upwards.

Birth Control Pills Tend to Intensify PMS

Most women with a history of PMS would be wise to avoid oral contraceptive pills for at least two reasons. First, they contain synthetic progesterone (progestogens) which can depress the pituitary gland and stop it from producing its own progesterone. Second, while progestogens replace progesterone in some of its functions, they do not work as well in the progesterone receptors throughout the body and in the brain. These receptors are very precise and will only accept the real thing. Progestogens are like keys that fit the progesterone receptors but cannot open them or make them function.

This is why PMS will frequently worsen in women who take the pill. The pill is a major cause of PMS and a reason that PMS is now widespread. On the other hand, the new birth control pills are low dose, and some women with PMS do seem to feel better on the pill.

Hormonal Problems Are Common After Tubal Ligations

Some women who have had a tubal ligation, in which the fallopian tubes are tied to prevent conception, may later experience symptoms of PMS, premenopause, or both. Though some research suggests that women have no side effects from tubal ligations, there are many women who disagree.

Physicians who believe that side effects result after a tubal ligation have different opinions on why this is so. Some think these adverse symptoms are due entirely to the surgery. Others feel the onset of PMS-like symptoms may be partially due to life stresses at the time of surgery or to the hormonal upheaval of pregnancy and delivery, frequently occurring at the same time the tubes are tied.

Dr. Nils Lauersen suggests that 15 percent of women who have tubals will experience side effects of heavy bleeding, increased pelvic pain, or posttubal ligation syndrome (PMS or premenopausal symptoms). Another source suggests that up to 60 percent of women will experience premenopause within six to seven years, depending on the type of tubal ligation surgery done.

This means that a woman who has a tubal ligation at age thirty may find herself having subsequent hormonal problems, either immediately afterwards or by age thirty-six or so. Some researchers have suggested that older methods of performing tubal ligations may damage the ovarian artery that runs close to the fallopian tube. The surgery lessens or cuts off the blood flow to the ovary, causing a decrease in pituitary hormone stimulation to the ovary and a lessening of either estrogen and progesterone production, or both.

Dr. Sandra Cabot, an Australian physician and naturopath, in her book *Don't Let Hormones Ruin Your Life*, has a chapter called, "Surgical Sterilization May Be More Than You Bargained For." She states, "It is a pity that women undergoing or considering tubal ligation as a method of contraception are not always advised of all its possible long-term effects." She describes the different types of tubal ligations and concludes that the use of falope clips and filschie clips are the safest techniques. She mentions that it has been shown that blocking the blood supply to the ovarian artery causes high blood pressure in the ovary which can result in damage to the ovarian tissues. This may lead to poor ovarian function and affect the normal production of the sex hormones estrogen and progesterone.

For more information, see the separate expanded chapter on tubal ligations and the bibliography for a list of publications, which Dr. Cabot has written on hormonal problems.

PMS and Hysterectomy

Some women who didn't previously have PMS may start noticing cyclical problems after a hysterectomy, even when only the uterus is removed. So it's surprising that doctors often suggest a hysterectomy as a cure for women with PMS. Women think losing all their reproductive organs and not having periods would be absolutely wonderful, and, indeed, some women are lucky in their response to this surgery. Surgery may sometimes stop their PMS symptoms.

On the other hand, a hysterectomy may make the problem a lot worse, compounding it by adding estrogen-deficiency symptoms. Curing PMS by having a hysterectomy is a lot like playing Russian Roulette, and the odds are not good because some women have infinite difficulty adjusting their hormonal treatment afterwards.

Serious research papers has suggested hysterectomy and oophorectomy as a cure for very severe PMS. I believe this a very drastic solution which may worsen the problem, not cure it. The thesis behind this suggestion is that if women don't have ovaries, they won't ovulate, and they can't possibly have PMS, which is not true. Women can have cyclical PMS-like symptoms even if they don't ovulate (for instance, girls with PMS who cycle, but don't ovulate or menstruate a year or two before puberty; older women with PMS who have amenorrhea and don't ovulate; women with PMS who have had hysterectomies; and some rare postmenopausal women who don't have periods but still have cyclical PMS-like problems into old age).

Generally, if you already have severe hormonal problems, the less you do to irritate your hormonal set-up the better, though hysterectomy does have its place. An excellent book on this subject is *Hysterectomy: Before and After*, by Dr. Winnifred Cutler. Also read the separate chapter on hysterectomies in this book.

The Connection Between PMS and PPD

Women with PMS are very prone to having a hormonally-induced postpartum depression after pregnancy, and tend to experience quite characteristic pregnancies. One group experiences one or two trimesters of feeling exceptionally well (after the first twelve to sixteen week period of nausea). This is because their progesterone levels are very high after the sixteenth week. The other group may have difficult pregnancies, with toxemia, depression, migraines, or other complications. A history of toxemia or pre-eclampsia is very common in women with PMS.

Women with both types of pregnancies have an increased tendency to have postpartum depression. This can be mild to severe, lasting from a few days or a couple of weeks, to months, or years. Some women have postpartum depression that never seems to lift.

Just as there are different types of depression in general, different types of depression are experienced after childbirth. Symptoms of postpartum depression range from the relatively mild and short-lived "baby blues" to very severe and possibly long-lasting psychosis. Some women may need treatment with antidepressants.

If a woman has postpartum depression after one child, it does not necessarily mean she will have it after the next. But there are some women whose postpartum depression worsens with each child.

Read the separate chapter on Postpartum Depression for more detailed information.

Summary

Women who are going through PMS can lead pretty miserable lives for part of every month. They are often embarrassed by their behavior, and when their behavior improves about the time their period begins, they deny that the awful symptoms ever happened. They have an irrational hope that next month will be different, but find that when the second half of the cycle rolls around again, the same old process repeats itself. Because this denial mechanism is so strong, many women don't seek treatment until their symptoms are chronic and the effect on their life is serious.

May I encourage you to read the treatment section in this book and do something about your PMS. Your life and, consequently, the lives of those who love you and live with you can be greatly improved.

CHAPTER 6

The Birth Control Pill

Gina came to see me on the advice of her mother, a counselor who had heard me speak on the radio. Gina was depressed and very hostile, and the hostility was directed specifically towards the mother who had been so concerned about her. Gina spent most of the interview telling me about this terrible woman who had brought her into the world, but the conversation didn't seem quite rational. The mother seemed very nice.

The only factor I could see was that Gina was taking the birth control pill, and when I talked to her about the effect the pill sometimes has on the mind, she decided to go off of it, and see if she felt less depressed.

A couple of months later, I met the mother again, and asked her diplomatically how her daughter was doing. She didn't know what Gina had said to me, but told me that Gina was a different person now that she was off the pill, and they were getting on much better.

Gina didn't need hormonal treatment after stopping the pill. Her body came back to normal just by stopping it. Unfortunately, some women don't return to normal after taking the pill. The pituitary doesn't seem to function properly again, and they only find relief from their symptoms by taking hormonal-replacement therapy.

Fascinating History of the Pill
The history of the discovery of the birth control pill as told by Paul

Vaughan, a medical journalist, in *The Pill on Trial* makes for fascinating reading. Vaughan was at one time the Chief Press Officer for the British Medical Association. His book was the first one I read in the early seventies that pointed out that it was the progestin portion of the pill that caused depression.

The Pill Intended for Birth Control

The pill, of course, was produced in a concerted effort to find a new form of birth control—not for purposes of relieving the hormonal symptoms of PMS or menopause. The history Vaughan depicts is interesting because it shows the basic problem with the pill—the reason it causes PMS, and the reason it often makes PMS sufferers worse. It is made from synthetic hormones that do not exactly match the body's own hormones.

Margaret Sanger played a leading role in the history of the pill, urging the research biologist Dr. Gregory Pincus to find a new approach to contraception in the 1950s. Mrs. Stanley McCormick, a widow with a great deal of money, was to provide the funds for the research.

At the time, injections of the natural hormone progesterone were being used as a means of preventing women from ovulating. Progesterone had been synthesized from a sow's ovaries about a decade before this by a chemist named Russell Marker. Estrogen had also been isolated about that time, and was being used to treat women with dysmenorrhea (painful periods). Estrogen was also found to prevent ovulation. Professor Fuller Albright of Harvard had talked of birth control by hormonal therapy as early as 1945.

Hormones were still being manufactured from animal sources, and what was needed was a cheap and convenient way of manufacturing them in bulk. Russell Marker, a professor of organic chemistry was an extremely clever chemist, though he had a very touchy personality and had difficulty maintaining personal relationships. He stormed out of several jobs. With backing from the drug company, Parke, Davis, & Co., Marker produced a steady flow of material about the chemistry of steroids, which included the sex hormones.

Marker wanted to find a new source for the commercial manufacture of sex hormones, and he began this search in 1939. The best source he had found, to date, was a substance called sapogenin, a form of which—

sarsapogenin—was found in the sarsparilla plant. But the yield was too small to have any commercial value, so he set about finding other plants of the sarsparilla family. He felt the most likely place to find them was in the subtropical southwest of the United States and in Mexico. In 1940, Marker spent his summer vacation searching for the plant, and enlisted other botanists to help him. He apparently sifted through five tons of tropical greenery and found a plant that yielded the most sapogenin in the form of diosgenin. Its name was *cabeza de negro*, a species of wild yam.

When Marker tried to find someone to provide the capital to produce progesterone from diosgenin, he found a lukewarm response because Mexico was so far away and there was a war on. He left his teaching job and went off to Mexico City to synthesize progesterone from the wild yam plant. When he had a considerable amount, he went to a small pharmaceutical company in Mexico City called Laboratorios Hormona, run by two immigrants from Europe, and offered them four and a half pounds of progesterone, worth tens of thousands of dollars at the then current price. Marker and the two pharmacists went into business partnership and incorporated as Syntex, SA. Subsequent production of progesterone was slow to start, and tension grew between the three partners until Marker walked out yet again, taking the notes of his laboratory process with him.

A Hungarian, Dr. George Rosenkranz, continued the work Marker had begun at Syntex, and produced both progesterone and testosterone, and an adrenal hormone, desoxycorticosterone. Another chemist at Syntex, Carl Djerassi, produced the estrogens—estrone and estradiol. By the early fifties, Syntex had become the major supplier of synthetic hormones to drug houses in Europe and America.

However, there was a serious problem to overcome—progesterone, whether from animal or plant source, was ineffective when taken by mouth. At the time, it had to be given by injection. To make a birth control pill, an oral form of progesterone was needed. A chemistry professor at the University of Pennsylvania, Professor Max Ehrenstein felt that one could change the structure of progesterone and yet not change its effects.

In 1950, Carl Djerassi from Syntex, tackled the problem of creating synthetic progesterone that could be taken by mouth, the step that would lead directly to the production of the pill. The first progestagen he produced was norethisterone, a powerful testosterone derivative. At the same time, G.D. Searle & Co., in Chicago, produced a similar progestagen to norethisterone, called norethynodrel.

The Basic Problem with the Pill

At this point in the story, Vaughan points out that the progestagens and the estrogenic compounds which were in the classic birth control pill are not natural products, but synthetic adaptations with subtle variations. He says that though the differences may seem trivial on paper, they may produce gross differences in effect in the body, where the machinery is too intricate and too sensitive to be misled.

Though the pills have changed over the years, using less hormones, and, in some cases, progestagen only, they still have the same problem that Paul Vaughan described in 1970. They have molecular variations that may cause side effects in the body, including lowering of mood.

This thesis fits in with the suggestions of Drs. Katherina and Maureen Dalton in England—that while progestagens prevent ovulation and cause sloughing off of the lining of the uterus, they do not function properly in the progesterone receptors in the cells. Progestagens are like a 'key,' which fits in the progesterone receptor 'lock,' but will not 'open' it. While the progestagen is in the 'lock,' there is no room for the progesterone molecule to fit, and the overall effect is to lessen progesterone levels. Also the progestagens are very potent and may overpower the pituitary function either temporarily or permanently. This is similar to taking thyroid medication, where, above a certain dose, the pituitary may shut down, and become lazy, so that when a person goes off the thyroid medication, the pituitary function does not return.

Therefore, at one level or another, the pill may inhibit production of the body's own sex hormones, leading to a lowering of mood and the side effects of irritability and anger (and other emotional and physical symptoms) that often result from taking progestogens.

A Caveat

Having said all this against the pill, it seems as though some women do lose their PMS symptoms while taking the pill, which is why some doctors automatically put women on it. Some women also find the pill wonderful if they have painful, heavy periods, and wildly irregular cycles. Most of the women I have seen with congenital hormonal problems have had mainly adverse reactions to the pill; and I advise women that if they are subject to PMS, they probably would be better to avoid the pill and other progestagens.

CHAPTER 7

Postpartum Depression

*D*enise didn't know what depression was until her new baby was about four months old. She was sitting in her chair one night, watching television, when she felt a total body change come over her, and she soon went into a deep depression.

Nobody in her family could understand it. She and her husband had wanted the baby. The pregnancy had been fine. There seemed to be no reason why Denise should be so depressed.

It was very hard for Denise to tell anyone, even her husband, how dreadful she felt. At times, she was so angry with him and the baby that the idea of murdering them kept entering her mind. It seemed impossible to control her thoughts, and because these evil thoughts kept coming back, she felt she was going insane. It was as though she was floating outside her body watching herself—a spectator, alienated, and out of touch with reality. She felt spaced-out, exhausted, and anxious; and she was beginning to lose hope of ever returning to normal.

Denise found a sympathetic ear with her physician who had just had a baby herself and knew from experience that some mothers go through a hormonal imbalance for a while. She told Denise that she had PPD (postpartum depression).

The doctor put Denise on natural progesterone and checked her thyroid. Sure enough, Denise had borderline low thyroid, a temporary result of the dramatic changes which occur during pregnancy and delivery. The doctor said Denise might also need a little estrogen and progesterone, as well as thyroid, and, perhaps, an antidepressant. She could keep breastfeeding while on progesterone, because it was metabolized so fast, it didn't reach the milk. But if she went on estrogen or the antidepressant, she would probably have to stop breastfeeding. Fortunately, taking progesterone and thyroid were enough in Denise's case to effect a big change in her outlook. Within a couple of months, the worst was over, and she was able to go off the hormones.

Hard to Find Help with PPD

It's even harder to find enlightened treatment for postpartum depression than it is for premenstrual syndrome. The subject of PPD is barely dealt with in most baby care books. Unlike PMS which only occurs part of the month and allows a woman to function normally for most of the time, PPD is continual and without relief. It sometimes affects a woman almost twenty-four hours a day, if she has trouble with insomnia.

If a woman has not had PMS, and suddenly finds herself with severe PPD, the unexpected emotional mood swings are terrifying. She may feel as though she is living on an island on some other planet and has lost contact with the real world. Coupled with a loss of feeling, a numbness, and an inability to reach out in love to her husband and baby, this can be an incredibly painful and lonely experience.

Women with PPD frequently find themselves unable to feel anything emotionally, and it is common for them to think they don't love their husbands and that they want a divorce. The husband is often hurt and bewildered, when he becomes the target of the woman's irritability and anger.

Varying Types and Depths of PPD

According to Dr. Katherina Dalton, there are varying stages of depression after childbirth.

The Baby Blues—About half of all women suffer from this mild form of PPD, which only lasts a few hours, a few days, or a couple of weeks, and occurs shortly after delivery. It is a temporary, short-lived condition that goes away relatively quickly and is soon forgotten.

Other women suffer from extreme fatigue for the first few months of their baby's life. With a new baby, this makes life especially hard for a while. A woman may feel as though she is walking through wet concrete, but this feeling usually goes away with time. It is not accompanied by the terrifying emotional problems of serious PPD. Along with this deadening fatigue, some women also have drying of the vagina and low sex drive due to the low estrogen levels which occur after delivery.

Postpartum depression, with its exhaustion, irritability, depression, mood swings, and anger, occurs in one out of ten women. Generally, PPD begins some time during the first year after the baby is born, and, frequently, is triggered by the return of menstruation or when the mother stops breastfeeding. The intensity and length of PPD varies with individuals. While it is usually self-limiting (which means it will go away, whether treated or not, within a few months or a year), there are cases in which women have unresolved postpartum depression for many years and never fully return to health. Many women say their health broke down after a certain pregnancy.

PPD occasionally happens a long time after the delivery. I saw a woman who had no problems with her hormones until her baby was twenty-one months old. She had been breastfeeding her child, and menstruation had not returned. At twenty-one months, she weaned the child and her periods returned, bringing severe PPD and a breakdown of her immune system.

Postpartum psychosis, occurring in one in 500 to one in 3,000 women, is relatively rare but extremely severe. Such women are obviously mentally ill and may have delusions, hallucinations, mania and agitation, and deep depression. They may be suicidal or murderous. The life and safety of their babies or other members of the family may be at risk, and appeals for help should be taken seriously.

The Picture Puzzle of PPD

Dr. Alexander Hamilton, a San Francisco physician, divides PPD into two general levels, which he calls the lesser and major syndromes.

The Lesser Syndromes

These syndromes are very common and will be experienced by one third to a one half of all new mothers and one tenth of all women having their second child.

I. **Maternity Blues**—occurring day three to day ten after delivery. Symptoms include weeping episodes, insomnia, and exhaustion.

2. **Postpartum Depression**—mild to moderate depression, apparent three or more weeks after delivery. Incidence is one in ten births. Symptoms include gradual personality change, feelings of alienation, wish to divorce, problems with rearing children.

The Major Syndromes
Each of the major syndromes are characterized by inability to handle stress, apprehensiveness, sensitivity, anxiety, and fear.

1. The Early Agitated Syndrome or Puerperal Psychosis
Onset, postpartum 4-20 days. The symptoms include confusion, delirium, hallucinations, delusions, extreme bipolar mood swings, sudden mercurial changes, and potential violence. Possible cause—temporary low adrenal function because of sluggish pituitary function following childbirth.

2. The Late Depressive Syndrome/Severe Postpartum Depression
Onset three weeks after delivery. The symptoms include, insidious, slowly increasing depression, accompanied by many physical symptoms, suicidal tendencies. Possible cause—low thyroid production because of low pituitary function following childbirth.

3. The Late Mercurial Syndrome/Postpartum Psychotic Depression
Onset three to four weeks after delivery; may evolve from the other two syndromes. Moderate to severe symptoms include confusion, dullness, slow thinking, punctuated by unpredictable, explosive episodes of psychosis, with extreme agitation, hallucinations, auditory hallucinations which seem like commands, bizarre thinking and behavior, frequent amnesia about behavior. Violence, suicide, and infanticide are real concerns.

Symptoms of PPD

Agitation	Alienation	Anger
Anxiety	Ashamed	Crying jags
Confusion	Delusions	Depression
Dizziness	Drying of vagina	Euphoria
Fatigue	Fear	Forgetfulness
Futility	Guilt	Hair loss
Hallucinations	Headaches	Hopelessness
Inability to concentrate	Insomnia	Irritability

Lack of energy	Lack of motivation	Loneliness
Low self-esteem	Low sex drive	Marital conflict
Mood swings	Obsession	Panic attacks
Paranoia	Sadness	Strange thoughts
Suicidal tendencies	Swollen feet	Trance-like
Violent thoughts	Vomiting	Weak
Weight gain	Weight loss	Worry

What Happens Hormonally After Delivery

Dr. Hamilton describes the precipitous drop in serum levels of estrogen and progesterone soon after delivery, from the very high levels of pregnancy to being almost absent by the end of the first week. There is a latent period, the three-day interval after birth when symptoms are rare.

About day three, levels of bound and free cortisol drop dramatically to about a third of the predelivery levels. Levels of thyroxine also typically drop below normal, reaching a low about three weeks after delivery. These drops in hormone levels vary with the individual, though they are fairly common to all women.

Dr. Hamilton treats PPD as an endocrine problem, not as a typical depression, and designs the treatment, according to the timing, type, and severity of the symptoms.

Unpredictable Incidence in Individuals

Women often wonder, "If I had PPD once, will I get it again?" I recently saw Susan who had such a terrible time with her first child, that she decided against having any more.

Actually, unless there is a strong familial history of PPD, the incidence may be fairly random and, therefore, unpredictable. A woman could have several pregnancies without PPD, and then suddenly get it with the next child. Another woman might have PPD with her first child and dread the second, but find, with great relief, that it doesn't happen the second time around.

But, overall, women who have a history of PPD in the family, and have had it themselves, are more likely to get it again. There are some women who have severe PPD after each child, and it worsens as they get older, never fully resolving.

Those Horrible Feelings

The hardest thing for women to cope with is the emotional consequence of PPD. They feel spaced-out and alienated from those around them. They are sure that no one really understands what they are going through, and they are sometimes too ashamed to discuss their real feelings with their husbands.

Panic attacks, frequently occurring at night, along with inability to sleep, create a high level of fear and anxiety. Women may find themselves incomprehensibly sad, inexplicably angry with their husbands—alternately weeping uncontrollably, then hostile and angry. Hostility towards their baby may sweep over these women, and the urge to do the child bodily harm makes women extremely fearful and guilt-ridden. Sometimes, they become preoccupied with thoughts of gloom and death. They feel powerless to control these feelings.

Complicating the problem, most of these women are quite aware that these emotions are abnormal, but they still blame themselves. Their rational self can acknowledge that they have everything going for them—a loving husband, a beautiful new child—but they are unable to pull themselves out of the morass of depression. Sometimes they even see the PPD as a judgment on something they've done in their past. This can happen particularly if the PPD is a result of a terminated pregnancy.

Women feel that if only they had a little more self-control, they could overcome this hostility and pull themselves out of the depression, but trying to control it rationally just doesn't work. They are "out-of-control," and need sympathy, understanding, and medical help.

It Can Happen to Anyone

There is no particular type of women who is predisposed to have PPD. While family history is a factor, it can happen to any woman—regardless of age, race, social standing, religious affiliation, or previous psychiatric good health. It happens whether the child is wanted or unwanted. It is a physiologically-based problem, which happens as a result of the extreme hormonal changes during pregnancy, and it is not "just in the head."

Two Types of Pregnancy

Generally speaking, there are two distinct types of pregnancy prior to

PPD. In the first type, women may feel great during the second or third trimester. If they have previously suffered from PMS, they may find that, after the initial morning sickness, they felt the best in their lives during the rest of the pregnancy. It is normal for women to feel wonderful during pregnancy, with a characteristic glow of contentment. It's a time when, ideally, they should have fewer physical and psychological problems, and fewer allergies and infections. Unfortunately, some women who have a wonderful pregnancy, may experience PPD after delivery.

In the second type of pregnancy, women may feel sick all the way through and be troubled with depression or physical symptoms, such as breakthrough bleeding, nausea, and premature labor pains. Their physicians may be concerned about their high blood pressure because of possible pre-eclampsia (borderline toxemia). There is also a high incidence of PPD after such a pregnancy.

Both extremes of pregnancies—good and bad—may lead to PPD.

Massive Physical Changes in Pregnancy

During pregnancy, the uterus changes from the size of a small pear to the size of a football, including baby, placenta and fluid. The skeleton and body cavities are pulled out of shape, and the amount of blood which circulates is doubled, and consequently, the heart, liver, and kidneys have to work much harder.

Hormones Rise in Pregnancy

When a woman becomes pregnant, the body also goes through massive hormonal changes. For the first twelve to sixteen weeks, estrogen and progesterone are produced in the ovaries, at higher levels than normal. Then, the placenta produces thirty to fifty times the normal amount of estrogen and progesterone. (Other sources give a much higher figure.) Prolactin levels, which prepare the breasts for lactation, also rise, and so does adrenal hormone production. Four other hormones are produced only during pregnancy, including the major one, human chorionic gonadotropin (HCG). As mentioned before, if all goes well, women will blossom with the increased hormonal activity. But if the hormone levels don't rise properly, women can be miserable during pregnancy.

It has recently been discovered in Japan, that progesterone has an

MAO-inhibitor effect during pregnancy, which means that progesterone inhibits monoamine oxidase in the brain, countering depression the way the antidepressants Nardil and Parnate do. Dr. Maureen Dalton also believes this is why progesterone plays a role in lowering high blood pressure and preventing toxemia in later pregnancy.

Hormones Drop after Delivery

As mentioned earlier, after the baby and placenta are delivered, the levels of estrogen and progesterone suddenly plummet—estrogen to about 1/200th of the pregnancy levels, progesterone to zero within a week. Prolactin is still produced at high levels while the woman breastfeeds, and these high levels help inhibit the pituitary stimulation and ovarian production of estrogen and progesterone. Prolactin not only inhibits the pituitary precursor of progesterone—luteinizing hormone (LH)—but thyroid stimulating hormone (TSH) levels may also drop, because LH is chemically similar to part of the TSH. Changes in TSH levels may result in temporary thyroid problems. The four unique pregnancy hormones disappear completely, and cortisol levels also plummet.

All of the changes that take place throughout pregnancy are supposed to return to normal levels within six weeks. It is no wonder that some women don't pull out of these massive changes in their body's chemistry without problems. In fact, some women, during severe labor, actually suffer damage to their pituitary glands. Sheehans and Simmonds diseases are disorders that result from internal chemical injury to the pituitary because of pregnancy.

The Woman with PPD Needs Support

A woman's husband and family need to realize that PPD is a real problem, and that it can be a terrifying experience for the new mother. She needs to be able to talk about what she is experiencing in a nonjudgmental environment. She already feels alienated, confused, estranged, and even insane. It is hard for her to make decisions, and her family may need to help her get medical attention and follow it through. Treatment for PPD may involve several hormones and is outlined in other chapters.

CHAPTER 8

Thyroid Problems

Doreen's family includes several women with thyroid problems. Her grandmother had a goiter, and her mother, one sister, and a cousin are taking thyroid medication. Doreen started her periods late, at about age sixteen, with severe menstrual cramps. Sometimes she would go three or four months without a period and then have an extremely heavy one. Because of her family history, she had often been tested for low thyroid, but the tests always came back within the normal range, though borderline low.

She had trouble becoming pregnant and, like her mother, had two miscarriages. When I saw her, she had a six-month-old baby and was suffering from severe postpartum depression after having borderline toxemia during her pregnancy.

In Doreen's case, her thyroid seemed to be the main culprit. She was suffering from extreme exhaustion. Her hair was very dry and fell out easily. She felt the cold terribly, and her basal temperature was low.

When she went to the doctor, her thyroid tests were low this time, but she probably had been suffering from a subclinical hypothyroid condition all her life. After a few days of being on thyroid medication, she said that, impossible though it seemed, she was already feeling better.

The Thyroid-Ovary Team
The thyroid and the ovaries are indirectly connected to each other

through the control of the hypothalamus and pituitary glands. All the subordinate glands—thyroid, ovaries, adrenals, and pancreas—function more as a team than as individual units. Therefore, when one gland doesn't work properly, there is a tendency for the other glands to sympathize.

They are also directly connected to each other because the thyroid puts out a releasing factor that signals the hypothalamus to initiate the menstrual cycle. So the thyroid has a measure of control over the ovary. Conversely, the ovaries produce a type of thyroid.

Menstrual Problems Common with Low Thyroid

Women who have thyroid disorders frequently have associated menstrual problems, such as irregular cycles, painful cramps, heavy bleeding, premenstrual syndrome, endometriosis, infertility, infrequent ovulation, habitual miscarriage, difficult pregnancies, toxemia in pregnancy, postpartum depression, and premature menopause. The thyroid disorder affects women differently, just as PMS produces varying sets of symptoms in different women.

Sometimes, when a woman has PMS or postpartum depression, the major gland at fault is the thyroid. Often, when it functions at a subclinical or borderline level, nothing shows up in the normal thyroid tests. Some women lose their hormonal symptoms simply by treating the thyroid problem. Other women need more than one hormone.

But, of course, women with thyroid problems are a subgroup. Not all women with PMS also have thyroid problems, just as not all women with thyroid problems have PMS.

Subnormal Thyroid and Family History

There are many possible symptoms resulting from low thyroid, and some of the symptoms of PMS and thyroid are the same—for instance, depression, migraines, skin problems, aggression, and fatigue. But the patterns of the symptoms are different, and the overall profile is quite distinct.

A low thyroid condition can cause a wide range of symptoms, such as: feeling the cold excessively, extreme fatigue, loss of hair and eyelashes; brittle hair and nails, lizard-like skin, eczema and acne, headaches and migraines, depression, repeated infections, respiratory disorders, anemia, diabetes, heart problems, menstrual difficulties, edema in the face and ankles, and skin problems.[1]

At least half the women I see with hormonal problems have at least one close relative (frequently their mother or sister) who have a diagnosed thyroid condition, and many have several family members with thyroid problems. Often, because of their symptoms, physicians have suspected these women might be low thyroid, and have already done blood tests. Sometimes the tests did detect a problem, and those women are already taking thyroid medication.

Other women's tests show up as normal despite a family history or suspicious symptoms. Even if the levels are borderline low, they are not considered low enough to treat.

In other cases, the woman is resistant to her own thyroid, which means she apparently has enough, but it can't be used. She may be producing antibodies against the thyroid, and these are blocking the thyroid cell receptors and interfering with the function of the hormone in the cells.

Blood Tests Not Always Reliable

Many physicians are unwilling to treat a thyroid problem unless it definitely shows up in blood tests, despite the fact that research has shown blood tests are not always conclusive.[2]

This can be very frustrating for the woman whose hair is falling out and who is dying on her feet from fatigue. She may have strong, obvious symptoms of hypothyroidism, but be unable to secure treatment because the bloodwork is normal or low normal.

Testing One, Two, Three

When thyroid problems are suspected, physicians usually order a thyroid panel. This test shows blood levels of the different hormones produced in the bloodstream by the thyroid gland. Doctors often check the pituitary hormone, thyroid stimulating hormone (TSH), to see if it is high. The thyroid panel may be normal, but if the TSH is high, it means that the pituitary is producing high levels in an attempt to try to stimulate the thyroid to produce more thyroxine. In this case, the thyroid is functioning at a low level.

Doctors may stop with these tests, if they are normal. However, relying on these tests may cause the physician to miss a condition called thyroiditis. This is an inflammation of the thyroid, which causes the body to produce antibodies to fight the infection. The antibodies, in turn, attack the thyroid gland and also block the production of thyroid hormones in the bloodstream and in the cells.

The onset of Hashimoto's thyroiditis, as this disease is called, is slow. In the early stages, a thyroid panel may show high, low, or alternately high and low levels; but often the levels are normal. The thyroid gland may be rather swollen or have nodules on it, or it may feel normal.

A test for thyroid antibodies will show positive for thyroiditis, though the level of antibodies may fluctuate from test to test, and the intensity of the symptoms may not correspond with how high or low the antibodies are.

It may also be helpful to test the level of TRH, the hypothalamic releasing hormone that notifies the pituitary to produce TSH. Sometimes this hormone will show low when the others don't.

Six Common Denominators
In the 1930s, Dr. Broda Barnes completed a Ph.D. in physiology, specializing in the thyroid, and later taught endocrinology at the University of Chicago. Subsequently, he also did an MD, and found in his medical practice that many of his patients had low thyroid problems, though their symptoms varied a great deal. Dr. Barnes found six common denominators in his mild cases of hypothyroidism:
1. Subnormal temperature (below 97.8° F)—sufferers feel the cold deep inside, especially the hands and feet.
2. Fatigue, particularly on rising and in the afternoon with more energy at night.
3. Drowsiness
4. Depression
5. Female problems
6. Recurrent infections

Common Symptoms
Symptoms often found in people with subclinical low thyroid include:
Allergies
Arthritis

Asthma

Brittle and ridged nails

Cold extremities

Colitis or constipation

Confusion, inability to think clearly, lack of concentration, poor memory, Slowness in speech or movements, slurred speech

Decreased sweating

Depression, and other emotional problems, including paranoid thoughts, even psychosis

Diabetes or hypoglycemia

Dry, coarse, rough, scaly skin

Dry, brittle hair, fine hair, hair that falls out easily

Energy pattern—a tendency to wake up slowly, fatigued in the afternoon, and feeling best at night after 8 p.m. (night person)

Excessively high or low blood pressure

Fatigue, listlessness, languor, indolence, lack of endurance, muscle weakness

Formication or crawling feelings on skin

Headaches and migraines

Heart irregularities—high cholesterol, rapid or slow pulse rate, palpitations, murmur, mitral valve prolapse, family history of stroke or heart attack

Hoarseness

Inability to tolerate extremes of temperature

Insomnia

Irritability

Low sex drive

Menstrual cramps, excessive flow, irregular menstruation, infertility, habitual miscarriage, toxemia in pregnancy, endometriosis

Peripheral neuritis, carpal tunnel syndrome-like symptoms

Recurrent colds

Respiratory problems—tonsillitis, sinusitis, ear, and mastoid infections

Skin problems, such as boils, eczema, psoriasis, and acne

Slowing down of the circulation, which may cause fluid retention, and edema of the eyes and ankles

A list of symptoms is by no means an adequate basis for diagnosis. However, a woman with hormonal problems who has a group of these symptoms may be a likely candidate for hypothyroidism. As with PMS, remember, nobody has every symptom, and some have only a few.

The Basal Temperature Test
Dr. Barnes developed the basal temperature and basal metabolism tests for low thyroid (but found the latter to be unreliable). Because of his influence, the basal temperature test was featured in the *Physician's Desk Reference* and was used for years to detect low thyroid problems.

When blood tests came into prominence, the basal temperature test went out of fashion. Stress, anxiety, allergies, low pituitary or low adrenal function, and slower heartrate from athletic exercise can also lower the body temperature. Nevertheless, the basal temperature test is still helpful in pointing out the likelihood of a subclinical thyroid problem.

How to Take Your Basal Temperature
Dr. Barnes felt that the best time for taking this test is immediately upon awakening in the morning. Shake down a basal thermometer and put it on the bedside table the night before. As soon as you awaken, put the thermometer under your armpit for ten minutes by the clock. Oral temperatures are often misleading because any sinus or respiratory infection will elevate the temperature of the mouth.

The normal basal temperature is between 97.8°F and 98.1°F. If your temperature is consistently below 97.8°F, you may have low thyroid activity.

Another method of taking the basal temperature is to do it at about 8:00 p.m. when the thyroid levels are at their highest.

A ten-day average for taking your temperature is recommended, but it is a good idea to take your temperature for a whole month. Women who menstruate should note the results particularly on the second and third day of their period because their temperature fluctuates throughout the menstrual cycle.

The APICH Syndrome

Imagine your body as a complicated engine with many different pieces making up the whole. The body, functioning at its best, is like a well-oiled machine, but, like a machine, parts may have been poor to start with (heredity) or wear out later. When the parts break down, the whole machine doesn't run properly. Sometimes the problem is fairly simple and easily fixed. At other times, more than one part goes wrong, and the problem is more complex and difficult to repair. The APICH Syndrome is a hormonal disease in which more than one gland is not functioning properly.

The name APICH was coined by Drs. Nathan Becker and Phyllis Saifer from the Bay Area in California. It describes a polyendocrine, immune system dysfunction. Polyendocrine means that more than one endocrine gland is affected. The immune system is frequently affected as well, leading to accompanying allergies and respiratory symptoms.

According to Drs. Becker and Saifer, ten times more women than men suffer from the APICH Syndrome. I see many women who identify very strongly with the description of this disease.[3]

The Body Turns Against Itself

Women with the APICH syndrome have an infection resulting in inflammation of one or more of their glands. They may have thyroiditis (inflammation of the thyroid) and, along with it, oophoritis (inflammation of the ovaries). The body produces antibodies in order to protect itself against the infection. Unfortunately, these antibodies, produced by the body for a good purpose, can turn against the body and damage it. A similar process occurs with rheumatic fever, where antibodies which the body produces to fight the infection, may damage the heart valve and produce heart disease later in life.

With thyroiditis and oophoritis, the antibodies attack the thyroid and the ovaries on three levels—in the gland itself, in the bloodstream, and in the cells (the antibodies block the hormone receptors).

Hashimoto's thyroiditis may cause, alternately, hyperthyroidism (high thyroid levels) or hypothyroidism (low thyroid levels). Thyroid blood levels may fluctuate high to low, but eventually the levels settle to low. Frequently, however, the thyroid blood panel and TSH are normal. The thyroid size may be normal to somewhat enlarged, and nodules may be present.

The onset of this disease can be very slow and symptoms may take years to appear.

Symptoms of the APICH Syndrome

Women with the APICH syndrome may have multiple and divergent symptoms, including:

Afternoon fatigue	Allergies	Autoimmune disease
Black under eyes	Bladder frequency	Blurred vision
Candida	Coarse skin	Colds
Depression	Difficulty swallowing	Edema or swelling
Eye sensitivity	Headaches	Inappropriate fatigue
Irritability	Low blood pressure	Low temperature
Menstrual problems	Mood swings	Morning fatigue
Nasal congestion	Needs to sleep a lot	Night person
PMS	Pallor	Photophobia
Poor concentration	Premature gray hair	Respiratory problems
Ridged nails	Ringing in ears	Short-term memory loss
Sleep disturbances	Sore throat	Suicidal tendencies
Thin, brittle hair	Weight fluctuation	

Intolerance to temperature change—chills easy, wilts in hot weather

History of the APICH Patient

Women with these symptoms may also show certain tendencies in their history, such as:

- a family history of thyroid disease, goiters, thyroidectomies or irradiation of the thyroid
- acne
- alcoholism
- eczema
- endometriosis
- fibrocystic breasts
- hypoglycemia
- irradiation for acne, thymus, birth marks, tumors
- juvenile onset diabetes
- pernicious anemia
- postpartum depression
- psychiatric problems
- mitral valve prolapse
- mononucleosis
- nervous breakdown

- rheumatoid arthritis
- tonsillitis, tonsillectomy
- toxemia in pregnancy

Footnotes

1.   Anyone who suspects they might be hypothyroid, should read *Hypothyroidism: The Unsuspected Disease*, by Dr. Broda Barnes. It goes into detail on the many symptoms of low thyroid disease. Though it was published in 1979, it is very readable, and much of it is still relevant.

2.   Broda Barnes says that the ideal test for thyroid function is not even possible because the amount of thyroid hormone needs to be measured on the inside of each cell in the body, an impossible task because there are billions of cells in the body, and analyses could not even be done with computers. See *Hypothyroidism*, pp. 36, 37. Dr. Barnes also says that all the tests done by measuring the amount of thyroid in the gland itself or in the bloodstream don't do what counts—measure what is available and working in the cells. These attempts are something like trying to work out what a thrifty man's spending habits are by looking at what he has in his bank account. How much thyroid there is in the thyroid gland or bloodstream tells us nothing about how much thyroid is spent in the cells. *Ibid.*, pp. 41,42.

3.   "Allergy and Autoimmune Endocrinopathy: APICH Syndrome," by Phillis L. Saifer and Nathan Becker was published overseas in a collection of medical articles. I do not know the source.

CHAPTER 9

Premenopause and Menopause

*A*nn had always been a fairly easygoing person with mild PMS. She took her pregnancies in stride and was only mildly tearful for a couple of hours after her delivery. It was a dreadful shock to her at about age forty-eight, when her emotions suddenly seemed to fly to pieces. At that time she was still having infrequent periods, with a light flow. She often felt hot, particularly at night, and she would occasionally wake up soaking wet. She found herself crying easily and becoming overanxious about small issues.

She had other unusual experiences. Sometimes, if she suddenly rose from her chair, she felt dizzy and had to grab onto something to keep from falling over. She began to think she was getting arthritis— her joints were stiff with fleeting pains that darted from one joint to another. She told her husband. "I not only ache in the joints, but right in the middle of my bones, between the wrist and the elbow and mid-thigh."

When Ann became increasingly confused and started crying all the time, her husband, Jim, began to worry. Maybe she was getting Alzheimer's disease. But when she became so morbid that she kept talking about wanting to die, Jim was frightened enough to call their family doctor.

"My wife suddenly seems to be losing her mind. She's going to pieces emotionally and physically. I'm worried sick about her. She's always been so calm and normal."

Her physician could tell something was wrong as soon as he saw Ann. Her skin was pale, her face drawn, and there were black hollow circles under her eyes. Her hair seemed dull and lifeless. Her digestion appeared disturbed, and she was losing weight.

Some physicians might have put her on tranquilizers or sent her to a psychiatrist. Ann was fortunate that her doctor recognized she was probably going through menopause and needed medical attention.

Not the Same for Everyone

Menopause takes place when a woman's ovaries run out of eggs and estrogen-producing cells in the ovaries, and stop producing major levels of estrogen. This is not usually an abrupt cessation. More commonly, estrogen levels tend to drop slowly from the mid-thirties onwards. Symptoms can be subtle, gradual, abrupt, mild, or severe. At one end of the scale are the women who have no symptoms, and at the other extreme, women can be totally dysfunctional. In the middle, the intensity and type of symptoms can vary tremendously.

Whether to Take Estrogen—a Vital Decision

Whatever a woman's symptoms may be, **every woman needs information about menopausal changes because the health consequences are so vital in later years.** Many women don't want to take hormones at menopause, but that may sometimes be a poor decision.

Many women want "to go through menopause naturally." It sounds like a nice idea, and it's a possibility for a significant number. But those who do it should know why they are doing it, and whether they are making the correct decision. Sometimes the cards are stacked against a woman going through menopause easily, for various reasons—genes, hormonal make-up, early diet, physical habits over the years, and past sicknesses. Women who give up estrogen because of side effects may only need some adjustment to their medication.

A woman who grits her teeth through night sweats and joint pains, determined never to go on hormones, may be making a great mistake. Also, women can have severe, hidden, physical effects, such as heart disease and osteoporosis, but no obvious symptoms until a fairly late stage.

In Denial

Sometimes, ignoring the issues of menopause is a refusal to face the fact that we're getting older. For many women, aging and losing their attractiveness is synonymous with losing their power. The idea of being dependent on hormones also makes them feel they are giving up control.

The change of life is a fact of life, and it's no use denying it because you don't like the idea of getting older. The big question is not "Will you age?" but "How will you age?" Who wants to spend her sunset years lying on a couch or lining up at doctor's offices and visiting hospitals, wishing they would die. You could, if you don't take time to inform yourself about these issues.

The Age of Poise

There are many things about menopause that make it a positive change—a time to look forward to, not dread. Many women in their forties and fifties start a new and happy phase of their lives. They no longer have to nurture their families and are able to spend time developing their own individuality and talents. They often flourish physically and have high levels of energy. It's the age of poise.

Obvious, Vague, and Hidden Symptoms

But this is not always so. Some women have an extremely difficult time going through menopause. They may suffer from all sorts of symptoms, including unpleasant emotional effects from the loss of estrogen in the brain, resulting in inability to think clearly, memory loss, depression, and fatigue. Their symptoms are so obvious, that they naturally seek help.

For other women, the effects of menopause are vague and insidious, and the onset of symptoms is hidden and gradual. Many perimenopausal women have gradual onset of estrogen-deficiency problems, including osteoporosis and heart disease, which are often not discovered until it's too late. Over half of all women die of heart attacks, and they are more likely to die during the first one than men, because they have narrower blood vessels.

Osteoporosis (brittling of the bones) is the third leading killer of women aged sixty and over. When women fracture their hips in old age, it's not that they fall over and break their bones. Their bones break, and then they fall over. Many do not survive a year after such a fall, due to the formation of blood clots in the lung or pneumonia from prolonged bed rest. The dramatic rise in incidence of heart disease and osteoporosis in postmenopausal women is directly related to estrogen loss at menopause.

Making an Intelligent Decision

Every woman needs to be able to make an intelligent decision about whether she should take estrogen after a certain age. She needs to find out what will happen to her if she requires estrogen and doesn't take it. What are the benefits and risks? Does estrogen really cause cancer? Are nutrition, herbs, and exercise adequate?

Most Women Better Off on Estrogen

Studies show that the majority of women would be better off to take hormonal-replacement therapy long-term. Unfortunately, women are not always told why this is so, because some doctors don't have time to spend with them individually. Many women stop taking estrogen because they are tired of having periods past menopause (they don't need to have them), or because they have side effects (adjustments can be made). Or they think they are through the worst of menopause and no longer need estrogen. They do not know that when they go off estrogen, it's not long before the benefits disappear.

Things Are Different Now

Things have changed for women this century. Because of birth control, they have fewer pregnancies and more periods. They ovulate more often and use up their eggs and estrogen-producing cells faster. This is probably a main reason estrogen levels begin to dip in the mid- to late-thirties.

Added to this is the fact of increasing longevity. The average woman may now live thirty years or more past menopause—a long period of time without adequate levels of estrogen.

The Process of Menopause

In order to begin understanding the health issues a woman faces at menopause, let's briefly review the process of change from puberty to menopause. We mentioned in the chapter on the endocrine system, that before a female baby is born, all the eggs she will ever have are already present in her two ovaries. At birth, a baby may have from 500,000 to 5,000,000 eggs in her ovaries. (These figures vary according to the source of information.) Probably, women are born with different amounts of eggs, and this may depend on a genetic factor.

From birth, the eggs begin to die off. By puberty, the numbers are down to about 200,000-300,000 eggs. They lessen each menstrual cycle, when, not just one or two, but from twenty to several hundreds of eggs are used up in the production of estrogen. Only one or two eggs per cycle come to maturity. The rest die. Likewise, the estrogen-producing cells in the ovaries are gradually used up.

Estrogen Gradually Declines Before Menopause

As mentioned, in previous ages, women had more pregnancies and fewer menstrual periods—only about fifty in their lifetime. Now, women have fewer pregnancies and more periods—about 400 periods in their lifetime. As you can see, ovulation causes the loss of hundreds of eggs, month by month. This must make a considerable difference to some contemporary women whose estrogen levels go into an earlier decline than they might have in previous generations, a decline which may gradually become more noticeable from their thirties onwards. They may not actually go through menopause until their forties or fifties, but the gradual decline in their estrogen levels may begin ten or fifteen years before their periods actually stop.

The Age of Menopause Varies

The average age for women going through menopause naturally is about 51.4 years, but a small proportion of women at both ends of the scale end their periods earlier or later. About 7 to 10 percent of women spontaneously and abruptly stop their periods in their thirties. I have met women who stopped menstruating as early as ages 27, 28, and 31. Their mothers and grandmothers stopped at a similar age, so there is, no doubt, a genetic factor.

At the other end of the scale, a small number of women stop their periods around age sixty. Diet can affect the age the periods begin and end, because menstruation is not triggered until a woman's body achieves a certain proportion of body fat. Therefore, women who eat more animal fat tend to start menstruating earlier and to finish later than those who are on a vegetarian diet.

Surgical Menopause

Many women go through "premature menopause" after having a tubal ligation which may damage the ovarian artery, and by reducing the blood flow, lessen the levels of FSH and estrogen. Other women become premenopausal or menopausal after having the uterus removed. Approximately half of all women in the U.S. have a hysterectomy by the age of sixty, and the average age for hysterectomy is thirty-five. Many of these hysterectomies are probably unnecessary.

While it is obvious that women losing one or two of their ovaries will suffer from estrogen deficiency, it is also true that women who have just the uterus or even a fallopian tube removed may go through premature menopause. At one time, women were told that if a portion of one ovary was left after a hysterectomy, they would produce adequate estrogen until menopause.

This is not always true. During removal of the uterus, a portion of the uterine/ovarian artery is severed, which means up to 65 percent of the blood flow to the ovary is diminished. Since hormones travel through the blood stream from the pituitary to the ovary, this can make quite a difference in the estrogen levels of some women.

A Process, Not a Point

So, while the average woman may have periods until her fifties, many women will start the process much earlier for one reason or another. While they may not actually stop their periods until ten or fifteen years later, they may suffer from a gradual hormonal decline, and may drift into a chronic depression, with low self-esteem, headaches, anxiety attacks and sleep disturbances while they still have relatively regular menstrual cycles. Often they will have bleeding irregularities of some sort. The emotional problems are the most troubling for women to deal with, but the hidden physical processes can also be very devastating.

The Wellspring Runs Dry

Estrogen has had a lot of bad press and has been treated as an enemy rather than a friend. But think for a while on those attributes of spirit and body that make a young woman beautiful and feminine—energy and joy, soft skin, lustrous hair, clear eyes, good muscle tone, strong bones, and healthy teeth. Estrogen, with its 300 functions in the female body, is largely responsible for these qualities, and is the most important hormone for a woman, just as testosterone is for a man. It makes sense that when estrogen starts to decline, a woman is profoundly affected in many ways.

Dr. Norman Beals likes the illustration his physician father taught him. In 1628 a group of physicians met at a conference in Paris to discuss the female disease in which "the wellspring dried up." These physicians noted how women's bodies began to crumble from the inside out, affecting their skin, their bones, their mucous membranes—in fact, all their tissues. The symbolism of the drying up of the wellspring is a good description of the ravages of menopause. The Bible, similarly, describes a woman's reproductive system as a fountain. At menopause, the fountain often runs dry.

The Salmon Run

Add to this the illustration of the salmon run. The salmon make its dramatic struggle upstream against all odds. It arrives at the place where it was conceived and, then, spawns and dies, and the cycle begins again.

If you think of a woman as a biological organism, it's as though, once she has had her children, nature loses interest in her. Her estrogen production drops, and she begins to return to dust, literally to begin the process of aging and death. Her skin and hair dry; her mucous membranes—linings of the nose and mouth, esophagus, intestinal tract, bladder, and vagina—thin and become irritated; her bones crack, crumble, and begin to disintegrate. Her cardiovascular system loses its elasticity, and the cholesterol level rises. Muscles become stringy. Joints become swollen.

The process is gradual. No one ends up a pile of dust, and it doesn't happen in six months. But, while the picture is exaggerated, the direction is accurate. The picture of some poor woman falling to pieces before your eyes is rather amusing, and a lot of women laugh at the idea, whenever I speak on this subject. But some women suffer from these universal aches and pains, and it's no joke.

Nature's Provision Doesn't Always Work

Nature provides for the production of lower levels of weaker estrogens after menopause through the breakdown of ovarian and adrenal androgens, and these should ideally be adequate for the nonmenstruating woman. But this is only really successful for women with superior genes, who have had good dietary and health habits throughout their lives, particularly in childhood.

Another factor that is frequently out of a woman's control is the amount of stress in her life. Grief over loss of a spouse, involvement in a driving accident, being a victim of violent crime, and other emotionally draining experiences around menopause may exhaust the adrenals, which are not meant to handle stress for long periods of time.

The ovary is made to last about fifty years at the most. The adrenals may function optimally another twenty years, if you are lucky, says Australian physician, Sandra Cabot. This is not so bad if you only live a short while. At the height of the Roman Empire, women only lived to an average of twenty-three years. At the turn of this century, women only lived to an average of about fifty. Now the average age is over eighty. Of course, the picture of the average age in women is distorted because of deaths at birth, childhood, adolescence, and during childbirth. There have always been old women. But Dr. Cabot says that in the year 2050, the world will be full of little old ladies, and, under present conditions, half of them would have broken hips.

Postmenopausal health—how you will feel and function after your late fifties—is a vital concern for all women.

The Three Stages of Menopause

The perimenopause (the whole process) often begins in a woman's late forties, though it can happen much earlier. Often women begin menopause about the same time as their mother, and they may experience menopause similarly, as far as symptoms are concerned.

There are three general stages:

1. Premenopause

A woman who did not have previous hormonal problems may begin to notice premenopausal changes between the ages of thirty-five and forty-five, or even younger. As her ovaries gradually decrease in function, her periods may become irregular, infrequent, or more frequent. She may have a period two or three weeks apart, then another six to eight weeks apart. The flow may also change, with lighter, more watery bleeding, and less clotting because of reduced progesterone. A woman may bleed very heavily, with clotting for one or two days, and then have several days of spotting. Another may have spotting prior to menstruation for several days. Sometimes women experience the onset or worsening of PMS at this time. Others have a gradual decline in mood, and experience mild depression, low self-esteem, crying spells, anxiety, sleep disturbances, and frequent fatigue.

2. Menopause

Menopause occurs when the ovaries run out of eggs, and the periods stop completely which, for the average woman, happens about age fifty-one. When periods have stopped for a full year, menopause is considered complete. However, a woman should use birth control faithfully for about two years after her periods have ended, to avoid a possible pregnancy.

A blood test of the levels of FSH (follicle stimulating hormone) may confirm that a woman is through menopause. FSH is very high before puberty and after menopause. Once the levels are over forty, a woman is considered menopausal (though this does not mean a woman could not suddenly ovulate and become pregnant). FSH levels may go up to over 100. Some people believe the norms for FSH are far too high, and that women are actually estrogen-deficient at much lower levels.

3. Postmenopause

After menopause is complete, a variety of physiological changes take place—lasting about three years for some women, in others less. An average woman, ending her periods at age fifty-one, may experience hot flashes and vaginal dryness from age forty-eight on, and start having bladder problems (burning, infections, urgency, frequency) by age fifty-four, followed by the onset of osteoporosis and heart disease by age approximately fifty-eight.

What Is Happening?

Around menopause, the ovaries begin to fail as estrogen cells and eggs diminish and the period finally ceases. Low blood levels of estrogen may cause the pituitary to compensate by producing very high levels of FSH at this time. Ovulation may cease, but estrogen levels could stay very high for a while, while progesterone production is minimal or nonexistent. At this time, women may have very heavy periods and may need progesterone to avoid hyperplasia (heavy buildup of the lining of the uterus).

Women who go for months at a time without periods also probably need progesterone. If they are producing high levels of estrogen at this time of their lives, and are not ovulating, they will develop endometrial hyperplasia, and are at risk of developing endometrial cancer.

How Long Does Menopause Last?

The time that it takes for a woman to complete the process of menopause may vary a great deal. Perimenopause can begin and end quickly; a woman may just suddenly cease having periods and have no other symptoms of menopause. Or, at the other extreme, menopause can be a process lasting thirty-five or more years. Some women experience hot flashes years before their periods cease, and still have them in their seventies.

The Passage Through Menopause

The average lifespan for American women has increased dramatically over the last few decades, with the result that a larger number of women are facing the changes associated with menopause and are confronted with its problems.

While most women, today, expect to go through menopause,

their individual passage through it varies tremendously. The following are examples of the variety of ways in which women experience menopause:

The Fortunate Few

Some women live their whole lives without knowing what hormonal problems are all about. They breeze through their periods, don't experience premenstrual syndrome, have little trouble during or after pregnancy, may go on the pill, have a tubal ligation, or a hysterectomy—all without side effects. About one in ten women go through menopause overnight, just stopping their periods and having no associated symptoms. They are the fortunate few.

The Average Experience

The typical woman experiences some discomfort through menopause and is aware of hormonal changes in her body, but these changes do not disrupt her life. Her periods may be late or early, short or long, light or heavy; they may stop and start spasmodically, or vanish for months and return. Such a woman may experience some discomfort from hot flashes and have depression, mood swings, insomnia, and loss of sexual drive. The average woman may have completed menopause in a couple of years.

Women Who Have Had Hormonal Problems Before

Other women may have had hormonal problems, starting with PMS, from puberty onwards. Their mothers and grandmothers had it; their sisters, aunts, and cousins all have the familiar pattern of cyclical symptoms before their periods.

Some women who suffer from years of PMS go through the transition of menopause very easily; but for some PMS sufferers, menopause marks a worsening and deepening of the hormonal problems they've battled for many years.

A Drastic Change

Some women have sudden and drastic menopause at a younger age than usual as a result of one or more of the following reasons:

I.   Having a hysterectomy or ovarian surgery (removal of ovary, uterus, tubes, or any combination).

2. Having a tubal ligation (some methods seem to lead to premature menopause). Other abdominal surgery that affects the ovarian blood supply can also trigger problems.

3. Ovarian failure (8 percent of women experience spontaneous menopause before the age of forty for genetic reasons, and others go through it as a consequence of autoimmune disease).

4. Chemotherapy, used in treating cancer, can throw a woman into menopause; as can Tamoxifen, used for breast cancer.

5. The use of Lupron and Synarel to treat endometriosis puts women into instant chemical menopause, and the effects are occasionally permanent.

The Late Shocker

Some women who have never experienced PMS or postpartum depression and who are going through menopause "naturally," are unpleasantly surprised, at about age fifty, by strong hot flashes, night sweats, fatigue, muscle aches, and a host of other physical problems. Emotional problems, such as depression, irritability, anxiety, and phobias, may also occur, and the mental anguish can be severe. Menopause can also herald the onset of alcoholism, and a few women may attempt or achieve suicide.

Some Typical Perimenopausal Symptoms

Changes in bleeding, heavy bleeding, irregular cycles, missed cycles, light bleeding, clotting

Anxiety, fear, depression, irritability, anger, rebellion, crying jags, panic attacks

Fatigue, loss of energy

Low self-esteem

Suicidal ideation

Inability to tolerate frustration

Inappropriate emotional responses

Low noise tolerance

Sleep disturbances, insomnia, sleepiness

Inability to concentrate, confusion, short-term memory loss

Drying and thinning of the gastrointestinal tract—constipation, ulceration, stomach pain, colitis, diarrhea, gas

Bladder infections, frequency and urgency of urination, burning, incontinence

Vaginal dryness,

Low sex drive, painful intercourse, reduction of fantasy, lack of lubrication during sex, diminished orgasms, lessened skin response

Hot flashes, night sweats, chills

Dizziness

Low blood sugar, trembling

Numbness, tingling, crawling feelings on skin

Dry, wrinkling skin, loss of collagen, sagging breasts

Dry, thinning hair, growth of facial hair, male pattern of hair on body

Brittle, slow-growing, and grooved nails

Osteoarthritis, bone thinning and loss, loss of height, shifting joint pains, joint degeneration, backache, midbone pains, muscle cramps and spasms, muscle weakness, and loss of strength

Rapid heartrate, palpitations, heart pain, increased cholesterol, high blood pressure, shortness of breath

Headaches, migraines, nausea

Dark, gloomy circles under the eyes

Weight loss or gain

The Hot Flash

Most women will have hot flashes during menopause—some say two out of three, others three out of four, others nine out of ten. Half the women lose them in a year. A third lose them in two to three years. Other women may have them for five, ten, fifteen, or even twenty years. Two to three percent have them until the day they die.

Some women have flashes three or four times a day. Others have thirty, forty, or more a day, one after the other. Some women feel the flash mainly in the face, some from the chest up, others from the feet up. Hot flashes last from a few seconds to five minutes. They vary from a mildly warm feeling to very uncomfortable, profuse sweating, followed by chills. They are often associated with dizziness and palpitations.

Hot flashes are usually worse at night, developing into night sweats. Some women become so badly soaked that they have to change clothes and bedding more than once each night.

Hot flashes may be due more to changes in levels of luteinizing hormone (LH) or norepinephrine than a lack of estrogen. But women born without ovaries or those with nonfunctioning ovaries do not experience hot flashes. Giving estrogen usually stops hot flashes, so the theory is of little practical consequence.

Osteoporosis and Osteomalacia

Osteoporosis is brittling of bones, and osteomalacia is loss of bone density. Both are common problems in postmenopausal women because of diminishing estrogen and progesterone levels and subsequent calcium loss. Women who are most at risk for osteoporosis are those with a strong genetic factor, those who ate a lot of high protein foods in their early years, and those who smoke.

Diet all through life is important, but it is particularly important when young because one starts to experience calcium loss much earlier. Women who eat large amounts of animal products, particularly in their childhood, teens, and twenties, pave the way for bone problems in later years. When more than 15 percent of the diet consists of protein, the kidneys require seven times as much water as normal to excrete it. So minerals in the bones, including calcium, are flushed out with the urine, and this bone damage from calcium loss is irreversible.

Vegetarians, by contrast, tend to have sturdy bones. In countries where the diet is low in dairy products and meat, the incidence of osteoporosis is also low. Interestingly, women in these countries are on a relatively low-calcium diet.

Smokers have lower estrogen levels because smoking causes the liver to metabolize estrogen faster, and so they generally go through menopause three or four years earlier. If women who smoke take hormone-replacement therapy, they get little or no benefit from it, and will have a high incidence of osteoporosis. (Ninety-four percent of women with spinal collapse are smokers.)

Bone Loss Most Severe at Menopause

Bone-loss begins usually about age 35, when estrogen levels begins to drop, and women start skipping ovulation occasionally. But for many women the bone loss is most severe around menopause (especially during the first two to seven years after menopause). If a woman goes through menopause at age fifty-one, she may begin having fractures by age fifty-seven. Those who go through menopause earlier will get osteoporosis earlier.

The consequences are serious. A woman's health, well-being, and mobility in her later years may be ruined by crumbling of her bone structure. One in four older women can expect to suffer at least one broken bone as a consequence of osteoporosis. Osteoporosis afflicts up to a third of American women over the age of sixty and leads to 1.3 million fractures a year. Incidence of fractures rises dramatically with increasing age. By age seventy, 50 percent of all women will have had fractures due to osteoporosis. By age eighty-five, 33 percent of all women will have had a hip fracture. Among women with osteoporosis, 88 percent will experience a fracture at some time, and 98 percent will eventually have hip fractures.

Over 60,000 women a year die from complications of osteoporosis. A woman breaks a hip or leg because of bone weakness. She has surgery and bed rest because the break won't mend and then develops a blood clot in the lung or an infection, or pneumonia, which leads to death. Because of these statistics, many physicians feel most women should begin estrogen therapy at or before menopause.

Who Is at Risk for Osteoporosis?
Osteoporosis can occur in women of any size, shape, and color. But the following are particularly at risk.
- Slight, small-boned, fair-skinned women, particularly of Northern European or Asian descent (blacks have the least tendency, genetically, to osteoporosis)
- Women who have either a natural or artificial menopause, before the age of forty
- Women whose female relatives became shorter in old age (i.e., have history of osteoporosis)
- Women who were heavy meat-eaters in their childhood, teens, and twenties
- Women who have been on lots of diets, particularly high-protein diets
- Women on low-calcium diets

- Women who smoke
- Women who drink a lot of alcohol
- Women who drink a lot of caffeine
- Women who have a sedentary life-style (the bones need the pressure of at least two hours standing and exercising each day)
- Some women with thyroid or parathyroid disorders
- Women who use too high a dose of thyroid medication
- Women who use cortisone long-term
- Women with hormone imbalances that affect calcium absorption
- Women who use a lot of aluminum-containing antacids
- Women with periodontal disease

Marathoners at Risk

Women who are largely sedentary and exercise too little are at higher risk for osteoporosis. So are those at the other end of the exercise scale—the marathoners.

Studies have found that marathoners have a high incidence of osteoporosis because exercise reduces the proportion of their body fat. Since some estrogen is produced in the fat cells of the body, their estrogen levels diminish, and menstruation may cease. This leads to loss of calcium and brittling of the bones.

For proper calcium absorption, the bones need pressure, and women need to be on their feet at least two hours a day, preferably moving. Some women cannot do vigorous exercise because of the exhaustion that accompanies their hormonal problems, and walking with friends would be a good choice for them.

The Pros and Cons of Being Overweight

Obese women have an advantage against osteoporosis since they produce more estrogen in the fatty tissues than thinner women. Of course, overweight women also have a higher risk of diabetes, and heart disease. And it is the women with android obesity (fat around the middle) who produce unbound estrogens that are believed to be connected with breast cancer.

Women who are at high risk for osteoporosis should begin estrogen therapy at or before menopause to counteract bone loss, and most of these women need to take estrogen for life.

Alternative Drug Treatment for Osteoporosis

In the first printing of this book, I confused etidronate disodium, a drug used to reverse damage from osteoporosis, with fluoride compounds used for the same purpose. I had been told that fluoride compounds have been found to make the outer bone more brittle and more liable to splinter. I attributed the fluoride problem to etidronate disodium, and I regret the error.

While etidronate appears initially to reduce fractures and increase bone mass, Dr. John Lee says it interferes with the body's mechanism for producing new bone. Over several years, results are less impressive and fractures increase. For more information on osteoporosis, contact Dr. Lee for his book on progesterone and cassettes about osteoporosis. See address in "Further Recommended Reading," page 283.

Uterine and Endometrial Cancer

Many women who die from uterine cancer have never taken estrogen. Some have a genetic tendency to endometrial cancer. Others who ovulate infrequently are at higher risk for this type of cancer, because they produce high levels of estrogen but no progesterone to oppose the estrogen. Unopposed estrogen builds up the lining of the uterus and can lead to hyperplasia and subsequent precancerous or cancerous lesions. Women who ovulate infrequently should probably be on progesterone to counteract the effect of too much estrogen stimulation.

In the 1970s, incidence and deaths from cancer of the uterus showed an increase because women were given large doses of more potent synthetic estrogens continuously over a long period of time, without countering their effect with progesterone. Over a period of about eight years, taking estrogen without progesterone causes a buildup of the endometrial lining, and may bring on precancerous changes and, eventually, full-blown cancer. However, this type of cancer, caused by taking too much estrogen, is considered a "good" cancer, because it is rarely fatal and survival rates are very good.

The number of annual deaths from endometrial cancer is usually stated as around 3,200 to 3,900. A recent study from Duke University has suggested a substantial increase, but, at this point, most experts hold to the old numbers. There is no doubt that the use of with added progestin or progesterone. If she takes progestin in adequate doses with estrogen she will have less uterine cancer and be better protected against endometrial cancer than if she was not on hormones. It is thought that postmenopausal doses of estrogen encourages better health because the cells are strengthened, and the body becomes more resistant to disease.

Heavy Bleeding

Sometime during her menopause, it is common for a woman's period to become lighter and more irregular. However, many women have heavy bleeding, which is also considered normal because it is so common. Physicians like to check out irregular bleeding because of the association with endometrial cancer. Other reasons for bleeding abnormalities include:

1. Imminent or actual ovarian failure, when the ovary produces insufficient eggs or estrogen-producing cells. When ovarian estrogen diminishes, the pituitary gland puts out high levels of FSH to compensate. FSH overstimulates the ovaries, leading to **high levels of estrogen.** This builds up the lining of the uterus, and heavy bleeding is the result. While these women still ovulate, they may continue to have regular periods with a flow that is very heavy and full of clots because of high estrogen levels.

2. **Low levels of estrogen** can also cause breakthrough bleeding because the endometrium cannot adhere to the uterine wall, and the lining keeps sloughing off.

3. Heavy bleeding also occurs at menopause because women tend to ovulate less frequently. Periods may be relatively regular and normal, but ovulation is irregular. When a woman doesn't ovulate and **progesterone levels are low,** progesterone's beneficial changes are not made in the endometrial lining. This can lead to erratic, heavy bleeding and can eventually cause a precancerous condition.

4. More rarely, bleeding occurs because of **pituitary failure.**

Bleeding Irregularities

Bleeding irregularities around menopause should be checked. Spotting between periods, heavy bleeding and clotting, even a long time with no periods may be perfectly normal at that time of life, or they may mask a problem. It's best to be sure.

Postmenopausal bleeding should definitely be checked, particularly if you are **not** on hormones. However, remember that you can have endometrial cancer whether you bleed heavily, spot, or don't bleed at all. The amount of blood is not significant in itself.

If a woman is not on hormones and only has a period twice a year, it is best to see a doctor about the need for some progesterone in order to avoid hyperplasia. But if a woman is on the proper combination of hormones when she is going through menopause or in postmenopause, she may stop bleeding or just bleed occasionally, and this is all right. She must be sure that she is taking adequate amounts of progesterone, especially if her periods are absent or irregular.

If you are concerned, an endometrial biopsy, though uncomfortable, may put yours and your doctor's minds at rest.

Endometrial Sampling May Be Advised

When there are significant bleeding irregularities, physicians like to check the lining of the uterus to ensure that there are no precancerous changes from estrogen overstimulation. Therefore, physicians always want to do some sort of endometrial sampling. There are many types of samplings that can be done, and the methods change frequently in an attempt to simplify the procedure.

Currently, an extension of the pap smear is done with a tube inserted into the uterus where samples of the lining are removed. This is an office procedure, performed more often these days than a D and C, which requires a general anesthetic. Physicians check for abnormal cells and for signs of ovulation. If the endometrial biopsy is normal or if the endometrial changes are in the first stages, a woman will probably be given a course of progestin or progesterone therapy during the second half of the cycle. Estrogen may also be given if the problem is due to ovarian failure.

Women at risk may be advised by their physic an to have an annual endometrial biopsy of the lining of the uterus. Some researchers say that an annual biopsy is no longer necessary. A baseline endometrial biopsy may be advised before going on estrogen and progestin/progesterone therapy. Then, a woman may take the progestin challenge test once a year to check the condition of her uterine lining.

Endometrial biopsy may not always be perfectly reliable, according to Dr. Wulf Utian. He believes anything slightly abnormal should be checked further. A new ultrasound process done with a vaginal probe is being developed, and it can show up the thickness of the endometrial lining. Less than 5 mm. thickness is ideal. More than 8 to 10 mm. requires further checking.

The Progestin Challenge Test

Dr. Don Gambrell proposed the Progestin Challenge Test in which a woman takes Provera once a year—10 mg. a day for thirteen days. If she begins to bleed before the tenth day, her uterus is being over-stimulated by estrogen, a condition which is not desirable because too much estrogen can lead to hyperplasia and, eventually, cancer. If the woman begins to bleed after the tenth day, her uterus is probably fine. Her progesterone has been adequate and has been doing its work of opposing estrogen.

If a woman does bleed before the tenth day, she is given three or four months of cyclical progestin or progesterone, which, usually, displaces the hyperplasia. If she is already on hormones, the dose of progesterone is raised for a while.

You Don't Have to Have Periods After Menopause

Many women prefer not taking hormones because they don't want to continue having periods after menopause. They often don't realize that hormones can be taken in a way that eliminates the period. Doctors, today, tell postmenopausal women to take both estrogen and progesterone daily instead of cyclically to discourage bleeding each month. In theory, the progesterone will oppose the estrogen, and the lining of the uterus will thin out and even disappear. This is an ideal which may not occur without occasional breakthrough bleeding until a woman is a few years past menopause.

Recently a perimenopausal woman told me that her doctors said she **must bleed** each cycle on hormones. He was worried because he felt bleeding was the important indicator that there was no endometrial cancer. However, endometrial health is indicated, not by bleeding per se, but by the actual changes in the state of the lining of the uterus. If continual progesterone does its work properly, bleeding is not necessary after menopause, though breakthrough bleeding may occur; and, in fact, some doctors say quite a number of postmenopausal women do keep bleeding on continual low doses of progesterone.

What About Breast Cancer?

The possible connection between estrogen and breast cancer has been voiced so often, that many women are afraid to take it. Many studies show no causative link between estrogen therapy and breast cancer; some studies indicate that estrogen actually helps prevent breast cancer. Other studies suggest that estrogen acts as a catalyst—not causing breast cancer, but encouraging an already present cancer.

However, some studies do suggest that estrogen increases the incidence of breast cancer. For example, a recent study done in Sweden linked breast cancer with estrogen therapy. But the synthetic estradiol used there is not typically used in the U.S. for postmenopausal women, and the doses were much higher than those used here.

When I recently went for a breast check, my physician told me that even studies that do suggest a link between estrogen use and breast cancer don't show a big increase in the number of cancer victims. There would only be about five or six extra cases in 100,000.

Note that most breast cancers occur after age fifty-five, and only less than 20 percent of these women are on HRT, according to Gail Sheehey. She also reports that the average length of time women stay on estrogen is only nine months.[1]

Probably because some of the information is conflicting, women are still confused and concerned about this issue.

Better Protected on Estrogen and Progesterone

Dr. Winnifred Cutler believes women are protected over twice as much against developing breast cancer if they are on the correct estrogen and progestin combination. Dr. Don Gambrell's extensive research indicates that women on estrogen alone had a lower incidence of breast cancer than women who took no hormones; and women on both estrogen and progesterone had an even lower incidence. The present consensus is that estrogen does not **cause** cancer, but it may **accelerate** the progress of estrogen-dependent hormonal cancers.

Women who have estrogen-dependent breast cancers are taken off estrogen therapy and given Tamoxifen which strips the fat cells in the breasts of estrogen. Women on Tamoxifen often develop menopausal symptoms and suffer miserably.

There is no conclusive data for or against treating women with past cases of breast cancer with estrogen replacement therapy, though estrogen has been routinely withheld from these women in the past. This has been done on the presumption that estrogen therapy would cause a return of the cancer, not on the basis of actual studies, as I understand it.

The attitude towards women with estrogen-dependent and other breast cancers is rapidly changing. Some doctors are recognizing the problems these women face at menopause and are giving women with "cured" breast cancer low-dose estrogen-replacement therapy. These doctors believe they are better off on estrogen, and that it won't accelerate a return of the cancer.

Giving estrogen after curing breast cancer is a new trend, but at the North American Menopause Society held in September, 1992, many experts said that they were doing this; waiting one to three years after successful treatment of breast cancer to commence estrogen therapy. And some of these doctors were also sounding warnings about Tamoxifen, because of its side effects.

Taking hormone-replacement therapy after breast cancer may be a difficult choice; but, in the end, a woman must decide whether she can cope with her menopausal symptoms and their effect on the general quality of her life. (See the chapter on breast cancer for more details on this subject.)

Avoiding Infections

After menopause, estrogen deficiency may be responsible for vaginal and bladder infections. Both the vagina and the bladder are full of estrogen receptors, and these tissues can become quite fragile after menopause. Vaginal estrogen creams help prevent the continual recurrence of vaginal infections. Where there are recurrent bladder infections, but nothing shows up in tests, doctors should not presume the problem is cystitis, and these women should have a urology work-up.

Many women (perhaps 45 to 60 percent) have problems with

some degree of incontinence after menopause. This is a highly treatable condition, but women rarely seek treatment for it.

How Sexual Response Is Affected by Estrogen
Estrogen contributes to a healthy sex life by keeping the vagina supple. This hormone is responsible for maintaining the size, shape, and flexibility of the vagina as well as the thickness and lubrication of the lining. When estrogen supplies diminish, the vaginal tissues become dry, narrow, and less pliable. The vagina may shorten, and the entrance to the vagina may become so narrow that intercourse is painful or impossible. Estrogen hastens the blood flow to the pelvic area during sexual arousal, which surges through the tissues, causing the release of fluid into the vaginal passage. Estrogen also makes the skin, the nipples, and other sensual areas respond more pleasurably to stimulation. It also increases sexual response and the quality of a woman's orgasm.

Some women naturally produce estrogen in the adrenal glands in sufficient quantities to enjoy sex after menopause. Others, whose adrenals have been depleted by stress, may notice estrogen diminishing soon after menopause or within the next five to ten years. Women who have had a hysterectomy may notice dryness of the vagina almost immediately. To counteract these symptoms and to continue an active sex life, Dr. Lila Nachtigall advises that almost all women will need to take estrogen if they want to continue having sexual intercourse after age sixty to sixty-five.

Estrogen, progesterone, thyroid, and testosterone all have their role in a woman's sex life. Women who do not fantasize and have a low libido may need some testosterone to increase their sex drive. Some women with subnormal or low thyroid levels also have a low sex drive.

High levels of progesterone can reduce sex drive, which is why some pregnant women have a low libido (progesterone levels are high during pregnancy). But I have not heard complaints from women who take progesterone for PMS that it affects their sex drive adversely.

Sex After Hysterectomy
Some women who have had a hysterectomy will find their sexual

response diminishes as a result of the operation, either because of the loss of the uterus or damage to nerves during the surgery. If a woman has had a problem like endometriosis which made sex painful, a hysterectomy may improve her sex life. However, the cervix has nerve endings which fire the pelvic nerve and produce orgasm, and women who have enjoyed deep cervical orgasms prior to the surgery will lose this pleasure. (There are other nerve pathways to orgasm that will remain, but many women say the orgasms are not the same.)

This loss of orgasmic ability can be deeply upsetting, especially to younger women in the prime of their sex life. (Dr. Winnifred Cutler's book *Hysterectomy: Before and After* has an excellent chapter on this subject.)

Summary

Women in their thirties, forties, and fifties who are going through hormonal discomfort often have critical decisions to make at this time of their lives. Whether they should take estrogen or go through menopause "naturally" is one decision. For half of them, whether to have a tubal ligation or a hysterectomy is another.

I hope the information in this book will help them in their decision-making. For help on treatment, see the relevant section on menopause and estrogen therapy. For further information, see the Book List at the end of the book.

Footnote

1. Gail Sheehey, *The Silent Passage*, p. 20. She quotes Marc Deitch, medical director of Wyeth-Ayerst, which produces Premarin.

CHAPTER 10

Tubal Ligations

*N*ancy and her husband, Ron, decided that Nancy should have a tubal sterilization after she had her third child. The surgery was done the day after she had her baby.

Before the surgery, Nancy had never had anything but the mildest mood swings before her period. In fact, she had no patience with women who said they had PMS, and felt they were making a mountain out of a molehill.

But after her surgery, there were some gradual but significant changes in her cycle; and about six or seven years after the surgery, they became very difficult to tolerate. Also, her periods, which had been normal with only minor cramps, became very heavy, and she had significant pain on the right side before and during her period.

When she went to her doctor, he said these symptoms had nothing to do with the tubal ligation. His nurse practitioner however thought differently. She sent Nancy to me, and I showed her several books with sections on tubal ligations, and explained that her symptoms were, in fact, fairly common side effects of a tubal ligation.

I told her of a physician friend in southern California who told me, anecdotally, that about 60 to 70 percent of women who have had tubal ligations go through premature menopause six or seven years afterwards and have symptoms of declining estrogen and progesterone levels. I said that I found in practice that what he said was true; and that when I spoke publicly on hormonal issues, there was always a significant number of women in the audience who started having symptoms after they had a tubal ligation.

Nancy asked if reversal of the tubal ligation would set her hormones straight, and I told her I didn't know, but I doubted it. I thought that once the blood flow had been damaged, the remaining scar tissue would continue to cause problems.

When the doctor put Nancy on hormonal-replacement therapy, she soon felt a lot better.

Tubal Ligations, a Frequent Cause of PMS

About 650,000 American women have tubal ligations every year. Many of the women I see have had problems after a tubal ligation, and there is no doubt in my mind that sterilization brings on some degree of hormonal dysfunction in a significant number of women. Many women with no history of chronic depression or hormonal problems begin having problems after a tubal ligation, and it can be a very unpleasant awakening for them. I have heard such women say that they used to think PMS was just an excuse women used for their bad behavior. Now they realize that PMS is real, and they are furious that their physician told them there would be no side effects.

Some physicians attribute the side effects after a tubal ligation to the fact that the women have just been pregnant or have stopped taking the pill, both of which can cause PMS. However, many women I see waited for a year or so after being pregnant and were not on the pill prior to the tubal. It seems the surgery itself causes hormonal problems, and research studies and popular books seem to agree.

Problems with Tubal Ligations Are Nothing New

Many doctors still tell women that there are no side effects, and they will have no problems following a tubal ligation. But other doctors have been sounding warnings for years.

Ten years ago, Dr. Niels Lauersen wrote about this in one of his popular gynecological books. He quotes case histories in which women developed pain in the area of the fallopian tubes after the surgery, causing severe cramping prior to and during menstruation. He also mentions women whose periods became either much heavier or lighter, and who began to suffer from cyclical PMS or symptoms of premenopause after the surgery.

Lauersen says up to 15 percent of women who undergo tubal ligations report complications during the first month after the operation. Posttubal ligation syndrome (PTLS) side effects include pelvic pain, irregular menstrual bleeding, severe PMS, and galactorrhea (a milk discharge from the nipples). Sometimes the pain of PTLS is so severe that women undergo further surgery including hysterectomies.[1]

Lauersen says that tubal ligation should not be considered minor, inconsequential surgery. He concludes that the pain of PTLS is probably caused by nerve damage; and the PMS is probably due to a hormonal imbalance, caused by lessened blood flow to the ovaries, shrinking of the ovaries, abnormal ovulations, irregular periods, and, possibly, formation of ovarian cysts.

Australian Physician Discusses Tubal Ligations

Dr. Sandra Cabot, an Australian physician and a hormonal expert, has written some excellent books on hormonal problems.[2] She includes a whole chapter on tubal sterilization, and cites several research articles which discuss the side effects.[3]

Cabot lists the different methods of tying the tubes—cutting, tying, burning, or clipping them with metal or plastics rings or clips. She says the method which causes least problems is using clips on the tubes. Cutting, tying, and burning produce more side effects and are more likely to damage surrounding blood vessels, which affect blood flow to the ovaries. When the blood flow to the ovaries is diminished, says Cabot, the ovary becomes impaired and produces less estrogen. She believes the problem occurs because of damage to the blood supply to the ovary since the ovarian blood vessels run alongside the fallopian tubes on their way to the ovary and could easily be compressed or cut during surgery to the closely adjacent tube. This may lead to high blood pressure in the ovary which could result in damage to the ovarian tissues. She says that if this occurs, the ovary may not function normally and its production of estrogen and progesterone which need an adequate blood and oxygen supply may be lowered.[4]

Drs. Guy Abrahams and Joel Hargrove have completed a study on the hormonal effect of tubal ligations, saying that estrogen levels are raised and progesterone levels lowered.[5] I believe their conclusions fit the presupposition that PMS is caused by high estrogen and low progesterone, and I personally think that Dr. Cabot's view is more correct—that both hormones, particularly estrogen, are lowered.

Symptoms mentioned by Dr. Cabot as a result of tubal ligation are—fatigue, difficulty in losing weight, vaginal dryness, bladder problems, loss of libido, reduced orgasms, poor memory, muscle aches and pains, and more rapid aging of the skin—mainly due to estrogen deficiency.

Surgeon Resists Doing Tubal Ligations

Dr. Vicki Hufnagel, in her book *No More Hysterectomies*,[6] says her patients have to fight her to have a tubal ligation because she has seen so many side effects from this surgery. Patients, she says, complain of more severe cramps, heavier, longer periods, dysfunctional uterine bleeding, pain with intercourse, and other pain. Examination of the surgery site may show abnormal swelling or enlargement in ovarian veins, hormonal imbalances, and fistulas associated with endometriosis in the fallopian tube.

She mentions three main theories as to why tubals are a problem:
1. Tubal ligation destroys the blood supply to the ovaries.
2. Certain types of tubal sterilization procedures are more likely to result in endometriosis.
3. An increase in the blood pressure within the ovarian artery can create an estrogen-progesterone imbalance.

Dr. Hufnagel, like Sandra Cabot, prefers clipping the tubes closed, because there are fewer postoperative problems. Both women say that, in the future, more sophisticated methods of microsurgery may prevent these side effects from tubal ligations.

Conclusion

Women who think their menstrual problems started after having a tubal ligation are probably correct. If their symptoms are cyclical, with physical and emotional problems recurring before each period, they probably need to be treated with natural progesterone. If these symptoms occur most of the month, and indicate premenopause, they may need estrogen as well.

Footnotes

1. Dr. Nils Lauersen, Eileen Stukane, *Listen to Your Body*, Berkley Books, pp. 353-355.

2. Sandra Cabot, *Hormones*. See chapter on tubal sterilization. Dr. Cabot's books are all worth purchasing. She has several including a general book on gynecology and a book on menopause. They are available from Women's Health Advisory Service, P.O. Box 217, Paddington, 2021, NSW, Australia.

The FAX number is 0116123607247 and includes the country and city codes for Sydney, Australia.

3. De Stefano, *et al*, "Long term risk of menstrual disturbance after tubal sterilization," *Am.J.Obstet, and Gynaecol.*, Aug. 1, 1985, Vol 152., No. 7, pt. I, pp. 835-841.

"Factors seen as links to posttubal ligation syndrome," *Contraception Tech. Update*, Feb. 1986, Vol. 7, No. 2, pp. 13-15.

Cattanach, J., "Oestrogen deficiency after tubal ligation," *Lancet*, April 13, 1985, (1(8433) pp. 847-849.

Stock, R.J., "Sequelae of tubal ligation: An analysis of 75 consecutive hysterectomies," *South. Med. J.*, Oct. 1984, Vol. 77, No. 10, pp. 1255-1260.

Cattanach, J., "Post-tubal sterilization problems correlated with ovarian steroidogenesis," *Contraception*, Nov. 1988, Vol. 38, No. 5.

Templeton, A.A.,"Hysterectomy following sterilization," *British Journal Obstetrics & Gynaecology*; Oct. 1982, Vol. 89, No. 10, pp. 845-888.

4. Cabot, *Hormones*, p. 85.

5 But note that Dr. Joel Hargrove and Guy Abrahams say that progesterone is low and serum estradiol is high. See their study on twenty-nine women with posttubal ligation syndrome—"Endocrine Profile of Patients with Post-Tubal-Ligation Syndrome," *Journal of Reproductive Medicine*, July 1981, p. 362. I think that, in most cases, Dr. Cabot is more correct that estrogen levels drop.

6. Vicki Hufnagel, *No More Hysterectomies*, pp. 228-229. Dr. Hufnagel is a surgeon who advocates myomectomies instead of hysterectomies.

CHAPTER II

Hysterectomy

A my was a divorced, 44-year-old, teaching at a medical university when her doctor told her she had fibroids. He put her on shots of estrogen with no progesterone—a strange treatment since taking a lot of estrogen can make fibroids grow.

Amy's fibroids did grow, and she began to bleed continually. When she visited her internist, he told her that the fibroids had enlarged, and she should have a hysterectomy.

Amy didn't want a hysterectomy and, subsequently, went to five different OB/Gyns practicing close to the Medical Center. Each of them told her she needed both the uterus and ovaries removed, even though there was no known problem with her ovaries. The reason given was a common one—if the ovaries are left in, they can become cancerous. There is no real evidence that there is increased risk of this,[1] and removing the ovaries has a profound effect on subsequent hormonal production.

After hearing the same story from five gynecologists, Amy felt she had no choice but to have the hysterectomy and oophorectomy. After the surgery, she was given Premarin .625 mg., but this did not cover her symptoms.

I met Amy about ten months later when I took a lecture on menopause at the university's women's center. As she talked to me afterwards, she was crying uncontrollably because she was so terribly depressed. After the surgery, she had developed vaginal pain and was told she had granuloma of the vagina. She also had pains in the bladder, burning eyes, and shooting pains in the ears, besides crippling depression. She had been to a number of doctors since the surgery because of the physical and emotional problems she was enduring. No one had linked the symptoms she was having with the hysterectomy, or increased her dosage, or changed the brand or form of estrogen.

During this time, Amy even asked a referral service for the name of a menopause expert, and went to see him at the university hospital. An internist, who did an examination before the doctor arrived, said he only had to look at her to see she was estrogen deficient. Nevertheless, the menopause expert disagreed with the internist's opinion, and would not increase Amy's dose of Premarin, though he did give her some additional vaginal cream.

By the time Amy came to see me, she had doubled her estrogen on her own volition; and by simply increasing her dose, controlled her depression enough to stop her crying jags.

The next woman I saw that day also had a hysterectomy and oophorectomy. Her surgeon had given her 2.5 mg. of Premarin—four times Amy's dose. This lady seemed to be experiencing symptoms of overdose.

These two case histories illustrate the fact that while many women receive satisfactory treatment and experience success with taking hormones after a hysterectomy, many other women don't. Also, women are frequently treated according to the whim of the physician. Some give low doses only; some give high. Some are willing to experiment with hormones until satisfaction is reached; some are not. The treatment women may expect after hysterectomy is often not uniform.

Some Women Need Hysterectomies; Many Do Not

There is no doubt that some women need to have hysterectomies. But researchers have frequently emphasized that too many women are given hysterectomies—half- to three-quarters of a million women a year in the United States, alone. Doctors often have the attitude that when a woman is past her childbearing years, the uterus and ovaries have outlived their usefulness. They believe this, despite the trouble women have regulating their hormonal-replacement therapy after this surgery, even when only the uterus is removed; and despite the lowered sex drive many women experience after it. Though some doctors are very conservative about performing hysterectomies, others do it fairly routinely.

I am not a doctor, so what I say has to be taken in balance. Some hysterectomies are absolutely necessary; and I am sure that there are many women who have had heavy bleeding for years, who are thrilled to lose their uterus and ovaries. And many of those women may have adjusted well to taking hormonal-replacement therapy. But I can testify to the others who regret having had a hysterectomy because it marked the onset of their present symptoms of hormonal depletion.

Now, several years away from the surgery, their physicians have "forgotten" these women had a hysterectomy and believe their present symptoms are all in their heads.

It's not only male doctors who do routine hysterectomies. I recently talked to two women doctors who both ran menopause clinics. One was an OB/Gyn, the other a reproductive endocrinologist. Both performed hysterectomies and oophorectomies as treatment for severe cases of PMS. One would first give the woman Lupron to put them in chemical menopause for a year or two, to see how she would cope with menopause. These are both extremely severe solutions for these problems and could make things even worse for such women.

A Surgeon Defends the Uterus
Vicki Hufnagel wrote a book called *No More Hysterectomies* in which she deplores the number of hysterectomies being performed on women. Dr. Hufnagel's book has the ring of truth, and every woman contemplating hysterectomy would benefit from reading it. She explains why, as a surgeon, she feels far too many hysterectomies are being performed. For instance, she mentions that in 1983, 13,000 hysterectomies were given to treat PMS—rather drastic since there are other treatment options and hysterectomy can itself worsen PMS. Hysterectomies are generally done because of cancer (a valid reason), fibroid tumors, endometriosis, and prolapse (there may be alternative treatment for the latter three).

Rather than perform hysterectomies on fibroids, Dr. Hufnagel performed early myomectomies, a surgery where the fibroid is shelled out of the uterus. She felt that these should be done early on because once the fibroid grew to a certain size, hysterectomy might be inevitable. She also developed what she called female reconstructive surgery, a way to tighten up loose ligaments that caused uterine prolapse, another attempt to avoid hysterectomy. Unfortunately, in trying to challenge the system, she was accused of doing what she was fighting—unnecessary surgery.

It is interesting that in France, surgeons are well-trained in performing myomectomies, and hysterectomies are rarely done there for fibroids. By contrast, in the U.S., where performing myomectomies is more of a specialty, fibroids are a main reason for having a hysterectomy.

Reproductive Biologist Researches the Facts
Researcher Winnifred Cutler's book, *Hysterectomy: Before and After* is must reading for all women who are advised to have a hysterectomy or who have already had one. Here are some of the points that Cutler makes in her book:
- Fifty percent of women in the U.S. and Canada will have a hysterectomy (uterus removed) in their lifetime, compared with 10 percent in Sweden. In the U.S., the average age for premenopausal hysterectomy is thirty-five; in Scandinavia, it is forty-five. By the age of forty-four, 21 percent of women in the U.S. will have had a hysterectomy; 4 percent of women in six European countries. Half of the women over forty who have a hysterectomy will also have their ovaries removed.
- Immediately after surgery, women are often very happy that they had a hysterectomy, but as the years go by, the satisfaction rate drops drastically.
- The effects of a hysterectomy include: alteration in the hormonal environment, earlier aging, high risk of postoperative depression, deterioration of bone health, increase of atherosclerosis and coronary heart disease, reductions in sexual functioning (libido, arousal, lubrication, orgasm), increased urinary continence, premature menopause (where only the uterus is removed), instant menopause (when the ovaries are removed).
- Accumulating evidence shows that the role of the uterus and ovaries has been highly underestimated. The uterus plays a large part in keeping the ovaries working (so when they are removed, the cycling of the ovaries is affected). Also, the uterus produces hormones that affect brain function and help reduce heart disease. The ovaries are factories for hormones and many other substances.

- Dr. Cutler says that most of the information in her book has surfaced only since 1983, and is not yet disseminated to medical schools, medical practices, and health centers. She says that when women go to a doctor for help, even the well-informed physician may be limited in giving effective answers (partly because all the information is not yet collected).
- Avoid having a hysterectomy unless you really have to.
- Dr. Cutler has a helpful chapter called, "Sexual Life After Hysterectomy." I found this chapter interesting because I have counseled a number of women who wept over the loss of their sex drive after having a hysterectomy. Cutler says this is because of the loss of the pudental nerve in the cervix which fires at the height of lovemaking and provides deeply satisfying orgasms. Many women report a lessening of their orgasms after surgery. (On the other hand, some women who have suffered from horrendous pain stemming from gynecological problems report a dramatic improvement in their sex life after a hysterectomy.)

Difficulty in Treating Hysterectomized Women

In the treatment section for menopause in this book, there is a section that deals with "brittle menopause." Women who have had a hysterectomy and who have a real struggle balancing their hormones should read this section.

Footnotes

1. Winnifred Cutler believes that if you have a hysterectomy you should try to retain the ovaries. Many doctors will routinely remove them if a women is over forty or forty-five, for two wrong reasons: 1. they presume the ovaries are useless and produce no hormones; 2. they believe retained ovaries may become cancerous.

In answer to the first point, she says that while the ovaries stop cycling in 50 percent of hysterectomized women, they may keep cycling for years in the other 50 percent, and the hormones they produce are important.

The second point was based on published research that was reported wrongly. There is no increased risk for ovarian cancer after a hysterectomy. *Hysterectomy: Before and After*, pp. 104,105.

CHAPTER 12

Endometriosis

Sally suffered with PMS from puberty and always had severe stabbing pain and cramps with her periods. As she grew older, the menstrual pains worsened and lengthened, and she had heavy, clotting periods. It was difficult to become interested in sex because intercourse was painful. Not only did sex hurt, but she was also having great difficulty becoming pregnant.

Sally's fertility specialist suspected she had endometriosis because he could feel nodules on the underside of the uterus. He explained that endometriosis occurs when the tissue in the lining of the uterus, which is very similar to normal tissue, migrates through the fallopian tubes and adheres to the abdominal wall and surrounding organs, including the bladder, bowel, and the outside of the uterus and ovaries.

The doctor did a diagnostic laparoscopy, a surgery in which a small lighted scope is inserted through the navel to explore the abdominal cavity. He found that Sally had extensive endometrial tissue on the ovaries and bowel. He did laser surgery to remove as much of the endometrial implants as possible, and Sally was then able to conceive.

Over the next two or three years, Sally's cramps improved, and she did not have discomfort with sex; but, gradually, the symptoms returned. Her OB/Gyn said that endometriosis had a tendency to come back. He suggested having a hysterectomy, with removal of the ovaries. Sally thought this sounded pretty drastic.

Different Types of Menstrual Pain

Whenever the phrase PMS is mentioned, some people automatically think of menstrual cramps. Actually, many women with PMS do not have menstrual cramps at all; others do. The type of pain these women suffer is characterized by aching, bloating, heavy pain. They often remark that they feel as though their insides are falling out. Contrast this PMS pain with true menstrual cramps, in which knife-like, stabbing pains in the lower abdomen sometimes even radiate down into the groin and thighs.

Dr. Katherina Dalton says typical PMS pains are related to low levels of progesterone. She calls the stabbing type of pains spasmodic dysmenorrhea. Antiprostaglandins, such as ibuprofen, often help control these pains. Physicians frequently put women on the contraceptive pill for treatment, but this may worsen PMS symptoms.

Is There a Link Between PMS and Endometriosis?

Dr. Guy Abrahams has commented that in cases where severe cramplike pain is a major symptom of PMS, there is a very high incidence of endometriosis (approximately 56 percent). Dr. Nils Lauersen has treated many women with both conditions simultaneously. See *The Endometriosis Answer Book*, p. 143.

In my experience, and from conversations with several physicians, there does seem to be a strong link between the two conditions, because both seem to be caused by hormonal imbalances.

What Is Endometriosis?

Endometriosis occurs when tissue identical to that found in the uterine lining (called the endometrium) grows on organs and structures outside of the uterus itself. Note the following from *Consumer Reports*:

> Endometriosis is not malignant but it mimics cancer in the way it spreads and attaches itself to other organs, most commonly the ovary, bladder and bowel. This wandering tissue retains its uterine function and each month it bleeds in response to hormonal influences just as the uterus does. Also, as in the uterus,

this tissue releases prostaglandins which in the uterus help the uterus to contract. The action of these hormones causes a general menstrual pain in some women. The same pain is also found at the local sites of the misplaced tissue during menstrual periods. The bleeding at these sites may cause adhesions between organs which can lead to chronic pain and infertility in endometriosis sufferers.[1]

A Caution About Endometriosis

Endometriosis is a complex disease that can be very difficult to diagnose. It is mentioned here because there seems to be a link with PMS and, sometimes, low thyroid problems; though there is almost no literature saying this. This chapter can only deal with it in a surface manner.

Endometriosis can be painless or excruciatingly painful, and it can be a prime reason for infertility. Pain and infertility are two major reasons women seek help for endometriosis.

There are mild to severe forms and different types of endometriosis; and the lesions can attach to different organs and, in rare cases, travel into distant sites like the lungs and brain. Endometriosis tends to cause a reaction in the organ it attaches to. For instance, the appendix may atrophy because of it. Other sites of endometriosis may harden, and organs may adhere to each other. Rarely, endometriosis lesions can become malignant.

Also, a woman could lose a kidney, if lesions attach to the ureter; or she could potentially have a bowel obstruction, if lesions are on the intestine. She may lose an ovary if an endometrioma should burst (and some treatment suitable for other forms of endometriosis might encourage it to burst). Therefore, this is a complex problem, not one to be neglected, and a woman needs the continued care and supervision of a physician who is well-informed on the subject.

All available treatments only palliate the condition—a woman will probably have endometriosis for quite a few years. Each treatment, which varies depending upon the type and extent of the disease, the organ involvement, inability to conceive, and pain, and so on—may keep the problem at bay for a while, but it is likely to return. Keep in mind that any recommendations made in this chapter would only suit certain types of endometriosis and may be inappropriate for others.

Theories About Endometriosis

In the past, endometriosis was commonly called the career women's disease because it seemed to occur more in women who postpone pregnancy. It was believed to be epidemic because women have fewer pregnancies compared to previous generations—almost a curse for not having children. Another theory was that having sex during menstruation caused the endometrial lining to backflush through the fallopian tubes. These theories do not explain why it can occur in young teenagers before they have had sex. And note how both theories put blame on the woman for having the disease.

Since I first wrote my chapter on endometriosis, new information has been coming out about possible causes. According to an article in *Scientific American*, April 1994, the disease has been linked to dioxin exposure. Dioxins are pollutants made during certain industrial processes. There are various kinds, the most potent being TCDD. In a study by Rier, 79 percent of females in a colony of rhesus monkeys exposed to dioxin developed endometriosis. The more exposure to the pollutant, the more prevalent and the more severe were the symptoms. Other studies support these conclusions. Researchers are increasingly convinced that dioxins act as a hormone, a harsh, synthetic estrogen, which disturbs the immune system.

There seems to be a link between endometriosis and other immune system problems, including candida (yeast) infections. Among the many women I have seen who have endometriosis, there seems to be an unusual number with subnormal thyroid problems. However, I haven't seen this connection documented.

Some women develop endometriosis at the site of the surgery after having their tubes tied. The endometrial tissue apparently travels through the incision, and adheres to the outside of the tubes.

Retrograde bleeding through the tubes is not uncommon during menstruation, but not everyone who experiences it gets endometriosis. There seems to be an associated low immune system function in women with endometriosis, and this may be the factor that tips the scales in certain women.

Some researchers believe that initially endometriosis may be caused by low levels of estrogen, which results in an immature cervix, which makes it difficult for blood to escape and leads to retrograde bleeding.

128

Is There a Family History?

There seems to be a family history of endometriosis in some families. I know a family in which the grandmother had PMS-like depression even into her sixties and actually committed suicide while experiencing a cyclical bout of depression. Whether she had endometriosis is unknown, but likely; her daughter had endometriosis and had a hysterectomy after her children were born; her three girls each had PMS and endometriosis, and each had a hysterectomy after their children were born; the female great-grandchildren, being now of child-bearing age, are showing the same symptoms of PMS and endometriosis.

Adenomyosis

Adenomyosis is internal endometriosis, where the endometrial tissue migrates and grows into the muscles of the uterine wall, usually after a difficult pregnancy. Subsequently, menstruation brings severe pain, and often hysterectomy is the only cure.

PMS + Cramps May = Endometriosis

When reviewing a woman's medical history, if she has had severe, long-term cramping as a major symptom of her PMS, I think "endometriosis" and it often turns out that endometriosis is indeed the problem. But I have also counseled women who had severe cramping who did not have endometriosis, and natural progesterone treatment for their PMS sometimes helps this type of pain.

Early Warning Symptoms of Endometriosis

1. Menstrual cramps that become progressively worse as time passes
2. Ovulatory pain (mittelschmerz)
3. Painful intercourse
4. Infertility for unknown reasons
5. Bladder infections where tests and cultures repeatedly come out negative
6. Severe shifting pelvic pain a few days before and during menstruation
7. History of rupturing, bleeding cysts
8. Nodules on the uterus that can be felt by the physician
9. On examination, the cervical os does not line up with the vagina,

the urethra, and the anus. If it is out of line, it may indicate that the uterus has adhered to other organs

10. A sudden, chronic bout of midcycle or menstrual pain (which could, of course, be due to other causes)

Endometriosis Is Sometimes Difficult to Treat

Endometriosis is not a rare disease (it is estimated that 15 percent of menstruating women have it), but it can be difficult to treat. Women who have it from onset of puberty with severe pain have a long-term problem which will take skillful management over a period of many years. Different types of endometriosis are treated with different options, depending on the extent of the involvement, and the presenting symptoms. If a woman is trying to get pregnant, for instance, the birth control pill would not be a good choice for treatment.

Doctors may initially put young women on the pill or Provera continuously, and, for some, this will control much of their pain, though it may increase their depression. The doctor will also give medication to help with pain management if the hormones don't provide total relief. But doctors seem reluctant to treat young women with laser surgery or more potent hormonal treatment if the only symptom is pain. They are more aggressive about treatment, it seems, when the woman wishes to conceive and appears to be infertile. Then they may use either Danazol, Synarel, or Lupron temporarily to inhibit the production of ovarian hormones (particularly estrogen which stimulates the endometrial implants). The physician may use these hormones to inhibit the growth of the endometrial tissue for a few months and then do laser surgery to remove the lesions.

If women want children, they must have them quickly, or manage their endometriosis in the intervening years and hope they won't become sterile. Sterilization may come from adhesions or from the immune system response to the endometriosis which attacks the sperm.

Some of the treatments for endometriosis are exorbitantly expensive and may cause unpleasant side effects, including the symptoms of menopause, and, disappointingly, regrowth of the condition is common. Laser surgery to remove the implants is also available, and often used after hormonal therapy. None of these options is a problem-free solution, as we will see later.

After trying different options, some women opt to have a hysterectomy and oophorectomy to put an end to their pain. For some who are given a hysterectomy as a "cure" while still young, the subsequent problems of treating premature and instantaneous menopause may cause continuing problems. Another disappointment is that hysterectomy doesn't always remove the microscopic endometrial implants in the bloodstream; and estrogen-replacement therapy may further stimulate these implants and cause pain, though the doses are low and don't usually cause problems (there are differences of opinion about this).

A Silver Lining
But behind the black cloud of endometriosis, and despite frustration with treatment, there is a silver lining for many sufferers. Some with severe pain and infertility find relief from hormones and/or laser surgery, which lessens their pain, and they are able to have the children they desire.

Danazol—One Possible Treatment
Danazol, brand name Danocrine, is a gonadotropin inhibitor that blocks the production of FSH and LH and thereby inhibits ovulation and lowers estrogen production. Danazol shrinks endometrial tissue, suppresses ovarian production of hormones, and lessens the worst menstrual symptoms by creating a temporary pseudomenopause. Without stimulation by the ovarian hormones, estrogen and progesterone, the lining of the uterus shrinks. Danazol would not be suitable for all types of endometriosis, and some women would experience side effects that would exclude them from using it.

Treatment with Danazol:
Danazol has the following five functions:
1. It blocks FSH and LH, lowers estrogen production, and stops ovulation.
2. It blocks estrogen and progesterone receptors in the endometrial cells. The tissue is no longer stimulated, and begins to atrophy.
3. It inhibits the secretion of several enzymes involved in the production of estrogen and progesterone.
4. It alters the body's metabolism of estrogen and progesterone by

increasing their breakdown, and stops lesions from growing.

5. It strengthens the immune system to some extent.

Better Than the Pill or Depo-Provera

While the pill and Depo-Provera cause pseudopregnancy and reduce symptoms of endometriosis such as pain, they do not shrink the lesions as Danazol does. For women with certain types of endometriosis, Danazol is a miracle cure. Other women cannot tolerate the side effects, which may include weight gain, fatigue, weakness, dizziness, headaches, acne, increase in hairiness, oily skin and scalp, bleeding, spotting, pelvic pain, back pain, vaginitis, breast tenderness, swollen or decreased breasts (the latter temporary while on treatment), localized breast pain, painful lumps, muscle cramps, neck aches, hot flashes, depression, insomnia, anxiety, rash, and increased allergies. Adjustment of the dosage may help. On the positive side, sometimes when women are put on Danazol they lose their PMS symptoms.

Recent Hormonal Treatments

Analog hormones, such as Lupron and Synarel, are being used to treat women with endometriosis. These hormones work by throwing women into menopause temporarily, but the resulting estrogen-deficiency symptoms, such as depression, calcium loss and severe hot flashes, have dampened the results of using these drugs.

I recently saw a young woman treated with Lupron for endometriosis who had never been depressed prior to using this medication. She subsequently required psychiatric treatment, and her psychiatrist said her problem was wholly hormonal. While most women would probably not react this way to Lupron, the occasional woman will, because the finely tuned endocrine system is thrown out of gear. When women contemplate taking this medication, they need to weigh the possible side effects, because Lupron definitely throws a woman into chemical menopause.

Can Estrogen Be Given to Women with Endometriosis?

As women with endometriosis age, they may manifest the symptoms of perimenopause. Because estrogen proliferates the endometrial cells, it has generally not been given to women with endometriosis, and some women should not take it if their endometriosis is extensive.

Though hysterectomy and oophorectomy are not an ideal treatment for endometriosis, where this has been done, women are likely to develop osteoporosis if they don't take estrogen. Dr. Winnifred Cutler quotes Dr. Felicia Stewart as saying that hormonal-replacement therapy after a hysterectomy rarely causes any problems for women with endometriosis, but adds that adding plenty of progestin to the estrogen therapy will help avoid regrowth of the endometriosis. Some of the physicians I work with prefer to use estrogen and natural progesterone (instead of progestin), though this has not been studied as a treatment regime.

Whether women who have not had a hysterectomy, but who are suffering from premenopausal symptoms, can take estrogen is a difficult question. Some have taken a very low dose of estrogen with more than usual progesterone, but this is controversial.

Does Progesterone Help with PMS?
Information on whether women with endometriosis benefit from receiving natural progesterone therapy for their PMS is not available. Those with both PMS and endometriosis may receive some benefit from using natural progesterone, but they don't always. Some doctors I have worked with do give natural progesterone for the combined conditions, and it does seem to help some women and not worsen the endometriosis.

Laser Surgery Helpful
Women with visible, moderate to severe lesions of endometriosis, causing pain and infertility, may be candidates for laser surgery. After surgery, one or two courses of Danazol are often enough. The usual length of time to take Danazol is six months, but in extreme cases it can be given for a year. Listening to a lecture by a specialist on endometriosis, I was surprised to hear that the use of laser surgery and the combination of Danazol and laser surgery is not well studied.

Should You Have a Hysterectomy?
When a hysterectomy is performed on women with endometriosis, the ovaries are also removed because their continued production of

estrogen will stimulate endometriosis. This does not remove lesions in other parts of the body, or microscopic lesions in the bloodstream.

Note Nils Lauersen's comments that many doctors still hold to the old-fashioned view that a hysterectomy is the final answer for endometriosis; but he points out that because the lesions can exist microscopically in bladder, bowel, and lungs, hysterectomy is not the answer. He has seen women who go on estrogen having had a hysterectomy, and their endometriosis has subsequently regrown. Then they not only have the endometriosis but the results of the hysterectomy to deal with as well.[2] Lauersen says these women believed what they were told about the benefits of hysterectomy—freedom from pain and discomfort during sexual intercourse. He says that this is sometimes true. At other times, the symptoms worsened and became more numerous because of the effects of estrogen deficiency.

Dr. Winnifred Cutler also mentions the quite rare risk of having endometriosis return after a hysterectomy because of taking estrogen. She believes that taking enough progesterone to counteract the endometriosis, will prevent it from growing back.[3]

When May a Hysterectomy Be Advisable?
A hysterectomy may be advisable when:
1. Danazol or other hormone therapies do not work, and pain is debilitating
2. When laser or conservative surgery doesn't work
3. When more than one endometriosis specialist feels it may help
4. You have a physician who will help you control the menopausal symptoms that will result from this surgery

Footnotes
1. *Consumer Reports,* September 1990, p. 605.
2. *The Endometriosis Answer Book,* p. 197, 198.
3. *Hysterectomy: Before and After,* p. 163.

CHAPTER 13

Breast Cancer

One day, as Sylvia examined her breasts, she came upon a hard, painless lump that she had not felt before. Her doctor sent her to a surgeon, who biopsied the lump and found it was malignant, but self-contained, and performed a lumpectomy.

Sylvia was then put on a course of radiation and given Tamoxifen, a type of chemotherapy which suppresses the production of estrogen in the fat cells. The surgeon told Sylvia that there were estrogen receptors in the tumor that he excised. Estrogen, he said, might accelerate the return of the breast cancer, and this was the reason for using Tamoxifen.

Sylvia was forty-four and had her uterus removed at age thirty-six because of large benign fibroids, which had caused excessive menstrual bleeding. She had been experiencing symptoms of estrogen deficiency prior to the discovery of her cancer, but had not been on any estrogen therapy.

After she had been on Tamoxifen for a while, her menopausal symptoms became more pronounced. Her OB/Gyn told her that her vagina was as dry and fragile as that of a woman twenty years older than she.

But when she questioned her surgeon, he completely disregarded her hormonal symptoms and reemphasized the fact that she couldn't go on estrogen.

The Cancer Scare

Estrogen has received a lot of bad press concerning its possible connection with breast cancer. From time to time, the media puts out scare reports about women on estrogen replacement therapy having higher rates of breast cancer. Actually, there have been studies with opposite conclusions, proving that estrogen both increases and reduces breast cancer.

Other studies suggest that estrogen does not **cause** cancer but acts as a catalyst for preexisting breast cancers, particularly those containing estrogen receptors.

Putting It in Proportion

To balance this out, it's important to remember that cancer of all types and in **both sexes** is on the increase. Also, lung cancer kills more women than breast cancer—53,000 compared to 46,000, annually, according to present statistics. Also less than 20 percent of women take HRT for an average of nine months only, and the increase in breast cancer is fairly general among women over fifty to fifty-five.

Statistics Not As Bad As Forecast

In a recent UC Berkeley *Wellness Letter*,[1] the statistic that one woman in nine will get breast cancer was clarified. The article pointed out that **only at age eighty-five is the risk factor one in nine.** Actually, by age fifty, the risk is one in fifty; at age sixty, the risk is one in twenty-three; by age seventy, one in thirteen; by age eighty, one in ten. The article mentioned that these numbers have terrified many women and made them feel doomed. The American Cancer Society has heavily publicized the "one in nine" figure to convince more women to have mammograms. Sometimes the statistic is reported erroneously as saying that one women in nine already *has* breast cancer. Women need to know this, because these false statistics give women the idea that breast cancer is pandemic, fuels the accusation that estrogen increases breast cancer, and discourages women from taking estrogen.

Some Main Issues

The first one is: Will estrogen or estrogen/progestin-replacement therapy increase the risk for breast cancer? While studies have resulted in conflicting conclusions, the majority of current studies support the fact that it does not. In fact, according to Dr. Don Gambrell, women taking estrogen and progestin together are considered to be over twice less likely to develop breast cancer. Other studies say that estrogen-replacement therapy increases cancer in only five or six women in 100,000.

The second issue is a harder one to resolve: If I have a present or past case of breast cancer, can I then take estrogen with safety? Currently, the answer to this question is rapidly shifting. Some doctors are putting women on estrogen to counteract their postmenopausal symptoms one to three years after successful treatment of breast cancer. They believe the benefits of taking estrogen far outweigh the risk of getting breast cancer again.

The third issue is: What about Tamoxifen, a treatment that works by inhibiting estrogen in the cell receptors of the breast. If it is successful, doesn't that support the idea that estrogen stimulates cancer?

A Researcher's View

Dr. Winnifred Cutler, a reproductive biologist at the University of Pennsylvania, has studied a great deal of research concerning breast cancer and hormones. She takes the position that hormone-replacement therapy actually reduces the incidence of breast cancer. Those interested in the subject should read her book *Hysterectomy: Before and After*, pp. 135-37.

Here is a summary of her conclusions about breast cancer:

- Breast cancer is more an older woman's disease and is most common in the postmenopausal years, after age fifty-five, when the hormones decline.
- While breast cancer is said to be a very widespread problem for women, competent statistical studies have not been done to prove this.
- The chance of a forty-year-old woman getting breast cancer some-time in the following year is extremely low.
- About 40,000 women a year die of breast cancer as compared to 500,000 who die per year from strokes or heart disease (often directly related to estrogen loss after menopause).
- According to a study by Dr. Don Gambrell, women who are not on

hormones at menopause have over twice as much chance of getting breast cancer as those on estrogen-progestin replacement therapy.

- Women on estrogen-progestin replacement therapy have optimal breast health with a reduced risk of breast cancer. Women on estrogen alone have neither an increased nor decreased risk of breast cancer.

Fat and Unbound Estrogen Are the Culprits

Apparently, the incidence of breast cancer increases in women who produce higher levels of **unbound** estrogens rather than **bound** estrogens. These are much higher in postmenopausal women, especially in women who are apple-shaped, that is, overweight around the waist, rather than pear-shaped.

Men, generally, tend to get fat around the waist and stomach, yet keep their thin arms and legs. They are very susceptible to heart disease. Women, by contrast, tend to gain weight all over, particularly around the hips and thighs (pear shape). But certain women have the male type of fat pattern and gain weight around the waist (android obesity). These women are most at risk for breast cancer and also for heart disease.

After menopause, the ovaries and adrenals produce higher levels of androgens, the male hormones which break down into weak forms of estrogen in the fat cells. The more fat women have, the more of these unbound estrogens they are likely to produce. Some think that fat globules carry carcinogens through the bloodstream to the breast, where they stick to the estrogen receptors.

This is why, generally, older women over fifty-five who are fat around the middle are at highest risk for breast cancer.

Early Diet Important

Some researchers believe that diet during the early years prior to puberty determines the hormonal health of the breast. The nearer the diet is to vegetarianism, the less likely it is that breast cancer will develop. Women should particularly avoid too much fat in the diet.[2] They should eat adequate fiber and avoid salt, fat, and smoked foods. Excessively processed and fatty foods trigger most western diseases. In summary, women should eat less food, but more vegetables, fruits, whole grain cereals, and legumes. Smoking should be eliminated, and alcohol used only moderately.

Early diet can affect the age a woman at which a woman's periods begin and end, because menstruation is not triggered until the body achieves a certain proportion of body fat. Thin, active women tend to begin menstruation later. Women who eat more animal fat tend to start menstruating earlier and to finish later than those who are on a vegetarian diet. The more years a woman menstruates, the more likely it is that breast cancer will occur.

Reducing the Risk

- Eat a low fat, particularly low animal fat, high fiber diet. Fat intake should be less than 25 percent of your calories. Cheeses, for instance, which have most of their calories from fat content should only be eaten in small quantities and used only every third or fourth meal.
- Percentage of body fat ideally should be less than 25 percent.
- Body mass index (that is your weight divided by your height) should ideally be less than 25 percent).
- Waist-hip proportion should ideally be 75 percent, for example, a 30-inch waist and 40-inch hips. Over 80 percent increases your chances of breast cancer.
- Exercise aerobically (at least three times a week for 30 minutes).
- Stop smoking (ten or more cigarettes a day increases your risk).
- Reduce alcohol consumption to at least less than three drinks a week
- If you need to take hormones, even if you have had your uterus removed, both estrogen and progesterone taken together are best.

Other Factors

You should take into account other factors which increase the incidence of breast cancer. **Most of these, you can't control:**

- 20 percent of women who have breast cancer have a family history of cancer.
- Having had a previous case of breast cancer increases your chances of getting it again.
- Being black or white increases your chances—Asian, Hispanic, and American Indian women have a lower incidence of breast cancer—possibly because of life-style.
- Women over 5'5" tall are at greater risk of getting breast cancer.

- Having other cancers (ovarian, endometrial, bowel) increases your chances.
- Having atypical hyperplasia of the breast (fibrocystic breast disease, but the proliferative, not the nonproliferative type) increases your chance. (Ninety-five percent of women have fibrocystic breast disease, and most of it is benign.)
- Going through menopause later than age fifty-five increases the incidence.

Breast Examination and Early Detection

Self-examination of one's breasts, when done according to professional methods, is sometimes helpful in earlier detection of tumors. However, most of the time, early detection of breast cancer does not guarantee greater longevity.[3] Scientific literature suggests that the longer survival time may only reflect the earlier discovery of breast cancer, not an improved rate of cure. Breast cancer is usually slow-growing and may take twenty to thirty years to form.

Mammograms

Some researchers conclude that there is no value in routine mammograms before age fifty.[4] It has been shown that earlier mammograms do not increase the survival rate of women with breast cancer. Women in their forties who are at high risk because of family history may be an exception.

Exposure to radiation does increase breast cancer. However, today the newer mammogram detectors only use a quarter of a rad of radiation and are considered safer, since older machines emit more radiation.

If you decide to have regular mammograms, it is important to go to a breast-care center which specializes in mammograms and which has up-to-date equipment regularly tested for efficiency by outside inspection and well-informed, professionally-trained operators.

Instead of having routine mammograms each year, some physicians have a baseline mammogram done. This can be used later as a comparison if a problem arises.

Choose Conservative Treatment

Most breast cancer is considered systemic nowadays, which means that, in most cases, by the time it is a palpable lump, it has usually spread microscopically throughout the lymphatic system and has already metastasized at distant sites. This is why radical mastectomies—the removal of the entire breast and surrounding lymph nodes—often do not guarantee more longevity than a local lumpectomy.[5]

This is terrible when you consider the side effects of a radical mastectomy. With the removal of the lymph nodes from under the armpit, the lymphatic fluid runs down into the arm tissues and causes frequent swelling and pain. A woman cannot wear a blood pressure cuff, and the surgery may make her arm movement restricted. Researchers have known for decades that radical mastectomies make little or no difference in survival rates, yet this surgery is still commonly done. It is sometimes even performed on some women with high risk for breast cancer who don't actually have the disease yet!

Lumpectomy, the Treatment of Choice

Lumpectomy is the treatment of choice in most cases. Most of the 100,000 mastectomies performed each year in this country should not have been done. One *Science* article says:

> For many kinds of cancer it doesn't even make much difference what kind of treatment is used. Most studies seem to reveal no difference among the treatment outcomes.
>
> These conclusions are well illustrated in the history of breast cancer management. Between 1950 and the late 1970s dozens of studies compared the survival of patients treated with various kinds of surgery from radical mastectomy to mere "lumpectomy," with and without radiation or drugs.
>
> The results have shown little survival advantage for any treatment. Since the less radical treatments are just as helpful as the most radical, the trend has humanely been toward the less disfiguring procedures.[6]

Nevertheless, doctors remove local cancers in the breast because they may either grow into the chest wall or abscess on the surface of the breast. At that point, they become very difficult and unpleasant to manage.

If a woman has radiation with a lumpectomy, it is now considered that the lump is less likely to return at that spot (which doesn't mean it won't return somewhere else).

Tamoxifen

Tamoxifen is not a form of chemotherapy, but a nonsteroidal compound similar to Clomid, and is said to extend the survival rate of women with breast cancer considerably. Some consider it so successful that widespread research trials are currently in progress in which women with a high risk of breast cancer in their families are given Tamoxifen as a preventive treatment.

Women who are considering Tamoxifen should read the paper called "Tamoxifen: Special Considerations for Clinicians," by Dr. Leon Speroff,[7] because taking Tamoxifen has its pros and cons, like every other medication. Dr. Speroff concludes that Tamoxifen is **particularly helpful** for postmenopausal women with breast cancer which contains estrogen receptors. As women move further and further past menopause, it also seems to increasingly help those whose breast cancer is without estrogen receptors. It is, Dr. Speroff thinks, **less helpful for women prior to menopause,** and may actually accelerate certain estrogen-related problems. He appears to question the benefits of putting younger high risk women on Tamoxifen as a prophylactic because of these side effects.

While Tamoxifen functions as an estrogen **antagonist** in the breast cells, it also functions as an estrogen **agonist** in other parts of the body. In other words, in some ways it decreases estrogen, and in other ways it increases estrogen.

On the good side, Tamoxifen decreases estrogen in the breast cells and theoretically slows down the growth or return of breast cancer. There is a 20 percent increase in survival rate after five years on therapy, and the ten-year survival rate is even more significant. Tamoxifen also stabilizes bone density and increases the beneficial HDL cholesterol levels, effects which are toted as other major benefits of taking Tamoxifen.

On the negative side, however, taking Tamoxifen may increase estrogen stimulation of the vaginal and endometrial tissues, leading to an increase in endometrial cancer and endometriosis. This is more likely to occur in premenopausal women because many women who go on Tamoxifen end up experiencing an increase in their estrogen levels, and many stop ovulating. One doctor I met who had widely used Tamoxifen warned that the type of endometrial cancer produced with this drug was not the benign type seen with hormone-replacement therapy, but was often fatal.

Also, while doctors stress the estrogen-like benefits of Tamoxifen on the bones and heart, there are significant numbers of women who do experience severe estrogen-deficiency symptoms, such as hot flashes, nausea, vomiting, vaginal irritation, arthritis, and muscle cramps and pains (all classic menopausal symptoms).

Keep in mind that it is mainly postmenopausal women over the age of fifty who benefit from Tamoxifen. As with many other issues in hormonal health, women need to read significant articles and ask questions of their doctor, and, in the end, weigh the pros and cons before going on treatment.

Treatments Come and Go

The treatment of the moment is always a miracle cure, but only time will tell what the side effects will be, and, in the meantime, what will happen to you? Always remember that what was used for treatment ten years ago is now obsolete, and in retrospect may have been the wrong treatment, even though it may still be used. It's wise to be more than a little sceptical, remembering that often HMOs and other insurance companies may have more say in the treatment recommended than the clinician, and their information may be out-of-date. And, incredible as it seems, a doctor may be liable for not following a recommended course of treatment, even if he knows intellectually that the patient is not going to be any better off with the treatment and that her condition may actually be worsened.

Apparently, in Canada and Europe, large doses of Provera are being used in place of Tamoxifen with at least as much success. So Tamoxifen may not be the great cure it has been touted as. At the North American Menopause Society meeting held in September, 1992, it was clear there was a lot of concern about using Tamoxifen.

Many studies have been done on Tamoxifen, but more research is needed on its relationship to menopause and the use of estrogen.

Current Opinion Rapidly Changing

An OB/Gyn I recently spoke with said that the tide of opinion was turning concerning estrogen for past breast cancer patients, and some doctors are treating these women with estrogen for menopause within a year or two of successfully treating breast cancer. This opinion was ratified at the convention I mentioned above, as a number of experts in the area of hormone replacement therapy and breast cancer made this same statement. They felt giving estrogen did not increase the likelihood of the cancer returning, but significantly improved the woman's quality of life. Whether a woman would consider taking hormones might depend on how severe her menopausal symptoms were.

A Difficult Decision

Sylvia's story, at the beginning of this chapter, describes the plight of the woman who needs estrogen, but who already has breast cancer. Certain types of cancers can proliferate very quickly, during pregnancy, under the influence of high levels of hormones. When a woman has an obviously hormonally-related cancer such as breast cancer containing estrogen receptors, doctors treat it by reducing estrogen levels in the body. I have met many women who are suffering the symptoms of menopause because they are on Tamoxifen for breast cancer. Their physicians will not put them on estrogen. They may even urge removal of the ovaries in younger women who are more at risk.

Even if a woman has a breast cancer that is, apparently, without estrogen and progesterone receptors, specialists may be skeptical. They believe that even breast cancer without estrogen receptors may later produce a subset of the tumor that does have estrogen receptors in it. Also, when biopsies are done with electrocautery methods, they say the heat process can destroy estrogen and progesterone receptors. That is, the receptors may have originally been there, but were inadvertently destroyed. The patient with a breast cancer that does not have any estrogen or progesterone receptors may have a poorer prognosis because the cancer often is more aggressive.[8]

For some of these reasons, some cancer specialists put all women with breast cancer, with or without estrogen receptors, on Tamoxifen. They hesitate to put any woman with a current case of breast cancer on estrogen-replacement therapy, and think twice about putting anyone with a past case of breast cancer on it either. However, as mentioned earlier, the tide is changing on this. Some physicians believe the small amount of estrogen in postmenopausal doses can make a tremendous difference to a woman's general health and will not shorten the life expectancy as regards the cancer.

Footnotes

1. University of California at Berkeley *Wellness Letter*, Vol. 8, Issue 10, July, 1992.

2. Read Kristin White, *Diet and Cancer*, who says that throughout the Western industrialized world, colon, breast and prostate cancers are major killers. By comparison, breast cancer among Japanese women was rare for most of this century. She says, "Americans consume about forty percent of their calories in the form of fat, while the Japanese fat consumption accounts for only about 15 to 20 percent of their calories." Quoted from a section of her book reprinted in *Vegetarian Times*, September, 1984. White says that breast cancer takes several generations to develop, and early diet in childhood is critical.

3. "... some biomedical experts believe that the simple act of detecting cancer accounts for a longer survival time without enhancing the quality of life. They conclude that while the cancer is discovered sooner and at an earlier stage, this does not actually promote any greater longevity. Women still die of the disease at the same age, but now live with the fear and certain knowledge of their disease. Because the disease is detected earlier, they have the awareness of it but no guarantee of cure." Winnifred Cutler, *Hysterectomy: Before and After*, p. 138.

"There is no convincing evidence, as yet, of net health benefits, in terms of reduced mortality or morbidity, accruing to women of any age who practice BSE [breast self-examination] ... Whether unequivocal evidence of BSE effectiveness can actually be produced in the social climate of widespread BSE promotion is very doubtful. In the meantime, there are substantial risks, as well as many personal costs, for the overwhelming majority of young women who present with breast masses found by BSE, only to have unpleasant subsequent investigations reveal no pathology of significance." Frank, J.W., and Mai, V., "Breast self-examination in young women: more harm than good?" *Lancet* 1985 2:654-7.

4. Eddy, D. M., Hasselblad, V., McGivney, W., Hendee, W., (1988): "The Value of mammography screening in women under age 50 years. *JAMA* 259L10:1512-1519, Bailar, J.C. (1988): "Mammography before age 50 years?" *JAMA* 259:10: 1548-1549.

5. "The 'simple' solution of surgery—cut everything out, and you will get rid of the tumour as well as the problem—has been found wanting. ... Skrabanek finds the evidence that breast cancer cannot be cured with

present methods to be overwhelming. He comments that "it is surely complacent to continue our current practice of subjecting ... women with primary disease to a futile mutilating procedure," and quotes Lowe's assertion that survival is much more closely related to the intrinsic malignancy of the tumour than to early diagnosis and treatment." Skrabanek, P., "False premises and false promises of breast cancer screening." *Lancet* 1985; 2:316-20, and Lowe, C.R., "Breast cancer." *Screening in Medical Care. Reviewing the Evidence.* Nuffield Provincial Hospitals Trust, London: Oxford University Press, 1968:33—both quoted in "Breast Cancer: The Debates Continue," by Tony Dixon, *Canadian Family Physician*, Vol 33: April, 1987, pp. 817-818.

6.   Haydn Bush, *Science*, September 1984, p. 34.

7.   "Tamoxifen: Special Considerations for Clinicians," Speroff, Leon, M.D. Dr. Speroff has also written many other articles, including "Hormone replacement therapy and the risk of breast cancer." He is a professor of obstetrics and gynecology at Oregon Health Sciences University at Portland, Oregon.

8.   Answer by George E. Block, MD, "Questions and Answers," *JAMA*, October 4, 1985—Vol. 254, No. 13, p. 1817.

Comments on Article by Dr. Don Gambrell

Women who are interested in the subject of breast cancer should read the very significant article "Progestogens and Postmenopausal Women," *The Female Patient*, Vol. 17, April 1992, pp. 43 to 45. Dr. Gambrell says studies show that women who lack progesterone long-term are at higher risk for breast cancer. The greatest increase in breast cancer by age is between the late 30s and early 50s when ovarian estrogen is declining and women's cycles are more frequently anovulatory. He also says there is strong evidence that menopausal therapy consisting of conjugated estrogens does not increase breast cancer risk; and three studies show that there is a significantly reduced incidence of breast cancer in estrogen-progestogen users.

HORMONAL PROBLEMS

Section Three:
Case Histories

CHAPTER 14

My Own Story

I became interested in helping other women when I was in my thirties because of my own severe hormonal problems during the previous decade. I would like to explain the circumstances in some detail to show how difficult the problem was, and how hard it was to find any help.

I inherited problems with PMS—my mother and sister both had severe problems with it. My mother had terrible monthly migraines, and still gets them cyclically, long after menopause. Because she had a hysterectomy in her early forties and because she smoked for sixty years, my mother, who is now eighty-two, has osteoporosis. My only sister had severe PMS and says there were times when she was afraid to go out in the car because she was tempted to kill herself. She once broke her best china set throwing it at the dining room wall. She also has had a hysterectomy, and is presently taking hormones. My mother also had a goiter, and my sister had to have surgery on her thyroid.

I started having PMS at age thirteen when I started my periods. But, as a child, I was moody and experienced a lot of fatigue. At age eleven, I had mononucleosis that may have been the beginning of the terrible fatigue that plagued me much of my adult life. In my teens, I could easily sleep until noon. I struggled through the afternoon, feeling as though I could sink through the floor with fatigue. I was a night person, and woke up about eight at night. I also felt the cold to an extreme. I was unable to sleep at night unless I had a hot water bottle or an electric blanket. Without one or the other, I would wake up shivering from the cold. I had these symptoms of low thyroid all my life, though my tests were always normal until it was discovered in my mid-forties that I had thyroiditis. I experienced dreadful fatigue from childhood on; felt the cold deep in my bones; had dry skin, and my eyelashes kept falling out.

From the time I started my periods, they were extremely regular— twenty-five days each month, to the hour. I never missed one. My periods were light to moderate, and I had occasional cramping, but it was never what I would consider a major problem. My problems with PMS started at puberty, with PMS lasting about four days a month. It was short but, while it lasted, the sudden drop in mood was intense and frightening. I felt as though my emotions fell off a cliff, and the suddenness and violence of the change frightened me. But I was fortunate, even though it was severe, because it only lasted a few days a month. I first went to a physician for PMT (premenstrual tension, as it was called then), in 1961, at age seventeen and living in New Zealand. The doctor gave me Valium, but I decided not to take it.

I went to a private missionary college for five years from age twenty-one to twenty-six. I was responsible for my own financial support the whole time. I remember my constant struggle with chronic fatigue while there. The last two years of my stay there were especially difficult because I was an assistant dean of women and had to stay up late to lock the doors. I found it was hard for me to stay awake late (though much of the rest of my life I have had most of my energy at night).

I met my future husband, Des, while at the college. He was my religion teacher, and I became his secretary for one year. He was married to a wonderful woman, Gwen, who was desperately sick and dying from breast and bone cancer. She had great faith and a very strong will to live, and these attributes enabled her to survive several years longer than expected. About a year and a half before her death, Gwen and Des discussed the possibility of his getting to know me better, if I was interested, with a view to marrying me later. This may seem strange, but it's not unusual for dying women to let their husbands know they want them to remarry partly to provide for their children. Gwen was a very sane, unselfish person, and it was in character that she would initiate this.

Gwen felt that, because Des was a public figure, we would not have a chance to get to know each other after her death. She also wanted him to marry as soon as possible because there were three children and one was only three years old at the time. So, the three of us spent many hours together. Gwen was in a wheelchair, and the three of us covered hundreds of miles on pleasant walks. It must have been a very difficult situation for Gwen to be sick, to know that her life would shortly end, and another would take her place. But you would never have known it. Her patience and humor lasted right to the end, and she died radiantly after years of dreadful suffering, weighing only sixty pounds during her last three years. She treated me wonderfully, like a sister.

Gwen's passing was a terrible loss, particularly for her two older children. She was a mature Christian, able to look beyond her present problems, but the children took her death very hard. It seemed so unfair because Gwen was a loving, kind, patient and guileless person, with no enemies. She wouldn't hurt a fly, and yet she suffered terribly. It seemed so unjust to them.

Gwen died in April of 1970, and I graduated from college after five years of study in November of that year. A month before my graduation, Des received a request to go to Manchester University in England to complete a second Ph.D. In that month, I told my parents I was getting married, and then worked on completing my exams. I had done all my major subjects in my last two years and was practice teaching that last year. We had to get passports and make all the other arrangements necessary for such a trip, and I had to graduate. I married at 7:00 a.m. on the morning I graduated, and Des and I went away for a few days' honeymoon. A week later, Des's youngest child returned home after living with friends for a year, and that night we all left for England.

As you can imagine, I had been under a lot of stress, and in the months before I married, the stress had affected my periods. They suddenly became irregular—nothing drastic—twenty-three days, twenty-one days, and nineteen days. But I had been as regular as clockwork (twenty-five-day cycles) for thirteen years, and I thought there was something wrong. I didn't realize that the stress of my circumstances was causing the changes. I also didn't know that most women's periods weren't as regular as mine and, had I known, I wouldn't have worried about this slight irregularity. But because I didn't know, when I went to my doctor for a premarital check-up, I told her about the irregularity, and she suggested

I go on the birth control pill.

Before I married, I did have a couple of premenstrual upsets, but Des attributed my emotionality to the duress I was under. There is no doubt that the pill made me much worse. A week after we married, the youngest boy came home after almost a year away, and we flew to England. Des and I had our first real argument during the trip, while we were in Bangkok. The following day, I started my period. This cycle of argument and resolution was the pattern for the following years. I stayed on the birth control pill for about three months. Then, because I realized it was making me continually depressed, I went off it, and all hell seemed to break loose. My cycles changed completely and, from then on, they were rarely twenty-eight days and usually well over thirty days apart. I started having problems for at least two and a half weeks during the second half of the cycle, and sometimes as long as a month.

I found that my symptoms started, like clockwork, every twelfth day of the cycle. Right from puberty, I had always known when I ovulated because I had pain on the right side of my navel each twelfth day of the cycle. This timing of ovulation remained the same after I went off the birth control pill, even if I didn't bleed until the thirty-ninth day. Once I ovulated, I began my symptoms, and they would worsen until I began my period. The longer the cycle was, the longer my symptoms lasted, and the more intense they became. But, as soon as I began to bleed, the symptoms completely disappeared, as though a veil had been lifted, and I felt perfectly normal for twelve days.

Some women have worse PMS every second or third cycle, depending on which side they ovulate. My symptoms were always bad, though worse during longer cycles. The patterns of symptoms was predictable. On day twelve, I would feel a sudden change, as though someone had thrown a switch in my body, and I began to change. First, I became extremely irritable. Within a day or two, I became absolutely exhausted. Then I went into a gradually deepening depression where I would withdraw into sullen silences, punctuated by sudden uncontrollable outbursts of anger. I could never tell when these were going to happen and ended up retreating into my bedroom for hours and days at a time. I would shut myself away from my family because I felt violent, and I was afraid of what I might do or say. I became very volatile and angry. My skin, which had always been very clear, became riddled with acne after being on the pill. Just before my period, I felt emotionally as though I was about to fall off a cliff, and I became extremely suicidal. I also started to have severe cramps for the first three days of my period. I had cramps before but nothing like this. Nothing seemed to take the pain away.

But every month, as soon as I began to bleed and cramp, I felt instant emotional relief. Then I had eleven good days (apart from the three days of cramps). I felt my normal, happy self at that time. Looking back, I feel that something "broke down" in me because of taking the pill which has never been permanently resolved. I take hormones, and they make a tremendous difference; but, if I go off them, I quickly regress emotionally and physically. At this time, I was on a vegan diet and running five miles a day. I was doing everything I knew to be right, but nothing helped.

Going through this experience each month was like living on an unpredictable seesaw. My husband, with typical male logic said to me, "Why can't you decide in the good part of the month how you will behave in the bad part." I told him that if I always felt like I did in the good eleven days, I would have no conception of what the other part was like. I felt as though I was in a watertight compartment during the bad days, unable to imagine that I ever had any good days. It was like finding yourself in the path of a huge tidal wave, or a battalion of marines—you were defenseless, totally unable to respond normally or to pull yourself out of the depression.

My husband thought my behavior was a reflection of my personality—that I had hidden this side of my nature prior to marriage and was now revealing it. As for me, I didn't really know what was happening, and I was terribly confused. Inside I felt like a trapped animal, and the thought that this was going to keep coming back, filled me with panic. I couldn't control my feelings or my behavior, and I was terrified and guilty. It's very difficult to explain what PMS is like to someone who doesn't have it, but it is devastating to one's feelings of self-worth. You constantly ask yourself, "Who am I?" Am I the nice person who emerges at the onset of my period for eleven or twelve days, or am I the cyclical bitch? When you take a vote on yourself and the bad days drastically outweigh the good, it is very difficult to believe you have much value. This experience in my mid- to late-twenties was very different from the one I had at age seventeen, when the PMT lasted only four days a cycle. In my twenties, the problems lasted so long in the cycle (up to twenty-seven days before my period), that I could hardly think of it as premenstrual.

I started to question my marriage. I had thought that God had led me into marriage, and that I had done the right thing taking on the family, and suddenly it seemed like a disaster. I felt terrible that I was making everyone miserable when inside I wanted to be part of their healing. I did recognize that it had something to do with my menstrual cycle, but when I started visiting doctors, none of them believed that the problem was hormonal. All I knew was that it occurred between ovulation and menstruation, and I realized the pill was a large factor in my change of personality.

While we were in England, from 1970 to 1972, I began trying to get medical help. I had a recurrent pain mid-cycle on the right side. It was only mittelschmerz (pain at ovulation), as I found out later, but, at the time, I thought it might indicate a problem that could be the cause of my PMS. I kept going to doctors looking for the source of the pain. Maybe it had something to do with my emotional problems.

A couple of doctors thought that I might have appendicitis, and I went into hospital to be checked, but that diagnosis was ruled out. The surgeon sent me to a psychiatrist who told me there was nothing wrong with me, and that I needed to learn to like myself. Later, still in England, I had surgery, supposedly for polycystic ovaries. Doctors I visited later challenged this diagnosis. They said I didn't have the symptoms (I was extremely thin, had periods every month, and no male hair pattern on my body). The surgery, supposedly a wedge resection of the ovaries, didn't help my PMS symptoms at all—they returned immediately to my great disappointment. Twelve years later I had a triple surgery for massive adhesions, a result of the surgery in 1970 which, I feel, on looking back, was totally unnecessary.

After we returned from England to Australia, I continued trying to find relief during the years from 1972 to 1977. Then we moved to the United States in 1977, and I continued my search there, alternating mainly between internists, gynecologists, and psychiatrists. Since I came from a family with a history of depression, it was probably understandable that much of the treatment I received grew out of the assumption that I had endogenous depression. I was also told I was manic-depressive.

My second encounter with a psychiatrist was in Australia when we returned from England in 1972. This psychiatrist, Dr. P., told me I was transferring anger from my father to my husband and put me in a private mental facility for a month to stabilize me on Parstellin, a combination of an antidepressant, Parnate (tranylcypromine sulfate), which is an MAO-inhibitor and has certain food restrictions, and a major tranquilizer, Stelazine (trifluoperazine hydrochloride). The medication seemed to help during the first cycle, but didn't afterwards. Still, I continued taking it for about eight months. Then, by accident, I ate the wrong food (a raw fava bean), and had an immediate and violent heart reaction. My blood pressure fluctuated wildly—first soaring high, then low, and I felt I was dying. At that time, I was grateful for this adverse reaction. I thought it was God's way of taking me away from all my troubles. But I didn't die. I just had to go cold turkey off the Parstellin, which made me feel even worse.

Subsequently, I went on a series of medications—Valium, Librium, Tofranil (imipramine pamoate), Norpramin (desipramine hydrochloride), Pamelor (nortriptyline hydrochloride), and Elavil (amitriptyline hydrochloride). None of this medication helped my depression. In fact, some of it made me worse—more nervous, more anxious, more phobic. I often woke up in the night terrified. During those years in Australia, when I was on medication and my depression would get out of control, a local doctor friend would, occasionally, put me overnight in a private hospital.

I found that the majority of doctors I visited weren't really listening as I recited what was happening to me. They never recognized that there was a hormonal connection. I was told by one psychiatrist (I visited six through the years), that my problems were continual, not cyclical as I thought. He said my problems were connected to the stresses of early childhood and the circumstances of my marriage, and that I was being stubborn and not facing facts. I would go home and think about what was said, but I knew it wasn't correct. Whenever I didn't agree with the doctors' conclusions or asked questions, I was told I was being stubborn.

I found, over the years, that PMS is a disease that drops between the cracks separating different medical specialties. Most doctors would treat the individual symptoms—headaches, depression, skin problems, heart arrhythmias, seizures, bronchial problems, etc.—and miss the common thread, the hormonal imbalance. A family physician might send you to an OB/Gyn. He might put you on the pill, (which landed me there in the first place), give you a tranquilizer, or (as in my case) look for something that needs surgery. Frequently, women treated for the individual symptoms of PMS become treatment failures because the basic problem is hormonal.

If you mentioned you were suicidal, as I was for years, the OB/Gyn, trained mainly in surgery and obstetrics, might take fright and send you to either a psychologist or psychiatrist. The psychologist would want to know about your early childhood, and the psychiatrist would treat with psychotropic drugs. I have rarely met a psychiatrist who will acknowledge that there is such a thing as hormonal depression. It has always seemed to me that PMS is an endocrine problem and endocrinologists are the logical physicians to treat it. But in fact, they generally don't.

I was living in Australia, in 1974, when I received my first gleam of hope. Help came from reading three books, written by a man, and two women, each with different training. The man was a medical journalist; one woman was a physician in England; and the other a psychologist in America. I have always felt it was providential that I read these three books within several months of each other.

The Pill on Trial, by Paul Vaughan, said that synthetic progestins caused depression; *The Menstrual Cycle,* by Dr. Katherina Dalton, described PMS, and said there was a cure—natural progesterone. *The Psychology of Women,* by Dr. Judith Bardwick, said that estrogen was a mood elevator. These books confirmed my belief that my problem was basically hormonal and connected with taking the pill.

I had been telling physicians for years that this problem must have something to do with my periods, because it was so cyclical, but they always tried to convince me otherwise. "You just think you're all right half the month, but, actually, you are continually depressed. You just won't face up to the facts." I told a friend who taught physiology at the college where my husband taught what I had said to others repeatedly— "This has to have something to do with my periods." She lent me a book she used for teaching about menstruation, called *The Menstrual Cycle,* written by Dr. Katherina Dalton. This book helped me remarkably, because it was a book about PMS, and it described my problem exactly. When I read the case histories in that book, it was like reading about myself. At last, my problem had a name—premenstrual syndrome. I now knew that many other women had been through the same experience.

What's more, Dr. Dalton said there was a cure!—natural progesterone.

As I have already mentioned, I had known at seventeen that I had PMT. It was the same problem, but it had just become much worse over the years. The thing that made it hard to believe in my case was that it lasted so long each cycle. Doctors often say that PMS cannot last any longer than two weeks because there is a timed connection between ovulation and menstruation—the average is fourteen days, but it can, they say, range from ten days to sixteen days. I always started symptoms the same time each month—on the twelfth day. But the cycle varied a lot and could be thirty-four to thirty-nine days. I would have PMS for almost a month AFTER ovulation until my period began with eleven or twelve symptom-free days BEFORE ovulation. Even though some doctors felt I could not have PMS because it lasted too long each cycle, I have met other women who also had symptoms that lasted longer than normal.

Still living in Australia in 1974, I set about finding Dr. Dalton's recommended treatment—natural progesterone. This therapy is still largely unavailable in Australia. Another friend, a social worker, recommended a psychiatrist, Dr. M., because he had told her he had been reading material on hormonal problems. While Dr. M. had good intentions, he inadvertently made me worse.

Not knowing the difference between natural progesterone and synthetic progestins, (and the fact that the latter could make me worse), he arranged for me to be given Provera, medroxyprogesterone. I was given a 100 mg. injection and told to take 10 mg. per day for twenty days and then wait to bleed. I found out, like many women with PMS, that I was extremely sensitive to progestins. Provera sent me spiraling rapidly downhill emotionally within hours of the injection. At the end of the month, I was crying uncontrollably. When I went back to Dr. M., he sent me to an endocrinology hospital in Sydney. They told me that we were on the right track, but it was the wrong hormone. They put me on another progestin, norethisterone, 10 mg. a day.

I couldn't understand why I was feeling worse on the hormones, but was sure they were making me more depressed. I decided to go home to my parents in New Zealand, and while there I saw yet another psychiatrist, Dr. S. He told me my childhood and marriage were full of reasons why I should be depressed. At the time, I didn't understand why I was feeling worse and worse on the synthetic progestins, and I was terribly disappointed after finding such hope. But, fortunately, I had written to Dr. Dalton, who kindly wrote and told me I was on the wrong medication, and that progestins were not the same as natural progesterone. In fact, they lowered the levels of progesterone in the body and often made symptoms worsen. She told me it was the progestin in the pill I had taken at the time of my marriage that had exacerbated my PMS in the first place. This made sense to me.

When I went back to Australia, still feeling suicidal, Dr. M. arranged to have 400 mg. progesterone suppositories made especially for me. They did stop me feeling suicidal, though I had been given so much progestin that I now was having bleeding problems. I bled for fifty days continuously, stopped for a week, and then started again. About this time, I read an article on Provera injections. In Australia, they were giving them to female inpatients in mental facilities, as a convenient contraceptive, because their sex lives were so difficult to control. A 100 mg. shot, I read, would make a woman infertile for three months. I had taken a lot more than that. The article also said that women could have bleeding irregularities for up to six months after having a single shot.

I had only been on progesterone for three weeks, when Dr. M. received a report from the psychiatrist I had seen in New Zealand. As a result, Dr. M. said I did not have hormonal problems—I was manic-depressive. He said they were going to take me off all hormones, and arranged to send me to a gynecologist to help regulate my periods. Then I was to go on Lithium.

I told him that I had already been on Lithium, and it didn't help. Dr. M. said that when I was on it before, I did not have regular blood tests for lithium levels. He had me speak to his superior at the hospital, supposedly a world authority on bipolar disorders, who said I was indeed manic-depressive; the pattern was not classical, but occurred on a monthly basis instead. When I told Dr. M. I was sure I had PMS, he told me I was stubborn, refusing to face the truth about my background and the circumstances of my marriage.

I went, that day, to see the gynecologist Dr. M. had recommended. He wanted to take me off all hormones and let nature regulate my periods. I told him that I had finally found out what was wrong with me and had just found the proper hormonal help, and now they were going to whisk me off before I had time to see if it helped. I asked him if he had ever been depressed.

"No," he replied, "I have a very even personality."

"Well," I told him, "I have been terribly depressed for a long time. I was desperate when I came to see Dr. M., and he has made me much worse. You may both be responsible for my death if you take me off progesterone, and I don't get some help."

I went home that evening feeling very desperate and cried myself to sleep.

Amazingly, the next day, I was handed another significant book. Another scientist, at the same college where my husband taught, knew I was struggling with depression and showed me a book called *The Psychology of Women* that had just come into the library. It was written by Dr. Judith Bardwick, a noted clinical psychologist, who was a teacher at Michigan State University. Dr. Bardwick had been researching the subject of women's psychology and found that, to date, the most popular theory was based on Freudian penis envy. She thought this was ridiculous and wrote her book as an attempt to rethink the subject. Though based on limited research, much of the material stemmed from her remarkable intuition.

The book was largely about women's sexuality, but there was an excellent chapter on the physiology of women and its impact on a woman's emotions. In this chapter, Dr. Bardwick described how different kinds of contraceptive pill—the combination and the sequential—with their different proportions of estrogen and progestin caused different and predictable patterns of depression. I had been on both kinds of pill. The portrayal of the differences in their effects on depression matched my experience exactly. I had also read, as mentioned, *The Pill on Trial,* by Paul Vaughan, and *Women and the Crisis in Sex Hormones,* by Barbara and Gideon Seaman. Collectively, these books demonstrated and explained the problems associated with the progestin portion of the pill.

The combination pill, said Dr. Bardwick, contained both synthetic estrogen and progestins taken every day, though in different proportions—more estrogen, less progestin at the beginning of the cycle, more progestin, less estrogen in the last half. Women on the combination pill who became depressed would experience depression every day.

The sequential pill, no longer on the market, contained high levels of estrogen in the first part of the cycle, and progestins during the last part of the cycle. Women on the sequential pill who became depressed would have typical PMS—they would feel fine while on the estrogen and depressed while on the progestin.

Bardwick had also done research on women's moods in relationship to their normal menstrual cycle. She claimed that women, universally, felt at their best before ovulation, when estrogen is at its highest. Then, premenstrually, when estrogen levels were lower, women experienced their lowest mood and were more negative; had low self-esteem and more nightmares; recalled bloody, violent episodes in their lives; coped less well emotionally. Dr. Bardwick blamed PMS on a lack of estrogen. This was the opposite of Dr. Katherina Dalton's theory that PMS is caused by a lack of progesterone and an excess of estrogen.

I had tried progesterone and it only helped marginally (though admittedly the form I took it in was not the best). When I read Dr. Bardwick's book, it gave me another great ray of hope. Here was a logical expression of my problem and a possible solution. I went the very next day to my local family doctor, Dr. E. He was manic-depressive, himself, and has, sadly, since committed suicide. He was a very kind man. I remember his visiting my son night after night when he had a bad case of measles. Dr. E.'s own horrific depression made him very sympathetic, and he had been wonderfully sensitive to my problems, though he didn't think they were hormonal.

I asked him if I could try estrogen, and showed him Dr. Bardwick's book. I told him the book suggested that estrogen was what I needed. Most physicians would have said no because I was only twenty-nine at the time, had periods every month, and showed no obvious symptoms of estrogen deficiency such as hot flashes and drying of the vagina.

He responded, "Why not. It can't hurt you." He gave me a prescription, and I went on estrogen that day. It was a fairly high dose and it was synthetic estrogen, but it worked like a miracle. I had a very dramatic response to taking estrogen and felt better overnight. After I had gone off the birth control pill, I had acne for several years, and began having severe menstrual cramps. My hair was lank. I lost weight and looked emaciated. As soon as I went on estrogen, overnight my physical and emotional state changed for the good. My skin immediately began to clear up. I was never to return to having the acne problem I'd been having for the last four years. My cramps went away. Most important of all, the depression lifted like a veil.

In my case, I found estrogen was far more helpful than progesterone, though for years I have taken both in all sorts of forms. That wasn't the end of my troubles, however. I was supposed to be on both estrogen and progesterone to avoid endometrial cancer. I couldn't get natural progesterone in Australia, and found that taking any synthetic progestin, even in small doses, made me feel suicidal within a short time of taking it. I also found out a year or two later that I was taking too much estrogen. It gave me a strange feeling as though my head was expanding. About that time, I found a woman family doctor in Sydney whose husband was a university medical professor specializing in hormonal therapy. She formulated a pill that was tailor-made for me. But I found that even the low doses of progestin she prescribed made me depressed and suicidal.

I have been in contact with Dr. Katherina Dalton ever since, but decided to also write to Dr. Judith Bardwick some months ago to thank her for saving my life twenty years ago. *The Psychology of Women* was a landmark book, way ahead of its time. When she replied to my letter, Dr. Bardwick said that her colleagues at Michigan State University, at the time, thought her crazy to write the book, but tolerated her. Her subsequent efforts to help women with hormonal problems were bitterly attacked by feminists who thought that any admission that women had hormonal problems would set their cause back many years. This was unfortunate because Dr. Bardwick was right on the mark. This attack against her is typical of the attitude of women who don't have hormonal problems, and one of the reasons why the cause is no further ahead twenty years after Dr. Bardwick wrote her book.

Reading Dalton's and Bardwick's books, with their opposite conclusions so closely together in time, left me with an open mind. I realized, even then, that some women responded to different hormones. In many cases of classical PMS, women respond well to natural progesterone alone. I was unusual.

In 1977, my husband and I came to the United States to work, and I switched estrogens at that time. I had heard about Premarin from an American friend while in Australia. Because it was from a natural source (pregnant mare's urine), I thought it would be better. I never did quite as well, emotionally, on Premarin, but did not make the connection until much later. When I was counseling some years back, a woman said to me, "I've been on all sorts of estrogen, but whenever they put me on Premarin,

I get depressed." Something clicked in my mind, and I realized I had the same experience. I started asking women about this afterwards, and found that some women with hormonal sensitivities do feel more depressed on Premarin. A doctor explained to me that it was the "horse factor." He said that Premarin contains about seventy different estrogenic compounds, including equilin equine sulfate. Some of these estrogenic factors will not function in human cell receptors, and some women get side effects from taking Premarin, including depression. I have found that many women feel fine on Premarin and should stay on it. But if a woman finds that she has side effects from Premarin, she should simply switch to another type of estrogen.

In 1979, when I had been in the U.S. for two years, I developed endometrial hyperplasia because I had used high doses of synthetic estrogen in Australia for several years and had only taken progesterone intermittently. I had cryosurgery on the cervix and then I was fine. My doctor told me to go off estrogen and never to go back on it. In the seventies, there was a cancer scare about estrogen that has since subsided in informed circles.

About that time, my husband and I went to live in Washington, D.C., for a year. While there, I suffered severely from estrogen deficiency. I can remember feeling as though I had concrete in my legs, and it was very difficult to climb stairs. I was also extremely anxious. Photos show me biting my lip, because I couldn't stop it trembling while being photographed. Starting from the time I went off estrogen, I had a few rough years with a return of my PMS symptoms.

Back in California, two years later, I was spending part of each month in bed, withdrawing from family and visitors. I thought I could never go back on estrogen, so I found a "Books in Print" volume at a library and ordered Katherina Dalton's latest books on PMS. About the same time, I was traveling somewhere on a plane and read an article about PMS in *Family Circle* magazine, and made contact with PMS Action in Wisconsin. I went on their mailing list and, shortly afterwards, received notice that Dr. Dalton was going to speak at Stanford University in San Francisco in a few weeks. It was an amazing providence because Dr. Dalton didn't speak on this side of the country again for another ten years. I went to hear her with a friend, Dr. Myrtle Caton, who was a board-certified internist, about to go into practice again. She knew my problems, and was interested in the therapy. By another amazing providence, my husband and I were both invited to Europe and were going through London the next week. That was the only time I have been invited to go with him on a trip to Europe!

When Myrtle and I arrived to hear Dr. Dalton, there were probably over a thousand people there. She was about to go up onto the platform. I spoke to her and told her that I was coming to England the next week. Could I see her? She said she was booked for four months ahead. I was discouraged, but my husband was determined, and he went and visited her in London. She gave him a prescription for progesterone for me, which Dr. Caton was to monitor.

In September, 1982, Myrtle sent me to PMS Action where I trained as a PMS educator/counselor and began working with her. We cooperated in helping women—I did the preliminary workup and education; Myrtle did the physical exam and prescribed the medication. Unfortunately, after we had worked together a couple of years, she became seriously ill with an autoimmune disease and had to relinquish her practice. Then I had to branch out and find other physicians in the area where I live who were willing to treat PMS.

The physicians I have worked with, have been open, interested, and really concerned. Most of the doctors I have worked with weren't initially well-informed on the subject. I lent them the books I'd read, and together we built up information and experience, here a little, there a little, over the years. I found that what helped me feel better helped a lot of other women with similar problems. After having a premenopausal pap smear at age thirty-seven and going into menopause in my early forties, I started to read more about menopause and began helping older women as well.

At the end of 1983, when I was thirty-nine, I was having a lot of premenstrual cramps which lasted from ovulation till the end of my period. Progesterone was only minimally helping me at that time. My gynecologist, Dr. J., could feel what he believed was either an ovarian cyst or a uterine fibroid. It was located higher up in the abdomen than would normally be expected. An ultrasound confirmed a mass which could have been a fibroid or an ovarian cyst. We decided on surgery. I hoped I could have a hysterectomy and no longer have to have my nightmare periods, even though I knew that this is not necessarily a cure for PMS, and that sometimes women became even worse afterwards.

During surgery, Dr. Jones found I had massive adhesions from the surgery I had in 1970. They extended from the navel to the pubic bone and were all through the abdomen, particularly on the right side. The right ovary was pulled upwards in the abdomen, and the bowel and omentum were wrapped around it.

After the first surgery, I had a bladder infection, and I was put on sulfa and sent home. The infection worsened after I returned home, and at two in the morning, I had to go to the emergency room, where a nurse drew off 1,400 ccs. of urine. Two days later, I went back into hospital, and large amounts of urine (1,200 and 800 ccs.) were removed by catheter over the next couple of days. When the infection didn't improve with IV penicillin, an abdominal catheter was inserted into the bladder under anesthetic. When I came out of the anesthetic, a nurse put saline solution into the catheter to test it. I nearly jumped off the bed because of the pain. I was given iodine into the catheter so X-rays could be taken. This, too, was excruciatingly painful. I returned to surgery to be patched up, the third surgery in ten days. The surgeon was worried that he had penetrated the bowel, but, fortunately, he hadn't. Because of the adhesions, and the fact that my bladder was distorted from urine retention, the holes in the catheter were in the abdominal cavity. The surgeon stretched the ureter and patched me up, and after that I was all right for a while.

A couple of months after the surgery, I hit a real low, physically and emotionally, with my hormonal problems. I was almost back to the state I had been in those earlier years in Australia. I knew I had to get help or I was in dire trouble. I couldn't live feeling like I was.

Through the detective work of a fellow sufferer and friend, who had called around nationally to find a hormonal expert for her own problems, I went to Dr. B. in Los Angeles. I stayed there for a month, while he tried to get me stabilized on medication. He gave me shots three times a week with a combination of estrogen, natural progesterone, and occasionally a little testosterone. He also put me on thyroid therapy. I started on .1 mg. of Synthroid. At the end of a month, I felt no better, so Dr. B. raised the Synthroid. Within a couple of days I felt normal again.

From then on, I did a lot better but, unfortunately, I developed side effects from the thyroid. For a while, I was unable to take even tiny doses occasionally without getting a severe pain in the back of my head. I tried changing the type and dose of thyroid medication several times with no success.

Several years later, I had contact with Dr. C., an Australian OB/Gyn who specializes in menopausal problems. He was interested in progesterone therapy and came to the U.S. with his wife to visit me and attend a conference by Dr. Dalton. We all traveled to Texas and heard Dr. Dalton speak. But when Dr. C. and his wife returned to Australia, they found they could not import progesterone, as it was not approved for use over there, except under research conditions.

Dr. C. read about the work of Dr. John Studd in London—a former student of Dr. Robert Greenblatt from Atlanta, Georgia. Before his recent death, Dr. Greenblatt was a specialist in hormone therapy and had developed the use of the estrogen pellet implant. Dr. Studd was now using it at St. Thomas' Hospital in London as a treatment for PMS, because the pellets give a continuous output of estrogen and stop ovulation. Dr. Studd believed you couldn't have PMS if you didn't ovulate. [As I have seen a lot of women who don't ovulate and still have PMS, I don't think the theory is correct; though the treatment works.]

On a visit to Australia about five years ago, Dr. C. gave me my first estrogen implant, a minor operation, requiring only a local anesthetic. He made a small incision and used a trocar to implant the tiny pellet of estradiol into the fatty tissue of the abdomen (it can also be put in the buttocks). [At the time of writing, estrogen pellets are not approved for use in the U.S., apart from research projects, so I get mine from Australia. They last me about two three months, though they last some women for up to a year. Depending on the dosage in the pellet, more than one may be inserted at a time. My estradiol pellet was 100 mg., but most of those available in the U.S. are 25 mg., so surgeons here using implants under research conditions may insert several estradiol pellets and, at times, they also add a testosterone implant. Several small pellets are actually better for absorption than one large one, because they have more surface area. Approval for a gel pellet is expected within a few years.]

As with the patch, the estrogen in the pellet goes directly into the bloodstream and straight to the estrogen receptors in the brain. I find that taking estrogen via the implant is much better than using any other form. I always feel wonderful within a couple of hours of having the surgery.

Though reading my history may make it sound as if I had one long protracted battle, there were years in between when I did fairly well. But the estrogen implant helped me more than anything else, and I have felt a lot better in every way since I went on it. I also take oral estrogen.

I also have found out that I have thyroiditis with high antibodies against the thyroid, but I have often had side effects when I have tried taking thyroid. Also my adrenal hormones measure low. I am not taking either thyroid or any adrenal hormones for these problems, as I find that taking estrogen solves most of my problems.

Some Things I Learned from My Own Experience

Through this experience, I learned a lot of things about life spiritually and emotionally, but my concern here is what I learned about hormones:

- Hormonal problems are real medical problems which should be taken seriously as such. Diet and exercise alone won't cure severe cases.
- Some women with PMS receive tremendous benefit from taking progesterone, and others don't.
- Estrogen will help some women with PMS. Particularly women whose symptoms occur after the end of their period, a time when estrogen levels normally rise.
- Many women with PMS comes from families where there is a common incidence of thyroid problems—more often hypothyroid than hyperthyroid.
- Women with depression may have chronic depression or hormonal depression or both. These two categories of depression are quite different and respond to different treatments. Most of the books I have read on menopause say that depression at that time comes from sleep disturbances. I don't believe this is true. I think depression is a bona fide symptom on its own.

My Present Protocol

My present protocol, which works very well, is that I have an estrogen implant every three months. I also take oral Estrace (estradiol) daily after I have been on the implant for four to six weeks, as it begins to run out.

Taking the oral estrogen on its own without the implant would give me a measure of relief from symptoms, but it doesn't work nearly as well as the implant. If I use estrogen injections, they only last about five days (they are often given every month). I have tried to use the patch more than once, but, like many women, I get severe skin reactions to the gel. I develop lumps under the bandage the size of a baseball. (A new Band-Aid patch is being developed, that should solve the problems of the old patch.)

The implant works amazingly within a couple of hours of surgery (I have had about a dozen of them). Both physical and emotional symptoms disappear, and a feeling of well-being dominates. I get maximum benefits towards the middle of the time I have the pellets implanted. The implant wears off just as quickly. If I don't overexercise (i.e., mainly walk for exercise), it lasts for two and a half months. If I go to aerobics three or four times a week, it only lasts six weeks. So exercise "uses it up."

The day the implant runs out, I feel an immediate change and begin to have joint pains, headaches, abdominal pains, and stomach aches. These gradually worsen, and I begin to sink back into the emotional fog that I used to experience years ago. But all these symptoms disappear immediately when I get a new implant, and I feel a tremendous calm come over me.

Estrogen is the main hormone that helps me. It completely lifts my depression, anxiety, and the suicidal feelings I experienced came after I went off the birth control pill. Without estrogen, I get migraines, severe joint pains, and abdominal pain from my adhesions. When the estrogen kicks in, all my aches and pains disappear.

I also take progesterone from time to time to counter the effect of the estrogen on the lining of the uterus and the breasts. This brings on a period, and I don't feel as well at that time. But it's nothing like I used to experience in my late twenties. I find progesterone helpful for some symptoms such as joint pains. I am experimenting with using testosterone, which I have read can be used in place of progesterone/progestin (though there are few studies on this).

I have also taken Synthroid .1 mg. and Cytomel 5 mcg. at times, but my need for thyroid varies. I can take it for some months at a time and then not be able to take it for months because of the side effects. When I do need it, the combination of Synthroid and Cytomel helps immensely with fatigue.

As I look back over the years, I am grateful for the people who have spent much of their lives devoted to solving hormonal problems. I feel that without the information I gleaned from them, I would never have found help, and I really think that I would have taken my own life in the end. As it is, I don't get depressed or suicidal, and I am profoundly grateful for this. It is this gratitude that fuels my own desire to help other women suffering with these problems, and I know these women exist everywhere.

CHAPTER 15

Barbara's Story

*B*arbara, a cheerful forty-one-year-old dental hygienist, began noticing problems about six or seven years after she had a tubal ligation, which was performed the same day she delivered her second baby at age twenty-seven. Her family history was fairly healthy, with no serious hormonal problems on either the maternal or paternal side.

When Barbara's periods first began, they were regular, about twenty-eight days apart, but long—generally seven to ten days of flow. She went on the pill at age nineteen, and took it a couple of years even though it caused difficult side effects such as mood swings and bloating. Subsequently, she developed an ovarian cyst, which the doctor thought was connected to the pill. At age twenty-one, she used a Dalkon Shield which caused erosion of the cervix, and, two years later, a wedge resection was done on her ovary because of the cyst.

Her two children were born when she was twenty-five and twenty-seven. Both pregnancies were fine, apart from low blood pressure and frequent fainting spells. Both babies were delivered by C-section and, as mentioned, the tubal ligation was done after the second delivery. She had no postpartum depression with either baby, but she had problems breast feeding both children because, despite continual leakage from the breasts, she could not seem to satisfy them, and when she stopped nursing, the milk dried up overnight.

Barbara's problems gradually increased. Always a high-energy person prior to the tubal, she found herself frequently exhausted. She had severe, incapacitating migraines just before her period, and often had to be taken home when one struck. Her head and skin itched and crawled and was so irritating that she wished she could tear it off. She was having horrible panic attacks and suffered from allergies.

Additionally, she seemed to lose her sex drive, which had never been high; but now she had no libido at all, and tried to avoid sex since it was uncomfortable because of vaginal dryness. Despite the dryness, she had a constant, heavy, watery discharge, and had been treated for this with cryosurgery on the cervix, which did not relieve the discharge problem.

She also had a couple of other unusual problems—what looked like an open sore on the aureole, and a recurrently swollen Bartholin gland, which swelled to the size of a marble. The swelling only lasted about an hour at a time and then receded, which her physicians thought was very unusual because that type of lump usually remains swollen.

Barbara consulted a physician who prescribed a combination of Estratest and natural progesterone. The estrogen helped her vaginal dryness and fatigue and, with the progesterone, stopped her monthly migraines. The testosterone helped her flagging libido and low sex drive. Barbara had a tremendous response to hormonal therapy and felt like a new woman. She came into the office and gave me a grateful hug.

Because she had no family history of hormonal problems and had never really experienced them herself prior to the tubal ligation, she responded wonderfully well to treatment. Other women whose family and personal history have been replete with hormonal problems may have a less complete reversal of their symptoms.

CHAPTER 16

Cassandra's Story

C assandra, fifty-one, took hormones because she had been having hot flashes and was almost past menopause. She had been put on the most typical protocol of .625 mg. daily of conjugated estrogens and ten mg. daily of Provera. She took the estrogen from day one of the cycle until day twenty-five, and took the progestin from day fifteen to twenty-five. Then she would have a "pseudo" or induced period, after which she would begin taking the hormones again on the first day of the calendar month.

Doctors are comfortable using this protocol for hormone replacement because it has been widely studied for effectiveness at menopause. Researchers have determined exactly how much progestin is required to ensure that women don't produce excessive build-up of the lining of the uterus which results from taking estrogen. They know that women who took high doses of synthetic estrogens without any progestin in the 1970s had a slightly higher incidence of endometrial cancer. Taking low postmenopausal doses of natural estrogens with adequate progestin solves the problem of endometrial cancer.

However, Cassandra felt sluggish and slightly depressed on this conjugated estrogen/medroxyprogesterone combination. Her friend, Kylie, suggested that she switch to another estrogen, such as Estrace with natural progesterone. She also told her that since she was now probably through menopause, she could take both hormones every day. Soon, the progesterone would "cancel out" the effect of the estrogen, and Cassandra would probably cease menstruating. Kylie even gave her a sample of both hormones to try. Cassandra took the hormones and immediately felt better. She found she had more energy and her sense of well-being returned.

When she asked her physician to give her a prescription for this combination, he said he would give her the Estrace, but balked at trying natural progesterone. "We just don't know how much to give to make the beneficial changes in the lining of the uterus. There aren't any studies published on using natural progesterone after menopause." He put her on another progestin, which made her very irritable. For example, she was making a sandwich one day. The bread was dry, and the ingredients kept falling out. In a fit of impatience, she took hold of the sandwich, threw it on the floor, and stomped on it. She and Kylie laughed about it afterwards, but Cassandra didn't feel she could fight her doctor and ended up going back on Provera.

Cassandra's case is an example of a very mild hormonal problem, one that most women wouldn't even recognize. All they know is that they are slightly depressed and dissatisfied with their lives. One could hardly say they are sick, but, nevertheless, their lives are definitely affected and the consequences can be significant. Such women may think that the reason for their dissatisfaction is their marriage or job, when, in fact, it is a vague hormone-related problem. The right combination of hormones can improve a woman's emotional moods and, therefore, has a large part to play in her outlook on life.

In fact, some study has been done on natural progesterone for hormone-replacement therapy after menopause. It has been determined that 150 mg. taken twice a day for thirteen days a month, or 150 mg. taken every day are sufficient to make the changes. Dr. Don Gambrell, a noted hormone researcher, says that taking 25 mg. suppositories of natural progesterone twice a day for thirteen days a cycle is adequate.

Not only do many women feel better on natural progesterone instead of the progestin, progesterone is better for them physically. Studies done recently in Europe show that natural progesterone is probably more helpful with treating osteoporosis than estrogen. Estrogen helps the cells retain calcium, but progesterone actually builds up the matrix of the bone.

CHAPTER 17

Dana's Story

D ana, a thirty-six-year-old intensive care nurse and mother
of one, had mild PMS, but suffered dreadfully from
allergies. She came to me because of the difficulty she had carrying her
pregnancies to term. She believed she had thyroid problems, but was
having problems convincing some of her doctors of this.

Dana's mother had been on thyroid medication from the age of
eighteen. There was a history of Hashimoto's thyroiditis, as well as breast
and other hormonal cancer in her mother's family. The two oldest aunts
had short-term treatment for schizophrenia, which Dana thought might
have been a misdiagnosed hormonal problem. At fifty-four, her mother
had a hysterectomy because of precancerous lesions on her cervix. She was
presently having monthly shots of depo-estradiol (estrogen) and bimonthly shots of depo-testadiol (testosterone). Whenever her hormone
levels dropped, she became very angry and paranoid.

As a child, Dana was very healthy and rarely sick except with
occasional earaches and a bout of bronchitis at age eight or nine.
Secondary changes occurred with dramatic weight gain at age ten, but
Dana did not have periods until age sixteen. She had no other health
problems until she was about nineteen years old, when she had painful
tonsillitis with a temperature of 104°F. She was sick with this for about
six consecutive months and was on penicillin for most of that time. She
has since been told this was classic for Hashimoto's disease, which was

not diagnosed then. She had a tonsillectomy at age nineteen, and her headaches, which began at puberty, developed into severe migraines after this surgery.

Dana's periods were always irregular, and, at age twenty-nine, they became even more irregular, and she developed a male body hair pattern. Polycystic ovaries were suspected; and this was confirmed by tests, but the hormone levels were always within normal limits. Yearly prolactin levels were usually slightly over high normal.

At age thirty, she was put on Clomid for infertility. Despite increasing doses, her periods remained forty-five to sixty days apart, and her progesterone levels were always low. A year later, on the tenth day of her cycle, she had a laparoscopy and hysterosalpingogram, which were both normal, showing no apparent reason for infertility. By day forty-five, because her period had not started, she was given a shot of progesterone to bring on her period. She had no period, but ten or eleven days later, she had sharp pains in her left ovary. On examination, the doctor thought she was pregnant, but a blood test was negative.

When she was given Clomid the following month, she had an extraordinarily severe migraine that day and thinks she conceived at that time. This proved to be her only full-term pregnancy.

For the first three months of her pregnancy, she had very severe headaches, and her blood sugar was out of control. When the baby was twenty to thirty weeks, she became very tired, but this was understandable since she was working for five physicians at the time. At her thirty-week checkup, they found the baby had dropped, and her cervix was dilated. Bed rest was advised and she stayed in bed, on her left side, for about eight weeks. Labor was induced because the baby's heartrate varied so much, due to the cord being around the neck, though that was not known at the time.

After delivery, the baby developed thrush which lasted eight months. She was colicky, allergic, and failed to thrive, and Dana's health worsened. She became dehydrated and had gastritis, diarrhea, congestion from allergies, one or two migraines a week, bladder problems, and pain on intercourse, which was relieved after treatment for yeast infection.

When the baby was a year old, Dana was doing better on a yeast-free diet and taking Nystatin, but she still had a lot of diarrhea and stomach-aches, and her hair and skin were dry. It took several years until these problems were resolved.

Her second pregnancy was unplanned, and Dana conceived without medical intervention. She had less diarrhea because she continued on a yeast-free diet, and so felt better. At thirteen weeks, an ultrasound revealed that she had a blighted ovum, and she had a miscarriage twenty-four hours later, with heavy bleeding. She became anemic, and her gastritis and allergy symptoms returned. Within two months, she lost another ten pounds, bringing the total weight loss to thirty-five pounds in one year.

After the miscarriage, she went to Dr. Z. who had been treating her for the yeast problems, and he put her on thyroid. She had been a patient of Dr. S., a physician in the Bay Area, who referred her to Dr. B., an endocrinologist, because tests showed she had high ovarian and thyroid antibodies. Dana saw Dr. B. in 1988 and he increased her Synthroid. She was also taking a little hydrocortisone given to her by Dr. Z. Dr. B. thought she might have Schmidt's Syndrome and told her that the Clomid may have worsened this underlying thyroid problem.

For a year, Dr. B. managed her thyroid problems. Her periods ranged from thirty-seven to fifty-five days, and she had mild PMS. She controlled the migraines and the gastritis with the yeast-free diet, though both symptoms were still present. In 1989, Dana saw a gastroenterologist who determined by a stool sample that she had blastocystis hominis. A course of Flagyl cleared the bowel symptoms, but she had migraines the whole six weeks she was on medication. For the next six months, Dana felt the best since her baby was delivered in 1986. Her periods were thirty-three to forty days apart; the PMS was mild and mainly consisted of sore breasts. She craved alcohol, but had to limit it because it brought on migraines.

Early in 1990, her cycles suddenly lengthened to eighty days, then sixty days. Dr. B. increased her thyroid medication to .15 mg. One month later, Dana became pregnant. She went off all alcohol. During this pregnancy, she had severe fatigue, and her blood sugar dipped precariously low. She had one to three headaches a week. An ultrasound was planned for fourteen weeks as no heartbeat could be found, and the ultrasound confirmed that the fetus was dead. All tests were within normal limits.

Dana's blood sugar levels remained low after having a D & E. She saw another endocrinologist who told her she had no business taking thyroid. She told him that she felt healthier on thyroid than she had ever before, but he said her tests did not indicate she needed it. Dana agreed to lower the dose gradually and eventually went off of it and experienced a progressive return of her symptoms and severe PMS. Another physician who checked her for a pituitary dysfunction felt she could not have conceived if she had a pituitary problem. He did not object to her using thyroid, and wanted her to go back on Clomid.

From July 1991, Dana was off thyroid altogether, until I saw her in September 1991, and she had only had one period. Her migraines had returned, and her allergies were much worse. Repeated TSH tests were mainly normal, but one test was borderline high normal.

Dana went to yet another endocrinologist, who put her back on thyroid and explained that in the case of thyroiditis, blood tests can appear normal. "It's not whether you have thyroid in the bloodstream; it's whether it is available at cell level." Since she had been on thyroid and was so much healthier on it, we knew that she would feel all right again once she went back on it. She was also a candidate for progesterone therapy because of her PMS, but because her PMS tended to go away when she was taking thyroid, we thought she might not need the progesterone.

Dana's story is a good illustration of a woman who is suffering severe, incapacitating symptoms (in this case, of a thyroid problem), yet her tests are mainly normal. She is a very intelligent woman and has worked for years in the medical system. She understands how doctors' opinions differ even if they are trained in the same specialty. Her instincts told her she should be on thyroid, but the varying opinions of the specialists she went to confused her.

I find myself sympathetic with both the doctor and the patient. The doctor wants to go by the textbook. He is understandably cautious about giving out thyroid medication if it is not absolutely necessary; and he is aware that side effects can be serious. However, we have not seen any serious side effects when using small doses.

On the other hand, the physician doesn't understand how miserable women feel with their symptoms, which are very real whether the tests show normal or not. When a woman with problems like Dana takes simple hormonal medication, the effect can be dramatic, relieving a lot of symptoms. Given the choice, women with long-standing chronic problems prefer to take the small risk of side effects, because they feel so much better. In fact, they know their body works better with a little help.

Why is it that physicians will give out other drugs like antidepressants which can produce really serious side effects, but are so reluctant to prescribe hormones, which the body produces naturally?

Says Dana, "I used to think there was this large body of information out there that all doctors tapped into. But it's not like that. They all have their own opinions and prejudices. When you work as a nurse as I do, you realize that doctors are not infallible." She's looking forward to having another pregnancy soon, and has hopes of being able to carry the baby to term.

CHAPTER 18

Jeannie's Story

I was sitting in my office one day when a man knocked at the door and asked if he could speak to me about his wife. He was a Christian minister and had heard me speak about PMS on my husband's radio program, and he wondered if I could help her. She had been put on a series of antidepressants and was presently taking Parnate, a fairly heavy-duty medication which required certain food restrictions. So far, she had not improved, and the next step was shock therapy. Jeannie's husband was vague about her problems, so I didn't know if I could help her.

When Jeannie came with her husband to see me, she looked like a zombie—stricken, pale, and deeply shaken by her experience. She told me that her problems began when she had toxemia during her second pregnancy. Afterwards, she had severe postpartum depression and became anorexic with no periods for three years. Her doctors tried the pill and Provera, but she did not feel good on them, so they decided to leave her alone. She did not go on antidepressants then.

She had struggled with depression ever since, and it had worsened in her early thirties. With the depression, she was having strong hot flashes, night sweats, and panic attacks, with very heavy periods. One physician told her that if she weren't so young, he would have thought she was going through menopause. She had been put on a series of antidepressants—Tofranil, Prozac, Xanax, Pamelor—and was now taking Parnate. She actually felt a little better on Prozac; but her doctor was reluctant to keep her on it, because of the controversy surrounding it, and had taken her off of it. Jeannie was given a little Cytomel (thyroid medication) to boost the Pamelor, but the levels never rose to the therapeutic levels, so her psychiatrist put her in hospital and did a "wash out," taking her off of all medication. He told Jeannie that it would take three to four days for the medication to leave her system, but she became very ill with chronic fatigue, flu-like symptoms, forgetfulness, and weepiness. Her doctor put her back on Xanax and Restoril, and added Parnate at that time.

Jeannie's mother had suffered from hormonal problems with severe mood swings and outbursts of anger. She had been put on Valium, and her uterus was removed when she was thirty-seven. Later, her ovaries were removed, and she was very sick afterwards. Jeannie's mother, now aged seventy, told me she had osteoporosis and arthritis, and that her vagina was "raw." But the doctors had told her she could never go on estrogen as she had a stroke history. I tried to tell her that she might be able to go on the postmenopausal doses now. The strong stroke warnings had been related to high doses of synthetic estrogens such as those in the pill and the older forms of estrogen-replacement therapy. Now, a woman could have a blood test for her antithrombin levels, which indicates whether she is at high risk for a stroke. But, because she was frightened by what her doctor had told her years ago, the advice fell on deaf ears.

I believed that Jeannie was indeed going through premenopausal changes when she started having the night sweats and panic attacks, and these probably were initiated by the postpartum depression and amenorrhea following the birth of her second child. I sent her to an OB/Gyn, who would put her on hormones.

But Jeannie had to wait a month to get in to see this doctor, and, unfortunately during that time, she inadvertently ate the wrong food and had a violent reaction to the Parnate she was taking. She went to the emergency room with a terrible headache. Jeannie had been warned by her psychiatrist what to expect if she had an adverse reaction, and the symptoms were classic; but, amazingly, the doctors at the emergency room did not know what Parnate was! Nor did they consult with the pharmacist. When Jeannie tried to explain, the nurse who was attending her told her rudely to shut up. It wasn't that Jeannie was aggressive; by nature she was the opposite.

She was sent home without treatment, her headache worsening. When she called her psychiatrist, he told her the problem was related to the medication and she should go to another emergency room. While there, because she had a temperature, they thought she might have spinal meningitis, so they did a spinal tap. Unfortunately, the procedure was done too low in her spine, and she became temporarily paralyzed. The staff further worsened her headache by making her stand up and walk around too soon. She was given several strong medications for the terrible headache she had, including morphine, but nothing worked. At the same time, Jeannie was bleeding very heavily, and her doctors felt they could do nothing about that until they solved the other problem.

She was taken off all medication and sent home and, gradually, over about ten days, the headache subsided. She kept the appointment she had made with the OB/Gyn, and the doctor, a woman, was horrified at Jeannie's story. She planned a D & C and hysteroscope to find out what was causing the bleeding. Because of what had happened to Jeannie with the Parnate, both these procedures had to be done without an anesthetic, and this was excruciatingly painful.

Afterwards, having determined there was no major problem, the doctor put her on natural progesterone and, later, on estrogen. The progesterone helped stopped the bleeding, and the combination of hormones helped the other symptoms she had been experiencing. Jeannie had gone cold turkey off the Parnate, of course, and was on no other medication. Despite the severity of her problems and the hair-raising experience she had just been through, when I spoke to her a few weeks later, I couldn't believe the improvement in her physical and emotional health. Nor could her husband.

I don't want to convey the idea that Jeannie's terrible reaction to Parnate is typical. On the other hand, I had a similar reaction to it and nearly died. I think it is very unfortunate when women like Jeannie and myself who both had hormonal problems are automatically sent to a psychiatrist for treatment with potentially lethal psychotropic medication, which is not appropriate for this type of problem. How much better to try a woman with obvious hormonal symptoms on a small amount of estrogen and progesterone first, than to give them a heavy-duty drug like Parnate.

Women like Jeannie are not only given a series of antidepressants, but often they have had shock therapy as well. This method of treatment has come back into vogue. Anyone contemplating shock therapy should read Peter Breggin's book, *Toxic Psychiatry*, published in 1992. Breggin is a Harvard psychiatrist who is against the use of shock therapy and psychotropic medication, both of which, he believes, permanently damage the brain. His book is full of information explaining his position and is a must-read. Some may consider him one-sided because he seems to advocate using no antidepressants or antipsychotic medication, and there are so many people who seem to find relief through the use of these medications. Nevertheless, his book is very thorough and has the ring of truth; and the information in it should be taken into account if one is contemplating either shock therapy or heavy-duty medication.

I try to keep an open mind on this issue, since some women do seem to need psychotropic medication. I see women who have been definitely helped by medication such as Prozac and Lithium; others who get absolutely no response to such medication (as in my case); and others who have major problems after taking such medication. Jeannie's story is a good example illustrating what can happen when such medication actually makes a bad situation a lot worse.

CHAPTER 19

Laura's Story

*L*aura was about twenty-seven years old when I first met her. She was married to a minister and had two small children. Laura had had problems from puberty, which had been compounded by repeated surgeries and her pregnancies.

Her mother and maternal aunt had goiters, and the maternal aunt and a cousin had dermoid cysts, but nobody in the family had the severe problems Laura did.

Her periods were irregular—two months apart—and long and heavy—lasting two or three weeks. The excessive bleeding caused her to become very anemic. She was diagnosed as being hypothyroid at age sixteen, and was put on thyroid and the birth control pill. The thyroid medication made her feel better and gave her more energy, but after a year, the family moved and she stopped taking it. Sometime during her teens she was anorexic and bulimic, and her weight went down to eighty-five pounds. She drank heavily and describes herself as a borderline alcoholic.

Laura took the pill until she was twenty-three, when she was diagnosed with cancer of the cervix. She was having a lot of pain and bleeding with her periods; and at that time, she discovered she was sterile. Her uterus was tipped, and her fallopian tubes were blocked with endometriosis, so she had surgery to clear out the tubes in 1978.

She had many medical problems after she was married, including a disease in the glands in the groin, resulting in six or seven surgeries. She went on Clomid to help her ovulate, but didn't become pregnant while taking it. Later, in 1980, she was able to conceive and become pregnant. She described herself as very emotional during this pregnancy, but not enough to prevent her enjoying the pregnancy. She was toxemic at the end, and the pregnancy went three weeks over. She didn't dilate, and, because of this and the fact that she had a small pelvis, she had a C-section. After the surgery, she lost a lot of blood, was very anemic, and had very low blood pressure. She felt as though she was dying, and was extremely weak.

In 1982, Laura became pregnant again, and was very exhausted and emotional during this pregnancy. She did not have toxemia this time, but did have another C-section. She was RH negative, though it caused no problems. Initially, she felt better after this pregnancy than the first, but within a short time, postpartum depression crept up on her and she had great difficulty maintaining control.

Shortly afterwards, Laura thinks she had a miscarriage. She hemorrhaged for a week just like she did during her second labor. Afterwards, she had pain in the right ovary, and her gynecologist thought she had either a swollen ovary or a tubal pregnancy and put her on the pill because her condition was not clear. She saw another doctor who did an emergency laparoscopy and unfortunately punctured her ovary.

The ovary remained swollen, and Laura was told she had postpartum depression since she was hysterical and seemed as though she was on the verge of a nervous breakdown. In 1983, a doctor put her on 400 mg. of natural progesterone, three to four times a day. This apparently did not help and he wanted to put her on the pill, which she refused because of her prior bad experience with it. Instead, she took Librium and sleeping pills, worked on her diet, and took vitamins.

Her doctor told her that her ovary was larger than a golf ball. At the time, everything hurt and she couldn't have intercourse because of the pain. Her uterus felt as though it was falling out, and it even hurt her to walk. After she moved to Pennsylvania, her ovary and uterus swelled again and became excruciatingly painful. She also had severe pain at the site of her C-section surgery. She had no periods for three months, and her uterus was growing larger. A doctor said she needed a hysterectomy and that he would also check out her ovaries. He removed the uterus and fallopian tubes, but left the swollen ovary alone even though it was bigger than the other one. He found she had lacerations of the bladder which were causing internal bleeding, so he patched the bladder and repaired adhesions from previous surgery.

Some time later, the offending ovary was removed, and then the other ovary began giving her similar symptoms.

When I saw Laura, she had extreme PMS. She would cry, scream, become violent, and throw things. She described herself as nervous, jumpy, and irritable. She suffered from insomnia and was having night sweats and hot flashes every day.

I sent Laura to a doctor, who put her on a combination of estrogen, progesterone, and thyroid treatment. It was the estrogen which helped her most significantly. Eventually, it became necessary to have the second ovary removed. She moved away from California and some time later, her husband called me because she was having a return of her symptoms, had lost a lot of weight, and was under 100 lbs. She felt as though she was dying.

I suggested she go to a clinic in Atlanta, where I knew she could get an estrogen implant. Like me, she had an immediate response to the implant and found that it worked better than any other method of taking estrogen. The physician implanted five 25 mg. estradiol pellets and one testosterone pellet, and she felt immediate and dramatic relief.

Laura now lives in California again and does well as long as she has the implant every three months. She and I have a similar need for estrogen. The implant only lasts us less than three months, but while it works, it is wonderful. She also takes thyroid but gets no obvious benefit from progesterone so doesn't take it. She also takes Prozac which she says helps a lot with her depression. [I have also seen women who have had very adverse reactions to Prozac.]

Laura looks fine, and is able to work full-time. It is sad to see a woman in her early thirties who has had to go through such terrible problems most of her adult life. But Laura is grateful that eventually she found some help, and her family is glad that she is back to a relative normal.

CHAPTER 10

Lynelle's Story

*L*ynelle is an intelligent and fun-loving thirty-eight-year-old, and a single parent with two children. After an extremely difficult marriage, she divorced and returned to school to train as a nurse so she could support her family.

While at school in 1985, she experienced a series of episodes with such severe anxiety that her mother had to come and stay to help with the children. She was given Xanax, and the problem lasted a couple of months.

When she finished school in 1987, Lynelle went off of Xanax, a process she found difficult because of withdrawal symptoms. By then, she had two part-time jobs and loved both of them. She felt she was under no more stress than she had been before. In fact, her marriage had been so difficult, that life was much better than it had been, despite being very busy.

Lynelle had been on the pill for years. Her periods had been irregular from age thirteen, and she was prone to heavy bleeding. In the summer of 1988, just before the return of her symptoms in 1989, she had been put on a high double dose of a contraceptive pill to control her heavy menstrual periods. This medication could have been the cause of her later problems.

She had always been overweight, but her blood pressure remained low until four months before her anxiety episodes returned in 1989. Then her blood pressure went from 110/70 to 160/100, but this varied and sometimes would be quite normal. She went on hypertensive medication to control her blood pressure.

Her hair which had been hip length began to fall out and break at the ends. She did not have it cut, but it quickly became shoulder length and lost its fullness.

In 1988, Lynelle went on the Weight Watchers diet and lost forty-five pounds. Within three months of stopping the diet, she became sick with a virus, and the episodes returned. Whether this sequence was connected or not, she is not sure. Although she had been a vegetarian for nine years before becoming ill, after the onset of the "episodes," Lynelle found that the only food item she could digest was meat.

In February of 1989, Lynelle became sick with a bout of bronchitis that lasted three weeks. About that time, she started waking up at night with heart palpitations. She had severe stomachaches with cramping and sudden diarrhea. Her head would become dizzy, and she would feel so ill that she would panic. This made her heart "flip flop," and race at 120 beats a minute. Two or three years later, she still experiences this racing heart at times.

When the "episodes" recurred in 1989, Lynelle began to think she was going crazy. She experienced a lot of anxiety and fear, and once, at midnight, her neighbor had to drive her to the emergency room. She was diagnosed as having bronchitis, but the physician in attendance said that the bronchitis was not connected with the racing heart episodes. He told her she was having panic attacks, due to stress, and wanted to put her on Xanax again. She didn't want to go on Xanax because of the problems she'd had with it previously.

Lynelle continued to have the episodes and had to take two months off work. She took her children out of school, and went to stay with her parents for a couple of weeks. While in the Bay Area, she saw a physician who suspected her thyroid was not functioning normally. The results were low, but she was on the pill, which he thought could be affecting her thyroid levels. The physician told her her health was in a serious state, and she needed major help to recover. She had two choices—to give up work and stay at home, or take her children to live with her parents. He said she was having a type of nervous breakdown.

Lynelle stayed with her parents for a week, and then her mother returned home with her to help her for a while. Lynelle was unable to drive at the time, because a rushing feeling, caused by the motion, would come over her, but, gradually, this feeling went away.

Lynelle was told more than once that her problem was psychiatric even though many of the symptoms were physical. Because Xanax appeared to help when she was ill before, she returned to the same psychiatrist, who told her nothing was physically wrong; she was just doing too much. He told her to take Xanax whenever her symptoms occurred. He also tried to make her hyperventilate in the office, in an attempt to produce an episode; but she was unable to produce the symptoms on demand.

Lynelle wanted a second opinion and saw another psychiatrist for three visits. The psychiatrist just took the diagnosis of the first doctor, without doing a work-up. But she did refuse to treat her with any other medication while she was on Xanax. By this time, Lynelle was dependent on Xanax again and going off of it was difficult, because her symptoms returned. Lynelle continued with this psychiatrist for a while; but made no progress, so, after three or four months, she stopped seeing her.

She then went to a family doctor who had a perpetually dazed and sleepy look, who was always yawning as though there was not enough oxygen in the room. During her time with him, Lynelle was again rushed to the hospital in the middle of the night. The emergency room called the doctor, and he said it was just another panic attack. The attending physician in the emergency room examined Lynelle and said that, while some symptoms were symptoms of panic attack, some of them weren't. He felt her problems were basically physical and recommended another doctor.

This new physician was a kind, Christian man. He did all kinds of tests, and really tried to help, though Lynelle says that when he did her pelvic exam, it felt as though he were "digging to China." Tests that he ordered included one to see if she had a pheochromocytoma, a tumor on the adrenals that causes sudden adrenal surges. She had an upper G.I. series and a Doppler Echogram to check for mitral valve prolapse. These tests all came out negative.

Lynelle actually had an episode in the new doctor's office. Her pulse and blood pressure went crazy. The doctor went out of the room to get the electrocardiogram, and by the time he returned, Lynelle's vital signs were normal. He put her back on Inderol for her high blood pressure and left her on Xanax. A couple of times, he called his staff in to pray over Lynelle, which upset Lynelle as she wasn't a Christian. He also gave her books on the Bible, and told her that part of her problem was that she was spiritually deprived. She told Dr. M. how discouraged she was. "You don't know what to do for me, and I don't know what to do for myself." He asked her, "Is this the way you acted towards your father and your husband when you were angry?"

Dr. M. sent her for a full work-up by an endocrinologist who ran all sorts of tests from the adrenals up. Lynelle commented that all the endocrinologists she knew tended to ignore the ovaries. He told her that she was hypertensive, overweight, and that it was all stress-related.

Lynelle had begun to chart her symptoms, and their timing in relationship to her periods became clear. She called a hospital resource center and was given the phone number of a physician who specialized in PMS; but when she visited the doctor, the doctor said that she was not familiar with PMS. She did not do a physical exam, and suggested Lynelle take vitamin B6 and call back in a couple of months. As Lynelle was leaving the office, she asked the doctor if she might not have endometriosis or thyroid problems. The doctor replied that she didn't think she had either.

She sent her to another endocrinologist, who checked her thoroughly again. Two out of her five thyroid tests were abnormally high. The doctor said that the majority would rule, and the others were flukes. One wonders what would have happened if three out of five had been high.

At this point, her family physician, with a bit of prodding, agreed to give her some natural progesterone. I thought Lynelle had some esoteric thyroid problem, as yet undiagnosed (possibly Hashimoto's thyroiditis, because her thyroid levels seemed to go alternately up and down). But, since the episodes occurred premenstrually, I thought progesterone might help, even though she didn't have typical PMS. It did help, even though she only took a little.

Lynelle then went to a woman family physician who examined her and felt a lump on the ovary. She ordered a sonogram which showed an ovarian cyst the size of a pea and smaller cysts, which could have been endometriosis. She referred Lynelle to an OB/Gyn who said she could also feel the cyst on the right ovary. She recommended a laparoscopy. Lynelle was nervous about the risks of having an anesthetic with her palpitations and high blood pressure, and resisted following through for two months. Then she gave in and had the laparoscopy. By that time, there was no cyst on the right ovary and no endometriosis, but there was a cyst on the left ovary. The surgeon also noticed a hole in a ligament on the right side which could possibly have been causing Lynelle's pain.

For a month afterwards, Lynelle felt fine, and she had no actual episodes for about four months. But then she began to have horrible clots and hemmorrhagic bleeding with her periods. If she stood up, she would immediately flood, and the bleeding would last for days. The OB/Gyn put her on a progestin for three months. During that time, Lynelle had to go the emergency room for the bleeding, and so Dr. B. increased the progestin to several doses a day. She wanted Lynelle to have a laser ablation, to remove the endometrial lining from the uterus. Dr. S. suggested a hysterectomy, and sent her for a second opinion to yet another OB/Gyn. He didn't think she needed a hysterectomy but thought she might have another cyst and wanted to give her a shot of Provera. Lynelle didn't want that because she knew that the shot would wear off around her period, and she might have an even worse time when her period finally came.

Four months after the surgery to remove the cyst, Lynelle had a return of her episodes, with irregular heartrate, up to 120 beats a minute, every minute or so, for three hours at a time. After these episodes, Lynelle would feel terrible, as though a truck had run over her. Her family physician sent her to a cardiologist.

The cardiologist determined by giving Lynelle more than one Doppler Echogram that she did have mitral valve prolapse. She changed her medication, but Lynelle still had palpitations, so the medication was doubled.

During the next three months, she was sick three times—with stomach flu, and a respiratory virus that went from strep to bronchitis.

Now, Lynelle is far from cured, and still doesn't know what is really going on in her body. But she is taking natural progesterone for the premenstrual symptoms, and this helps her a lot. It keeps her cycles regular, it helps her sleep, and she has no horrible, heavy periods. It takes the edge off her problems. Also, because of the natural progesterone, Lynelle no longer has the extreme episodes.

Lynelle only takes 100 mg. orally every evening during the second half of the cycle. She would probably feel even better on more, but she can't afford it. I still believe that Lynelle has a thyroid problem, and have always wondered if she might have a tiny pituitary tumor that has not been found. The problem is, the many tests she has had have found very little. The two thyroid tests taken while she had episodes did show an abnormality in the thyroid levels. But, unfortunately, her problem comes and goes in surges. Physicians have tended not to take that fact very seriously.

I asked Lynelle if she felt that doctors had listened to her. She said, "Generally, no. Medicine is a profession just like any other field—some physicians know a lot and others are inept. You could put four administrators or four cooks on a panel and get varying answers to the same question. It's the same with doctors.

"Most people think, fallaciously, that doctors know everything. After all, they've gone to medical school and they have a license. Not only do the patients think the doctor knows everything, many doctors are convinced they know everything, too. Or, at least, they believe they have the capacity to know everything.

"They don't listen," she continued. "They just make conclusions from the bloodwork and the physical examination. If they can't SEE the cause of the symptoms, the problem doesn't exist. It doesn't really matter how sick you feel. If they can't measure or define the problem, they blame it on stress, or emotional problems that twist the patient's perception of what is going on. If a person also happens to be overweight like me, they are even more prejudiced. The fact is that though I went on Weight Watchers that time and lost forty-five pounds, I put it all back on, and since then, I have been unable to lose any weight on any diet."

Lynelle continued, "I think there is a difference between male and female personalities in medicine. A man is a man, whatever his profession, and a lot of men have big egos. You don't try to tell them anything in their area of expertise or they will be offended. Women are better at listening, generally. Sometimes, however, medical training changes that. The medical profession has, traditionally, been negative towards women. Some women during their training have almost taken on the personality of the male to survive.

"Of course," she concluded, "listening takes longer. Most physicians have the pressure of financial survival—costs of insurance, rent, telephone, and personnel. They cannot spend more than ten minutes with each patient. They have to make a decision on what is going on very quickly, and this is hard when symptoms come and go as they do with me. But, though I still don't know exactly what's going on, I'm fortunate that natural progesterone removes the worst of those dreadful episodes I kept getting."

CHAPTER 21

Sandra's Story

W hen I first met Sandra, she was on the verge of suicide. Her eyes were almost swollen shut, and she had tunnel vision. She was having occasional seizures. X-rays on her back showed her muscles were in knots.

She was molested by her father for several years. From the age of ten, when she commenced her periods, she rarely ovulated. She was told she would never become pregnant; and when she did, her physician was amazed, because he felt she never had adequate ovarian function. The pregnancy was very difficult, and after a difficult labor she was told she should never become pregnant again. A year after the delivery, she had a tubal ligation, and, afterwards, went into a severe postpartum-like pregnancy.

Sandy went to a psychiatrist who put her on medication, and she feels this made her even worse. She felt depersonalized, as though she was floating above, watching herself. After the tubal ligation, Sandy not only became constantly depressed, she also started having PMS. This was relatively short in the cycle, lasting about four days each time, but it was very intense, and Sandy frequently left home for a few days to spare her family from her violent anger.

When I saw her, Sandy had been going through depression and PMS for nine years, and it had worsened the last eighteen months. She had been to many doctors, and two of them said she had severe PMS. In pursuing this possibility, she came into contact with me about ten years ago, when I had just started counseling women. I was really out of my depth when I talked to Sandy. I have seen many women since with severe problems, but none as bad as hers.

Sandy told me later that she was planning suicide when she saw me, and that if I had so much as blinked in disbelief, she would have done it. I arranged for her to see a gynecologist the next day. I happened to be in the office the day she came and talked to her, but she was in such a state that she didn't know I was there. She has no memory of that day or even getting to the doctor's office. Dr. J. gave her a double shot of progesterone, a great leap of faith because he had only just started using progesterone as a treatment, and her problems were so severe. The shot made Sandy feel better immediately, and the effect lasted about six hours before fading; but it gave Sandy the conviction that her problem was indeed hormonal, and it strengthened her to keep trying.

Dr. J. told her he could feel a mass on the left side. I sent Sandy to an internist friend, Dr. C., because she had more experience with progesterone therapy. Dr. C. had another gynecologist examine Sandy, and he was unable to find any growth. They both presumed Dr. J. was wrong. Actually, he was right. There were two pedunculated dermoid cysts. The problem was they were floating in the abdomen and had changed position. The cysts weren't found again for three years.

Sandy's problems were very complex. In three consecutive Septembers, she was admitted involuntarily to a psychiatric ward for suicidal depression. Physically, she looked terrible—white, gaunt, as though she were dying, with eyes nearly swollen shut and muscles in knots. She also had migraines and occasional seizures.

Sandy became so desperate that she called every PMS center she could find in the States. A receptionist for a group in Las Vegas told her about Dr. B., a hormonal expert in southern California, to whom they sent their most difficult patients.

Sandy went to Los Angeles. and stayed there for a month to receive treatment from Dr. B., an experienced physician who worked with his physician father for a combination of sixty years with women with severe hormonal problems. He treated her with estrogen and thyroid, but her response to estrogen was always initially poor. It would send her immediately into depression, but later improve it. A genius with diagnosis, Dr. B. told Sandy what he thought was wrong with her—she was bipolar, had thyroiditis, and thalassemia (a genetic anemia among Mediterranean people—she is Greek). He thought she had a dermoid cyst because of her poor response to estrogen. She also had some sort of infection—her white blood count was extremely high. Later doctors thought it was caused by the floating cysts irritating the organs in the abdominal cavity).

When Sandy went to a psychiatrist to pursue treatment for being bipolar and was put on lithium, she had a severe reaction, but realized later she was actually reacting to an antibiotic. At the time she blamed it on lithium and went off of it. This was very unfortunate because her depression became a lot worse.

A few years later, Sandy started having extreme abdominal pain, and one day it was so bad that she rushed to the emergency room. When a scan was done, the cysts were seen floating around and pushing against the liver and kidneys. Her uterus, cervix, ovaries, and tubes were removed. Despite being on estrogen, progesterone, and thyroid, she went into a horrendous depression with long uncontrolled crying jags, and was put in a psychiatric ward two or three times more.

A psychiatrist said she was classic unipolar (the depressed side), and Sandra was put back on lithium, which helped to finally stabilize her. After this, she found out that several aunts and cousins in her family had suffered from this suicidal depression, and there had been a veil of silence in the family—a very great mistake as it caused her years of agony. Lithium causes her to be somewhat forgetful and slurs her speech. But it stops her terrible crying jags and the horrendous depression. She says she needs both the lithium and the hormones.

During this time, Sandy trained as a medical assistant and held a full-time job in a hectic practice. A very intelligent and capable woman, she showed incredible courage through the terrible protracted experience she went through. Most women would have killed themselves. She survived because of a rare inner strength and determination.

Although her symptoms appeared purely hormonal, it seems as though she had inherited depression, and this was always triggered by some hormonal event. Her problem was a combination of hormonal breakdown and depression, and both elements required treatment for full recovery. Because psychiatrists, as a group, don't really believe that hormonal problems cause depression, they usually only treat the one side of the problem, and frequently have limited results with antidepressants because they don't address the hormonal issue.

Section Four:
Treatment

CHAPTER 22

Diet

D iet is very important for women with hormonal problems because the cells in the body are dependent on good nutrition for good health and function. Poor diet may be largely responsible for the existing hormonal problem and certainly makes symptoms worse. Changes in diet make a considerable contribution to treatment for some women, particularly those with mild problems who have been on a poor diet for years.

On the other hand, severe hormonal problems probably won't respond to diet alone. The problems we describe in this book are endocrine disorders—chronic medical problems that pass the boundary between "natural" and hormonal treatment. A good comparison is the treatment for diabetes. At certain stages and with different types of diabetes, dietary change may be all that is needed to handle the disease. But, at some point or with certain types of diabetes, the patient needs insulin. Without it, they will die.

Women with hormonal problems may not actually die from their symptoms (though they might want to), but the analogy is similar. There comes a point at which diet and supplements are not adequate as treatment.

An Excellent Guide for PMS
Dr. Susan Lark has written two outstanding books, *The PMS Self-Help*

Book and *The Menopause Self-Help Book.* Dr. Lark is not only a physician, but she loves to cook. Her books are very practical and informative, and contain many recipes with step-by-step instructions for good nutrition, plus information on supplements, herbs and relaxation exercises that will eliminate or improve many women's symptoms.

Supplements and Diet Not Always Effective

In her practice in the Bay Area, Dr. Lark treats PMS with natural remedies, and rarely uses hormones. I am sympathetic with this approach and feel it is effective for some women. But, if after trying natural remedies, she meets with no success, a woman should not feel she has failed. The next step may be hormone-replacement therapy, and if she needs hormones, she should not be afraid to take them.

I have seen many women who are on a good diet, who take the right herbs and supplements, and are on a good exercise program. Yet, these measures have made little improvement in their hormonal problems. At my worst with PMS, I was eating an unprocessed vegan diet, taking herbs, and running five miles a day over a period of years, all of which did nothing to help my PMS.

Diet Is Important for General Health

The incidence of all chronic diseases, such as heart disease, hypertension, diabetes, and cancer, is much higher in western countries. Many studies have shown that, when people in other countries with a simpler, more natural diet emigrate to the United States, within a couple of generations, they begin to develop the diseases of the West. Breast and other cancers, heart disease, stroke, and osteoporosis have been strongly linked to a high-fat, high-protein diet, eaten in early childhood and the teen years. Diet in the adult years is also important, but the growing years are more important, and, unfortunately, what we ate in childhood was largely beyond our control.

The Best Type of Diet

What is the best diet for hormonal health?

The consensus of sixteen world committees on this subject is that we should be **largely** vegetarian, using natural, **unprocessed** foods, particularly **whole** grains, and peas, beans, and lentils, all of which are naturally high in vitamins B and E, and fruit and vegetables, which are rich in vitamins C and A. Though some vegetables need cooking because the starch is indigestible, raw food should comprise a large part of the diet. Foods high in animal protein, animal fat, other fats, salt, or sugar should be treated as concentrates and used sparingly.

Recent Chinese Study

The China Diet Study began gathering information on the life-styles of 6,500 Chinese adults, living in 65 countries, in 1983. This study is now in its final stages. It is the most comprehensive study ever done on Chinese people.

Highlights of this 920-page study show that:

1. Obesity has more to do with which kind of food one eats than how many calories one eats. Chinese natives eat 20 percent more calories than Americans do, but Americans are 25 percent heavier. This is because the Chinese eat three times the amount of starch and only a third the amount of fat that Americans eat. This is a more important factor than exercise.

2. Cholesterol levels in China are much lower than in America. The Chinese average is 127 mg. percent, compared to 212 mg. percent in the U.S.

3. For every heart attack in China there are sixteen in the United States.

4. Protein intake in China is one-third less than in America (64 gr. compared to 100 gr.).

5. Female cancers relate to diet. A childhood diet high in protein, fat, calcium, and calories promotes rapid growth and early onset of menstruation. This increases a woman's risk for developing cancer of the reproductive organs and the breast. Chinese women rarely get these cancers, and they begin to menstruate three to six years later than American women.

6. Osteoporosis is rarely found in China, though Chinese women eat only half the calcium that American women eat. Most Chinese eat no dairy products at all, and obtain their calcium from plant foods.

7. The Chinese diet is three times richer in fiber than the American diet, resulting in relatively low rates of colon cancer in China.

8. Iron-deficient anemia is rare in China, though their diet is mainly plant food, and they rarely eat meat.

Dr. T. Colin Campbell says these findings will challenge our traditional beliefs about protein, calcium, weight control, ideal cholesterol levels, dietary fiber, and vitamin requirements.[1]

Beware of Fads

There have always been many fads in promoting diet, just as there are fads in medical treatment. For instance, Adelle Davis wrote interesting and influential books on diet in the 1960s. Some of the theoretical material was very good, and many people still swear by it. Her books have many good points, and they recommend eating lots of fruits, vegetables, and unrefined grains. But the diet Davis recommended was extremely high in animal protein and fat. These are the very food items which lead to western diseases—heart disease, cancer, osteoporosis, diabetes, diverticulosis, and hemorrhoids.

The Error of the Four Food Groups

To show the power of a fad, consider how nutritionists swore by the "four food groups" as a theory of good nutrition for many years. Two out of four food groups were animal products—meat and milk, giving the impression that a person's diet should be 50 percent animal products.

Nutritionists have changed the four food groups theory because they now know that eating a lot of animal products leads to heart disease and all the other western diseases. Now they use the illustration of a pyramid.

Meat	Milk and Eggs
Grains	Fruits and Vegetables

The base of the pyramid is carbohydrates because, worldwide, more nations eat more grains than fruits and vegetables. Meat and dairy products have been put at the top of the pyramid. This illustration shows more clearly that animal products are concentrated and should be a relatively small proportion of the diet.

I like to reverse the triangle and put fruits and vegetables above carbohydrates. The pyramid then shows that people should eat lots of fruits and vegetables, then carbohydrates, then legumes, then concentrates such as meat and animal products, other high-protein and fat foods, sugars, and salt.

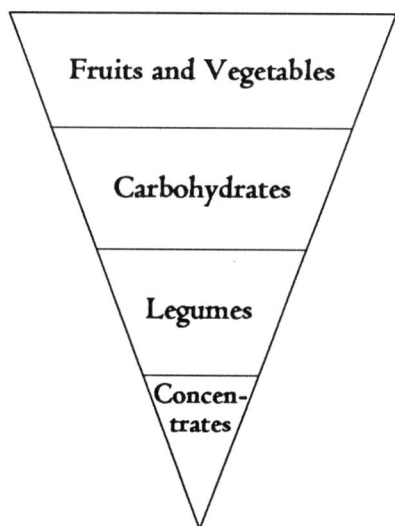

```
      _____
      \   Fruits and Vegetables   /
       \                         /
        _____/
         \    Carbohydrates    /
          \                   /
           _____/
            \   Legumes     /
             _____/
              \ Concen- /
               \ trates /
                _____/
                 \    /
                  \  /
                   \/
```

High Protein Another Fad

Emphasizing the need for protein has led many people to consume far too much of it, and because most high-protein foods are also high-fat foods, they eat too much fat. A lot of protein, especially from animal sources, is extremely difficult for the body to digest. The process of excreting proteins puts a heavy load on the kidneys, because so much more water is needed to excrete protein than other nutrients. Along with the loss of fluid, there is a loss of bone minerals which are leached out into the urine. This process then brings on early calcium loss and eventually paves the way for osteoporosis.

Meat, milk, and cheese are often recommended as good sources of calcium. Though they have much higher levels of calcium than nuts and vegetables, the high protein and fat in these products inhibits the absorption of calcium. Therefore, it is better to get calcium and other minerals, such as magnesium and potassium directly from fresh vegetables.

Vegetarian Fads

Vegetarians who avoid all the problems of meat can run into other problems with fads. For instance, it is easy to eat even more fat if you eat a lot of eggs, milk, cream, nuts, and avocados, and use refined or cold-pressed cooking oils.

When I first became a vegetarian in Australia, I attended cooking schools that taught people to cook appealing meat substitutes, such as "gluten steaks" (made from the gluten in flour). These gluten products, such as gluten mince or gluten steak, could be made to taste absolutely delicious.

In actual fact, gluten is a very poor protein made from white flour. It has less nutrition and fewer vitamins and minerals than white flour. Since it has no fiber, if people eat it day after day as a meat substitute, they are asking for trouble, and those who eat gluten regularly have been shown to have a higher incidence of bowel cancer.

Soybeans Killed the Cats

Other canned meat substitutes were made from soybeans and widely recommended as a nutritional breakthrough. You could buy chicken-like, beef-like, and turkey-like products. Since Australians eat a lot of meat, some people just substituted these gluten and soy products and ate them three times a day.

Local scientists on a college campus tried feeding the campus cats with these soymeat substitutes. The cats died one by one, and autopsies revealed that the undigested soymeat had backed up and solidified in their intestinal tracts. If you read the nutritional information on many of these products, you would be surprised at the chemical additives used to make them palatable. People who eat these products regularly have a higher incidence of pancreatic cancer.

Many vegetarians, thinking they are being smart in avoiding meat, would be better off eating a little meat, rather than these synthetic meat substitutes with their chemical additives.

Simple Common Sense Can Help You Avoid Fads
The few illustrations given above show how diet fads, which are popular for decades, can be dead wrong. Rather than promoting good health, they do the opposite and leave a trail of disease. How can you test each theory or fad and know quickly whether a dietary suggestion is good?

1. Eat simple, wholesome food—natural foods prepared in as natural a way as possible.
2. Avoid refined foods—that is, fats, grains, and sugars that have been processed. Simple sugars such as cane sugar, raise the levels of the blood fats (triglycerides) and increase the cholesterol.
3. Use high-fat, high-sugar, and high-protein foods as concentrates, sparingly, in the diet. Consider meat as a condiment.
4. Avoid or restrict anything else detrimental to health—such as alcohol, caffeine, and smoking. All of these substances increase glycogen in the liver and tend to cause blood sugar fluctuations. Caffeine also increases free fatty acids which accelerate the development of heart disease and diabetes.
5. Find out which foods suit your digestion. Avoid foods you are allergic to when possible.
6. Drink about eight glasses of water a day. People who eat a lot of fruit may not need as much. Note that the intake of huge quantities of water can be dangerous.
7. Try to eat quality food from good sources calmly, joyfully, and gratefully.

A Handy Summary
As far as the **type of food** is concerned, eat:

Fruit and vegetables
ABUNDANTLY
Whole grains and cereals
MODERATELY
Beans, peas, and lentils
OFTEN
Fats and concentrates
SPARINGLY

As far as **quantity** is concerned:

Eat like a **KING** for breakfast
Eat like a **PRINCE** at lunchtime
Eat like a **PAUPER** at supper
(Much of the food eaten after 5 p.m.
in the day is likely to be stored as fat.)
(For women with functional low blood sugar,
it may be better to eat smaller meals, including some
carbohydrate, every three or four hours.)

What Are Concentrates?

Concentrates are foods that are either high in protein, fat, or sugar. Concentrates include meat, butter, milk, cheese, salt, cream, cooking oil, margarine, nuts, sugar, candy, jams, honey, and yeast powder.

Nuts, avocados, olives, etc., contain high-fat levels. While the type of fat is not as saturated as that in animal products, it is still a concentrate and should be eaten sparingly. Avoid nuts that have been cooked in oil. It is best to eat freshly shelled nuts.

Public Enemy #1—Refined and Saturated Fats

Because of the affluence of the western world and the invention of refrigeration, fat intake has increased dramatically this century. Only a very little added fat in the diet is actually necessary for life. The body produces most of the fat it needs by metabolizing carbohydrates and sugars.

When thyroid or estrogen are low, cholesterol levels tend to increase, which is a major reason women with hormonal problems need to be concerned about their intake of fats. To summarize the following, eat less fat!

The Essential Fat

The only essential fatty acid that the body cannot make without a dietary source is linoleic acid (and arachidonic acid, but this is synthesized from linoleic acid in the body). The requirement for this fatty acid is small and easily obtained in a starch-centered diet (for instance, there is enough linoleic acid in three tablespoons of oatmeal to provide a day's need). There is very little of this essential fatty acid in animal products.

Therefore, most of the fat we consume is unnecessary nutritionally. We eat fat because it makes things taste good and satisfies hunger for a longer period of time. The main problem with fat is that it clogs the arteries.

Different Types of Fat in Your Diet

Generally, you can divide dietary fat into two groups—**A. naturally occurring fats** in food and **B. refined or processed fats** that have been altered by man. Both can create problems, but particularly the refined fats.

A. Naturally occurring animal and vegetable fats all contain saturated, polyunsaturated, and monounsaturated fats in varying proportions.

Saturated fats are mainly solid at room temperature. Sources of saturated fats are animal products, such as beef, pork, and dairy products. Chocolate, coconut, and palm oil are the only common plant sources that are rich in saturated fats. Saturated fats increase cholesterol.

Polyunsaturated fats. These tend to be more fluid at room temperature, and are found in high concentrations in vegetables, fish, and poultry. Polyunsaturates do not increase cholesterol directly in the body. They do, however, raise the LDLs. While all fats become rancid, polyunsaturated fats go rancid faster. In the body, they break down into free radicals, which are cells that tend to go berserk, metaphorically throwing a monkey wrench in the works.

Monounsaturated fats. They are in a liquid form. These are found in olives, peanuts, and olive oil and canola oil (the best oils to use if unprocessed).

It's the Proportion That Varies

Both animal and plant foods contain saturated, polyunsaturated, and monounsaturated fats, but the proportions are different.

Meat and animal products contain mostly saturated fats, some polyunsaturated fats, and very little monunsaturated fats. They also contain cholesterol, a waxy, fatty alcohol always found in association with other fat cells in the human body.

Plants contain mostly polyunsaturated fats, less saturated fats, and some monounsaturated fats. Chocolate, coconut , and palm oil are two plant fats that contain a high proportion of saturated fat. Olive, canola, and peanut oil are especially high in monounsaturated fats. **Plant foods contain no cholesterol.**

Fish contains mostly polyunsaturated fats because they would otherwise solidify in cold water. But **fish contains as much or more cholesterol as meat.**

B. Refined fats, also called hydrogenated fats

These are made by chemically adding hydrogen to vegetable oils, for instance, in making margarine. The hydrogenation process converts the oils into more saturated fats, which are solid at room temperature.

Margarine has been touted for years as better than butter in prevention of heart disease because of its "polyunsaturated" fats, but the process of hydrogenization makes the use of these fats very questionable. Such refined fats do not contain cholesterol, but they increase heart disease by raising the LDLs and triglycerides, and decrease the HDLs. To understand this, we need to understand how the body handles the digestion of fats.

Cholesterol and Triglycerides

To determine the amount of fat in your body, the physician will test the amount of cholesterol, triglycerides, and high, low, and very low density lipids (HDLs, LDLs, VLDLs) in your blood.

Cholesterol is a waxy, fatty, alcohol found in conjunction with fatty acids in the body. It is necessary for life and is produced in various places throughout the body. Therefore, it is not necessary to eat any added cholesterol. Eating large quantities of animal products causes the cholesterol to rise. The higher the levels of cholesterol, the more likely a person will be to have fatty plaques on the inside of their arteries and the more likely they are to have a heart attack from blockage of the heart vessels, or a stroke from narrowing of the blood vessels in the brain.

Presently a normal cholesterol level is 200 or less for women, (though closer to 150 is better). Levels below 130 can interefere with the liver's ability to regulate and convert hormones.

Triglycerides are fatty acids (saturated, polyunsaturated, and monounsaturated fats) that are formed in the body by the breakdown of simple sugars and complex carbohydrates. Simple carbohydrates and sugars raise the level of triglycerides higher than complex carbohydrates do.

Triglyceride levels are part of the overall profile of fats in your body and are frequently elevated in people with heart disease and diabetes.

Different Types of Fatty Cells in the Body

[While there are only a few types of fatty globules listed, there are many subgroups.]

The **chylomicron** is the largest fatty cell in the body with the thinnest protein coating. It is produced in the intestine from the breakdown of triglycerides. It contains 97 percent fat and 3 percent alcohol and is the most unstable of the fatty cells.

The **alpha globules** (HDLs, the good cholesterol) are the smallest fatty cells in the body. They contain both fat and cholesterol and have a heavy protein coating, which makes them the most stable type of fatty cell. HDLs act like a broom in the blood stream sweeping out excess cholesterol.

The **beta globule** comes in two sizes—large (VLDL) and small (LDL). These are larger than alpha cells and have a thinner protective coating. They are also much less stable than alpha cells.

The **large beta globule** is made up of twice as much fat as cholesterol. When there is an excess of large beta globules in the blood, the cholesterol levels will be elevated. That means you are eating too much saturated fat and cholesterol from animal sources.

The **small beta cell** is made up of twice as much cholesterol as fat. When there are high levels of small beta cells in the blood, triglyceride levels will be elevated, indicating a diet rich in calories from refined carbohydrates (refined grains and sugars).

Where levels of chylomicron and large and small beta fatty cells are high, they become unstable and dangerous, causing both the cholesterol and triglyceride levels to be elevated.

LDLs and, particularly, VLDLs, inhibit the effect of the HDLs and encourage the clogging effect of cholesterol. So, when your cholesterol levels are checked, the proportion of HDLs to LDLs is extremely important, and the doctor hopes to see high levels of HDLs in proportion to low levels of LDLs.

Summary on Fats

Some fats are definitely worse than others, but it is best to concentrate on decreasing overall fat intake. All fats, including cold-pressed vegetable oils, promote the growth of cancers in animals, and there is a definite link between breast cancer and intake of fat.

Meat eaters should cut down on their fat intake. But vegetarians should not think that because they don't eat meat, they can eat large quantities of hard cheese, cream, butter, milk, eggs, or salad dressings, margarine, and cooking oils.

At the other end, don't be too extreme. Some women who go on an extremely low-fat diet start to age rapidly. Because estrogen is produced in the fat cells, a nonfat diet can cause estrogen deficiency, which shows up as wrinkled skin, dull hair, and premature aging. Use some freshly shelled nuts and avocados.

Refrigeration and Milling Have Made the Difference

Keep in mind that today we are plagued with diseases hardly known before this century. Massive coronary heart disease, diabetes, and other western diseases were not the plagues of earlier generations. They have come only with the processing of foods, particularly grains, and the ability to refrigerate fats. Towards the end of the nineteenth century, white flour became a universal product because of the invention of the millstone. With refrigeration, it became possible to store animal fats for long periods of time, and so they became a much bigger part of the average person's diet.

Public Enemy #2—Refined or Processed Foods?

As whole grains are processed, the outer bran on the seed is discarded. With it goes most of the nutrients necessary for digestion. Most of the fiber is also removed, and fiber is necessary for rapid transit of food through the digestive tract. For both these reasons, refined foods put a heavy burden on the digestive system, and, eventually, cause a breakdown in health.

In countries such as Africa, where people eat a native diet with whole grain porridges, diseases caused by lack of fiber in the diet, such as bowel cancer, diverticulitis, hemorrhoids, and varicose veins are virtually unknown.

People who eat unrefined, whole grains can handle fat in the diet better, too, because the fiber in whole grains helps sweep the fat out of the system. (Unrefined grains are whole grains that have not been through the milling process.)

It is best to buy the grain yourself, and grind it as you need it. Like milk, grains will become rancid soon after grinding and should be refrigerated and used quickly. Even whole grains—bread without preservatives, flour, porridge, wheat germ, and bran will quickly go rancid on store shelves. That's why preservatives are often used.

Refined grains include white flour, white rice, white sugar, tapioca, glucose, flour, corn flour, gluten flour, pearled barley, white spaghetti, and all forms of white pasta.

Grains Are Good for Premenstrual Blood Sugar Problems

By contrast, a variety of whole grains is very helpful for women with hormonal problems. Eating some starchy food every three to four hours in the premenstrual week helps maintain a steady level of blood sugar. Since women have functionally low blood sugar premenstrually, eating frequent small meals with some carbohydrate or starchy type food can make a tremendous improvement. This practice can prevent violent emotional outbursts, the low blood sugar headaches, the unexpected crying jag that comes when a woman has not eaten for several hours. It doesn't require a huge meal. You can split your meals in half and eat more frequently. All it takes is eating a couple of crackers, or half a slice of bread, or some potato, or oat biscuits, etc. If women don't eat regularly, studies have shown that their blood sugar can drop precipitously, and it may take a week to raise it again.

Dr. Katherina Dalton has been involved as an expert witness in several murder trials involving women with severe PMS. She says that, in all cases, these women had not eaten for many hours prior to losing control.

Grains Contain More Magnesium

The element magnesium is especially important in the production of hormones and helps regulate the menstrual cycle. Animal products are especially high in calcium in proportion to magnesium and this high-calcium-magnesium ratio tends to interfere with the absorption of magnesium.

Dr. Guy Abraham's research showed that women who live in countries where calcium levels are high in proportion to magnesium (i.e., they eat a lot of animal products), are more likely to have PMS. For instance, Ethiopian women who consume large amounts of animal products have a greater incidence of PMS. Japanese women, by contrast, have a low incidence.

Grains are a great source of magnesium and their magnesium-calcium ratio is superior to that in animal products. Millet, for instance, has eight parts of magnesium to one part of calcium. Other grains have at least two parts magnesium to one part calcium.

Public Enemy #3—Refined Sugars

Many symptoms of PMS and other hormonal problems are caused or exaggerated by functionally low blood sugar levels. Women with PMS have strong food cravings for sugar, starches, chocolate, candy, caffeine, and alcohol, all of which raise the blood sugar. One might suppose that a high-sugar intake would help the problem. Instead, these substances cause the blood sugar levels to drop rapidly soon after eating, and this actually worsens the problem.

There are many different types of sugars in nature that are good for you. For instance, fruit is full of a sugar called fructose. But sucrose, (refined white sugar), is a concentrate that, if overused, can deplete your mineral supply, depress the immune system, and create havoc with your blood sugar levels. By easily satisfying the appetite but giving you only empty calories, sugar displaces more nutritious foods. Because sugar is bereft of nutrients to help in its digestion, your body has to call on its store of minerals in the bones and teeth. Thus it contributes to tooth decay and osteoporosis. Because of its high content of calories, eating too much sugar contributes to a weight problem. Refined sugar is converted into triglycerides (fatty acids) and these levels, in turn, may become elevated.

When you eat sugar, your blood sugar is swiftly elevated which may make you feel temporarily more energetic. However, the effect is brief, and soon the blood sugar slumps again. Complex carbohydrates (grains and starches) maintain the blood sugar better than simple carbohydrates (sucrose). Grains also contain fiber and nutrients which contribute to their digestion, whereas simple sugars don't.

Honey and raw sugar may not be much better than white sugar as they only have trace nutrients in them. All concentrated sugars should be used sparingly.

Public Enemy #4—Salt

Many other symptoms of PMS—such as varicose veins, closed angle glaucoma, and emotional changes caused by swelling of the brain—are caused by water retention, rather than by low blood sugar. Overuse of salt contributes to hormonal disorders by worsening bloating. Salt also raises blood pressure.

The adrenal hormone aldosterone regulates water retention and controls the sodium/potassium ratio. Premenstrually, this regulator often goes awry. Sodium is absorbed into the cell walls and attracts fluid, causing water retention.

Most vegetables and grains contain sodium, so adding salt to the diet is not generally necessary for nutrition. A little added salt may make food more palatable, and may also be necessary for people who are physically very active in hot weather. But you should beware of cooking with too much salt and adding it at the table.

Hidden Sugar, Fat, and Salt

Packaged and processed foods often contain high levels of hidden sugar, fat, and salt to make them tastier. It is a good habit to read food labels. Many packaged foods have white or enriched flour (white flour plus a few vitamins) or sugar as the first ingredient. Many others have high levels of added salt (sodium).

Summary

Make fruits and vegetables, whole grains, and legumes the staples of your diet. Eat fats, sweets, or salty foods only as concentrates—treats to be eaten occasionally. With daily, vigorous exercise, your health should flourish. In most cases, you will lose weight, your blood pressure will drop, and you will feel better.

But, remember, if you have severe hormonal problems because of a genetic inheritance, or as a result of hormonal interference, or surgery, you may find that changing your diet is not enough to relieve your symptoms.

Helpful Quotations

The Power of Prevention, Oliver Alibaster, pp. 219-220. "It is no secret that the modern American diet is mostly bad, and getting worse. Since the turn of the century, the consumption of meats, dairy products, refined sugars, and processed foods has increased tremendously, while the consumption of fresh fruit, fresh vegetables, milk, and grain products has steadily declined. This high-fat, high-sugar, high-calorie, low-fiber diet has resulted in an epidemic of degenerative diseases and cancer that have already affected or will eventually affect most of us in one way or another. These diseases are almost unknown in societies where the diet is low in fat and high in fiber, and they are increasing in countries like Japan as some Western dietary habits are adopted. The lessons are obvious."

Dr. C. Wayne Callaway, *JAMA*, October 26, 1984. "In 1980, the U.S. Department of Agriculture and the Department of Health, Education, and Welfare jointly published the "Dietary Guidelines for Americans," which stated: eat a variety of foods, maintain ideal weight, avoid too much fat, saturated fat, and cholesterol. Eat foods with adequate starch and fiber, avoid too much sugar, avoid too much sodium, and if you drink alcohol, do so in moderation. Subsequent reports of research, symposia, and expert panels have tended to support the overall message of the guidelines."

The best diet to avoid cancer: "Avoid fats, smoked foods, and salt, and drink alcohol only in moderation; eat foods that contain fiber; and eliminate such obvious lifestyle factors as smoking cigarettes." *Vegetarian Times*, September, 1984, pp. 23-26, citing *Diet and Cancer*, by Kristin White, p. 5.

Footnotes

I. *The China Diet Study*, (920 pp.) was discussed in an article, "Huge Diet Study Indicts Fat and Meat," by Dr. Hans Diehl, in *Lifeline Health Letter*, September-October, 1990. The points made in my book summarized his outline.

CHAPTER 23

Treatment for PMS

*T*reatment for PMS varies, according to the severity of each individual woman's problems. Many women with PMS may be able to control their symptoms with simple life-style changes. Others may need hormones.

Patience in Seeing Results

Many women find it difficult to commit long-term to the life-style changes necessary for success in treating PMS, because they don't see immediate results. It is important to realize that their symptoms have been out of control for a long time, and it may take several months to show improvement. While some women experience dramatic results in an amazingly short time, others have to wait three or four months for the direction and momentum of symptoms to change and for treatment to become effective. It is important to realize that what you do now will directly affect how you feel later.

Exercise and Relaxation

Daily physical exercise is always beneficial to general health. Some experts feel exercise helps PMS because it increases endorphins in the brain. Women with PMS have only 25 percent of the endorphin level of normal women, premenstrually. Some women find exercise helpful; others don't. Still others with PMS don't have much energy to expend on exercise.

Women should also relax as much as possible during the premenstrual week, avoiding stress. Dr. Susan Lark's book *The PMS Self-Help Book,* has excellent chapters on exercise and relaxation exercises.

Nutrition

The type of diet often recommended for women with PMS is high in unrefined carbohydrate and low in fat, refined sugar, and animal protein. (See separate chapter on diet.) It features lots of fresh fruits and vegetables. According to Dr. Guy Abrahams, a diet high in animal fat and high in calcium in proportion to magnesium may cause or worsen PMS. He recommends foods with a magnesium/calcium ratio at least 2:1 such as grains (the ratio in millet is 8:1).

Abrahams believes that women in Japan have little PMS because they have a low intake of animal fat. Conversely, women in Ethiopia who have a lot of milk and other animal products, have a high incidence of PMS. Likewise, in the West, women who eat a lot of animal products are more prone to PMS.

Hypoglycemic Diet

Physicians who prescribe progesterone treatment often feel that eating regularly is almost as important as the hormonal therapy. Women who have PMS often have functional hypoglycemia; that is, erratic blood sugar levels premenstrually.

A woman who experiences functional hypoglycemia may have sudden attacks of irritability. She may lash out in anger, and may have a pounding heart, anxiety attacks, or migraines. Many of the violent outbursts common to PMS are due to this drop in blood sugar. Often, when asked, women will admit to not having eaten for some hours.

One of the reasons for this is that progesterone helps metabolize sugar. In the cells, progesterone and gamma globulin share common receptors. Gamma globulin carries blood sugar through the blood stream. When progesterone is low at the cell level, blood sugar levels are affected; and when gamma globulin is low, women will have PMS and low immunity problems.

Since premenstrual hypoglycemia is only a temporary phenomenon, the results of tests for hypoglycemia are often misleading.

Eat Small, Regular, Frequent Meals

After ovulation and until the end of their symptoms, women with PMS should eat frequent small meals (as many as six a day), approximately every three to four hours to prevent low blood sugar attacks. Part of these meals should contain a portion of some complex carbohydrate, (starchy food)—for example, bread, wheat, rice, oats, or potato. Women need only eat half a slice of bread, a few crackers, a potato, or a small portion of rice. This will help keep the blood sugar levels constant.

Because refined sugar makes the condition worse, women are advised to reduce or remove refined sugar from their diets. Caffeine, alcohol, and nicotine initially cause higher glycogen levels in the liver, followed by a sometimes drastic drop in blood sugar. Therefore, it is advisable to stop smoking and cut caffeine and alcohol out of the diet.

Eating regularly and avoiding foods or substances that adversely affect blood sugar levels is very important, particularly for those women who have sudden rages, panic attacks, or drastic mood changes.

Vitamins, Minerals, and Herbs

It is more important to eat a hearty, healthy diet than to take vitamins and minerals which are processed and do not provide the same balance as vitamins found in natural foods. Still, some women seem to benefit from taking vitamins, particularly B-complex with vitamin B-6. However, the FDA warns against taking B-6 to excess, since taking doses as low as 50 mg. daily may cause peripheral neuritis. Once women become sensitive to B-6, even the low dose of B-6 in packaged cereals may cause overdose symptoms.

Women who get muscle cramps may benefit from potassium, magnesium, and calcium, since women with PMS are potassium-users. It may be necessary to occasionally take effervescent potassium, such as Klorvess, prescribed by a physician. A lower content of potassium is also available in salt substitutes and certain effervescent antacids.

Herbs such as vitex agnus castus, yellow dock root, burdock root, wild yam root, licorice root, fo-ti, pau d'arco, astragalus, dong quai, ginger, oatstraw, comfrey, nettle, raspberry leaf, squawvine, motherwort, horsetail, and red clover are all helpful. I suggest you find an experienced herbologist who grows and prepares organic herbs, rather than buying old herbs in a store. See book list at end of book for how to get the books of Rosemary Gladstar Slick.

L-Tryptophan

Two female physician's assistants in central California, researching PMS, compared their life experiences to see what they had in common, and whether the comparison would give them a clue about the cause of their PMS. The only common factor that they could find was that they both wet the bed until puberty. So they decided to study current research on the cause of late bed-wetting. They found that children who were late bed wetters had low levels of seratonin in the brain.

The substance melatonin is normally produced from seratonin overnight. Apparently, in late bed wetters, the low levels of melatonin stopped them experiencing rapid eye movement (REM) type sleep. They seemed to stay in stage four sleep where they were so deeply asleep, they were not wakened by the urge to urinate.

These two women concluded that PMS was related to low levels of seratonin and melatonin. Based on a questionnaire sent to 300 PMS sufferers, they found that although the national average for late bed wetters (male or female) was 1 to 2 percent of the general population, among PMS sufferers the average was much higher. In fact, in women with the most severe PMS, there was approximately a 36 percent incidence of late bed-wetting. Apparently whatever caused late bed-wetting, also affected PMS, at least in some women.

They discovered that lower melatonin levels directly affected the mechanism of ovulation, causing it to occur a couple of days earlier in women with PMS than those without it. Because of this, they theorized that PMS was not a hormonal problem but a sleep disorder—specifically a seratonin deficiency disease. Since seratonin and melatonin levels have a connection with the mechanism of ovulation, they reasoned that taking L-Tryptophan, an amino acid available at health food stores, might correct the PMS condition. Many women have found L-Tryptophan helpful, although the theory behind its use is probably too simplistic to cover all cases of PMS.

In 1990 an outbreak of an L-Tryptophan-induced syndrome caused the FDA to withdraw it from the market. It is widely believed, however, that the adverse reactions were caused by a contaminated batch of L-Tryptophan from Japan. The time may come when L-Tryptophan will be back on the market, perhaps under prescription. The suggested dosage was one or two 500 mg. capsules daily, with the dose raised, as necessary, premenstrually; limit five capsules per day.

L-Tyrosine is supposed to have a similar action to L-Tryptophan, and L-Phenylalanine may help depression. Both these amino acids are available in health food stores.

Primrose Oil

Great claims have been made for the success of primrose oil in treating PMS. Advocates for primrose oil say that either women's sensitivity to their own normal levels of prolactin or prolactin's action in reducing progesterone levels causes PMS.

Primrose oil contains an essential fatty acid (EFA) also found in mother's milk. This EFA is a precursor of prostaglandin EI (different from the one thought to be responsible for many menstrual cramps). It supposedly inhibits blood levels of the hormone prolactin. Apart from producing lactation after childbirth, one of the actions of prolactin is to reduce levels of progesterone. Black-currant, linseed, and borage oil apparently contain the same EFA.

Some women use primrose oil alone for relief from PMS. Others take it with progesterone to help relieve such symptoms as swollen breasts, bloating, and acne. Suggested dosage is six capsules daily for a couple of months, and from then on, three capsules daily.

Restrict Salt and Fluid

The sodium-potassium balance is altered in women with PMS, because, just before menstruation, the body cells absorb sodium more readily, which attracts fluid. Bloating is a universal problem in women with PMS, and the pressure of retained fluid causes many symptoms. All women with PMS should cut down on salt premenstrually. Be careful how much salt you consume in packaged and canned goods, and how much you add to your cooking or at the table.

Avoid Alcohol and Recreational Drugs

Many women, because of depression or stress prior to their periods, will try to use alcohol or drugs to alleviate those symptoms. In this way, they may also develop a habit of alcohol or drug abuse. Some recovered women alcoholics and addicts, who seek treatment for PMS, report that their past drinking or drug-using pattern was always cyclical, and their drinking or drug-using bouts paralleled their premenstrual stress.

A substantially large number of female alcoholics have PMS. Women seem to have an added craving for alcohol because their blood sugar is low premenstrually. They also have a lowered tolerance to both drugs and alcohol premenstrually, and many women cannot handle alcohol well before their period.

Alcohol may make you feel relaxed initially. It first stimulates the nervous system, but then depresses it; it also raises the levels of glycogen in the liver, sending blood sugar levels up dramatically, only to drop drastically, shortly thereafter. Because changes in blood sugar are so much a part of PMS, avoiding any substance that exacerbates the problem is most important.

Alcohol also tends to produce violent feelings. Many instances of physical violence toward either husband or children stem from a combination of PMS and alcohol abuse. It is sensible for women with PMS to cut down, or, preferably, eliminate alcohol entirely.

Some women with severe PMS may be tempted to use recreational drugs to alleviate the misery of their symptoms. However, the use of cocaine and amphetamines will further aggravate the endorphin depletion common in women with PMS, as well as undermine their general health. The habitual use of drugs like heroin can stop menstruation altogether. I recently saw a seventeen-year heroin user who did not menstruate most of the time she was on it, and who went into menopause after she went off of it at age thirty-four.

Restrict Caffeine

Caffeine, like alcohol, stimulates the central nervous system and then depresses it, raising the glycogen level and then dropping it. This can cause women to become irritable and worsens their PMS symptoms. Some women who are prone to headaches may find caffeine helpful at first, but the headache generally returns when the caffeine wears off. These women may develop the habit of drinking coffee, or taking other drinks or pills with caffeine in them. PMS sufferers are advised to either remove caffeine from their diet or reduce it drastically.

Resist Chocolate
Chocolate contains theobromine which is similar to caffeine, and has a high-fat and sugar content which tends to worsen acne. On the other hand, chocolate contains magnesium (the reason, say some experts, that women crave it). But it is better to get magnesium from other sources.

Diuretics
Diuretics are widely prescribed for PMS because of bloating but are generally not very helpful. They are usually unsuccessful in alleviating emotional symptoms connected with PMS. While diuretics cause some excretion of fluids from the body, using them is like dipping a teaspoon into a sea of fluid. If they are strong enough to rid the body of enough excess fluid to alleviate bloating, they also tend to cause excretion of minerals like potassium into the urine.

Herbs that may be helpful for their diuretic action are: uva ursi, buchu, chickweed, and cleavers.

Spironolactone, an Exception
Spironolactone is a diuretic which blocks the production of certain substances in the adrenal glands believed to cause or worsen PMS symptoms. Spironolactone is similar to progesterone, and functions like a hormone. Some women with mild to moderate PMS symptoms, including acne, may benefit from taking spironolactone alone. The usual dose is 25 mg. three or four times a day, taken during the time a woman has symptoms. Women with a history of breast tumors may wish to talk to their physician about using this diuretic, because it has been associated with increased breast tumors in beagles (a breed of dog which commonly has such tumors, anyway).

Spironolactone also helps some women with hirsutism, but the doses used to treat this are much higher—400-600 mg. daily. It is when Spironolactone is prescribed at such high doses, that it is more likely to have severe side effects.

Other women who use progesterone, but have problems with excessive fluid which the progesterone does not alleviate, may wish to take spironolactone as well. You will need a prescription for spironolactone from your physician (and it's expensive).

Antiprostaglandins

Research shows that some menstrual cramps are caused by prostaglandins (natural hormone-like substances in the body). Antiprostaglandins have been helpful in treating these types of cramps.

Some physicians treat PMS with antiprostaglandins because they think PMS and menstrual cramps are the same thing. If a woman has both PMS and cramps, antiprostaglandins may certainly help the pain.

Women who have uterine fibroids, often have a swollen uterus. The uterus produces prostaglandins and, when in a swollen state, it often produces higher levels, which may affect the hormonal cycling of the ovaries and cause PMS. If this is the main cause of PMS, antiprostaglandins may be helpful.

Bromocriptine

If a woman has a swollen pituitary or a tumor causing an increase in prolactin production, she may have symptoms of PMS. Where surgery is not indicated, medication with Parlodel (bromocriptine) to reduce the levels of prolactin may remove the symptoms of PMS. However, bromocriptine is not, generally, a treatment for PMS, and it has very strong side effects.

Progesterone Therapy

In severe cases, when PMS interferes with a woman's quality of life, and when symptoms fit within the classic patterns of PMS, patients often respond very well to cyclical progesterone therapy—just as a diabetic responds to insulin. While the exact cause of PMS is yet unknown, the role of progesterone seems to be involved because symptoms occur at the time when progesterone is normally high. When this hormone is supplied, the symptoms often disappear completely.

Note the Different Types of Progesterone

The female body produces two hormones—estrogen and progesterone. Progesterone is erroneously used as a generic name for all those substances that function similarly to progesterone. Many artificial hormones called progestins and progestogens have been synthesized in the laboratory. These substances are derived from progesterone, but may take on the characteristics of other hormones, including the male hormone, testosterone.

It is important to know the difference since progestins and progestogens often affect PMS sufferers adversely, while natural progesterone usually does not. Birth control pills, which contain progestogens (not natural progesterone), are often given as treatment to women with PMS. Occasionally they help, but most PMS sufferers should avoid them. Provera, the trade name for medroxyprogesterone, a progestogen, lowers both the ovarian and the pituitary production of progesterone.

Pharmacy Warning

When you receive your progesterone from the pharmacy, the package may contain a warning about possible side effects. You should understand that natural progesterone and synthetic progestogens are classified in the **Physician's Desk Reference** as the same substance. While they are all similar in composition, there are small physical differences which have a profound impact on some women's moods.

The warning you receive from the pharmacy contains all the possible side effects of all substances classified as progestational agents—natural progesterone, progestins, and progestogens. Some women who have used progesterone-like drugs, which are often more like the male hormone testosterone had a higher incidence of babies with birth defects. Natural progesterone is not known to produce birth defects.

A Typical Protocol for Taking Progesterone

If a woman has a regular twenty-eight to thirty-day-cycle, she probably ovulates about the fourteenth to sixteenth day. She may know this for a fact, since many women have ovulatory twinges or definite pain in the ovaries. Others feel the onset of their symptoms.

If a woman has symptoms from ovulation on, she should begin

taking her progesterone two days ahead of the time she expects her symptoms to begin. So, if she has a twenty-eight-day cycle, she would begin taking her progesterone on the twelfth or fourteenth day. To start, she could take a 100-200 mg. dose first thing in the morning and again between noon and 2:00 p.m. Often twice a day is enough, and taking the second dose five to six hours after the first may keep the progesterone high enough to see a woman through the whole day. But, if the symptoms return at dinner or late evening, a woman could take a third and even a fourth dose of progesterone. However, some pharmacists make a time-release capsule which lasts longer.

As the symptoms worsen towards the onset of the menstrual cycle, a woman might find she needs to raise the dose at that point. Raising it any earlier may bring on overdose symptoms such as drowsiness and euphoria. But keep in mind that Dr. Dalton believes it is important to take enough progesterone around ovulation to avoid having problems premenstrually and raising the levels of progesterone close to the period may delay menstruation.

Women should take their progesterone faithfully every day, trying not to vary it too much, since varying the dose and skipping doses may cause irregular bleeding and mood swings.

We recommend that women take progesterone until they menstruate, even if the period is a little late. Delay of menstruation commonly happens when women begin progesterone therapy. (Sometimes, the opposite happens and women get their periods early.) It is best not to worry too much about irregularities or changes in bleeding. Women can have bright red bleeding, black discolored bleeding, light bleeding, or heavy bleeding, but this is usually temporary and will go away as the body adjusts to the hormones.

Sometimes, if the endometrial lining has thickened previously, going on progesterone may cause very heavy bleeding. If a woman does hemorrhage, she may want to contact her physician.

A woman would stop her progesterone when she expects her symptoms to normally stop—when the period occurs, two or three days into the period, or at the end of the period. When a woman goes on progesterone, symptoms may be delayed. If prior to treatment you had symptoms until the first or second day of the flow, and now that you are taking progesterone, they seem to return during the period, you may take progesterone as long as necessary, but in most cases, go off of it by the end of the period. Then no progesterone would be taken until the next twelfth or fourteenth day (though there are exceptions to this rule).

Because of variations in the length of the cycle, the starting date may vary. When women have very irregular cycles, they would have to begin the progesterone at the first sign of symptoms.

Cancer Is Not a Problem

Many women are reluctant to take progesterone because of the fear of cancer in connection with taking hormones. Dr. Katherina Dalton makes the following points in her book *Depression After Childbirth*.:

- Progesterone has been used since 1934 and carefully monitored since 1948 without any serious side-effects.
- Progesterone is used for treating some forms of cancer.
- Natural human material is not cancer-producing. Insulin, for example, has been in use for over fifty years with no evidence of cancer production.
- The use of thyroid hormones produces no cancer risk. Thyroxine is given at birth to cretins, and continued throughout their entire life.
- The body can convert active hormones into inactive ones for waste disposal. In the case of progesterone it is changed to pregnanediol, which is excreted in the urine or feces.
- By contrast, man-made steroids and other drugs such as stilbestrol are not normally found in humans and the risk of cancer may result either directly or indirectly from the breakdown products formed when they are excreted. The body does not have the necessary chemicals to convert the progestogens into the same inactive agents and they are not disposed of in the same way as progesterone.[1]

Side Effects of Progesterone

Even when taking the correct progesterone therapy, some minor side effects may occur. They are frequently just temporary problems:

- **Spotting or breakthrough bleeding** at midcycle and in the premenstruum. Spotting may occur at ovulation if progesterone has been taken too early in the cycle, or if the uterine lining is already thick. If you start spotting premenstrually, you may stop the progesterone to allow your period to begin, but your symptoms may return. Often, spotting is a temporary problem and, after a few cycles of progesterone, will go away. Breakthrough bleeding sometimes indicates low-estrogen levels that cannot maintain the endometrium and easily slough off. It may indicate the need for estrogen.

- **Lengthening or shortening of the menstrual cycle.** Women usually take progesterone a day or two before their PMS symptoms appear, and stop taking it when the symptoms end, which is generally when their period begins, or one or two days into their period. Taking progesterone this way can cause the period to be delayed for a few days to a week. This can be adjusted in consultation with your counselor or physician, and often the cycle will stabilize after a few months. You may stop the progesterone earlier to avoid a lengthier cycle, but we do not advise this as often symptoms will return after progesterone has been stopped too early. However, you may go back on it during your period, if your symptoms return.

- **Missing a cycle.** Occasionally, a woman may completely miss a cycle or two, when she first goes on progesterone. This is nothing to be concerned about.

- **Initial heavier or lighter bleeding.** Women going on progesterone may have changes in bleeding. The first period may occasionally be very heavy. But, in general, the flow can become either heavier or lighter. The color of bleeding can also change. There is no need to worry about these temporary changes which tend to adjust after one or two cycles. Very rarely, a woman may lose the lining of the uterus all at once. It will look like a lump of liver, and while this may be frightening, it is not usually considered serious. If you are concerned, consult your physician.

- **Increase or decrease in food cravings.** Usually progesterone will help decrease food cravings, but a few women may find progesterone makes them hungrier. Generally, progesterone tends to normalize the appetite.

- **Increase or decrease in sex drive.** A few women find progesterone lowers their sex drive, which can be disappointing. But if they have been sexually overstimulated because of PMS, they may be happy about a return to normality.

- **Sore breasts or fleeting joint pains.** When beginning progesterone therapy, women may get relief from their PMS but may have sore breasts or fleeting joint pains instead. (I have read that joint pain is a side effect. I have never heard of anyone having it.) A few women feel faint. Younger women and those who have had no children may feel euphoric or have restless energy or mild cramps. However, women who have had children are used to having twenty to thirty times as much progesterone in their system for most of the nine months of pregnancy. For them, overdose is unlikely. We advise women to ignore these minor symptoms as they will probably disappear after a couple of cycles.

- **Allergic type reaction** may occur to the substance containing the progesterone or to progesterone itself. Some women are allergic to the wax in the suppositories. (They should switch to another method.) Other women get redness and swelling around injection sites, if they use shots. Typical symptoms of an allergic reaction can occur, including rapid heartrate and panic attacks. Some specialized allergy clinics can desensitize this allergy. Sometimes this reaction is due to antibodies produced by the body against progesterone. A physician I know uses injections of Depo-Medrol, a distant cousin of cortisone without the serious side effects, to destroy the antibodies.

- A very small minority of women with PMS depression experience a **worsening of symptoms** from taking progesterone. They will be unable to take it but may benefit from estrogen, with bimonthly or quarterly use of progesterone to protect the lining of the uterus. Some will feel this is not enough progesterone—however, I have found that many OB/Gyns with years of experience do this.

Pointers for Success in Treating
with Natural Progesterone

I. The Right Diagnosis

PMS symptoms occur cyclically sometime between ovulation and menstruation, and there is a time when symptoms are absent. Women who have symptoms for only a short time, about two or three days before their period, will feel normal for three and a half weeks out of the month. But other women have symptoms up to three weeks a month and only have one week without symptoms. When additional problems with low thyroid, menopause, and postpartum depression are involved, the PMS pattern may be less clear. Also, if a woman does not have PMS, but rather a chronic disease, such as nonhormonal depression or headaches, which occur at random times during the month and worsen at menstruation; she may not respond to progesterone therapy. Such variations and complications make it absolutely necessary to ensure that the diagnosis is correct.

2. The Right Hormone

Women must be certain they receive natural progesterone and not one of the many synthetics which may erroneously be called progesterone. The reason that most women with a PMS history do not tolerate the pill well is because of its synthetic progesterone-like hormones.

Natural progesterone is made from Mexican or South American wild yams or soybeans, and matches the chemical composition of the progesterone in your body. While progestins and progestogens are similar to progesterone in composition, they are not completely alike.

All the sex hormones, including estrogen, testosterone (a male hormone), and progesterone are similar, but there are small differences in their chemical composition. These "small" differences have profound effects. Consider the contrast in effect of estrogen, a female hormone, and testosterone, a male hormone.

Progestins and progestogens function similarly to progesterone in the uterus. They both cause the lining of the womb to thicken. When the levels drop, the lining of the womb sloughs off. However, progestins and progestogens do not function like progesterone in the progesterone receptors found in the brain and elsewhere throughout the body. In fact, these artificial hormones lower the natural progesterone levels in the blood, thereby worsening PMS.

3. The Right Dosage

The prescribing physician will determine the starting dosage on the basis of the severity of the patient's history—giving a lower starting dose for women who have never been pregnant; more for women who have been pregnant. The average dose ranges from one to three times a day, and may be increased or taken more frequently, if symptoms persist.

Your physician will determine your progesterone dosage, but you will probably have to experiment to find the correct amount for you. Dosage is very individual, and needs differ tremendously. This is partly because women vary in their ability to absorb and metabolize it. Dosage also depends on the method in which progesterone is administered, since different quantities of progesterone are put in different forms of medication—oral capsules in oil that are swallowed, oral tablets, suppositories, rectal fluid, injections, etc.

For instance, a single dose in the form of an oral capsule may range from 25, 50, or 75 to 100 mg. doses; the oral tablet may vary from 200 to 300 to 400 mg. doses, because of poorer absorption; suppositories range from 25 mg. to 400 mg.; a single dose of rectal fluid or injectable progesterone ranges from 2 ccs. (100 mg.) to 4 ccs. (200 mg.).

The normal range is to take a single dose from one to three times a day. However, it is possible that an individual who is sensitive to medication needs only a quarter of a normal dose. And some women who need more can take up to six doses a day (e.g., in the case of suppositories, 6 x 400 mg. = 2400 mg. per day).

When women take more progesterone and do not feel a corresponding benefit, there may be an absorption problem and alternative routes should be investigated.

If you are taking high doses of progesterone and getting no relief, this therapy may not be suitable for you. You should look at some of the other options later in this chapter.

4. The Right Frequency

The progesterone is taken at least twice a day—morning and noon. Women who begin taking progesterone should feel a beneficial effect within an hour or less, and feel it wear off after four to five hours (though some micronized forms of progesterone last up to twelve hours—ask your pharmacist about this). This is why it is best not to take it morning and night if only two doses are taken—the medication will wear off by the afternoon, and symptoms will return. This experience of feeling the symptoms leave and then return helps women work out how much they need. They need freedom to experiment with adjusting their own dosage.

We suggest you do not take more than a single dose at one time. If you need more, take it more frequently rather than in larger quantities. Allow a minimum space of an hour between doses, if using suppositories. The reason for this is that there is relatively little absorption of doses higher than 400 mg. in suppository form. Also, using more than one suppository at a time may hinder absorption because of the amount of wax.

If the dosage is raised during the cycle, it should stay at that higher dose until the symptoms would normally cease at the end of the cycle. For some women, symptoms stop at the beginning of the period; for others, symptoms continue to the very end of the period. The dosage should not be alternately raised and lowered, as this can cause spotting and bring back symptoms. An exception to this is when the patient has severe symptoms at ovulation but slight improvement later, lasting until the last part of the cycle (B pattern). Then progesterone can be effectively raised and lowered to cover symptoms. High doses may be needed prior to ovulation, and the dose may be decreased for a few days and then increased premenstrually.

Don't stop taking the progesterone suddenly or miss days in the last part of the cycle. This can cause breakthrough bleeding, or worse, a return of your symptoms.

5. The Right Form of Medication

Women vary in their ability to absorb progesterone and may need to experiment to get full benefit. If they have a correct diagnosis and experience some relief from taking progesterone, **they should pursue becoming as symptom-free as possible.**

Progesterone may be taken in a variety of forms—**oral capsules** in oil which are swallowed; **oral tablets** made of powder; **compressed wax suppositories** which can be used both rectally and vaginally; a **rectal fluid** used with a syringe; **powder capsules** taken under the tongue (somewhat bitter and ineffective); **pellets surgically implanted** into the fatty tissue of the abdomen or hip; **creams** and **oils** that can be rubbed on the skin (I have found these of dubious value, but possibly because of low doses—newer gels are in the experimental stage, and will be better). As a last resort, **intramuscular injections** can be given into the fatty tissues of the buttock; **Sublingual drops** have also been used, but, like the creams and oils, these have not been very successful.

In England, Dr. Dalton uses suppositories or injections or, for some women, implants. Europeans are accustomed to suppositories and take well to using progesterone this way, but this is not true in the United States, where women tend to find the use of suppositories distasteful. Dr. Dalton believes the oral route uses a completely different process which cancels the effect of progesterone, and she has never had much success with oral progesterone. However, in a recent seminar in San Francisco, so many positive results were reported from the use of oral micronized progesterone, that Dr. Dalton conceded that it might work. She is presently trying progesterone capsules in oil in England with marked success. Many women in the U.S. do find taking oral progesterone works as well, if not better than suppositories.

It is also true that some women become sleepy, and feel somewhat "drunk" or euphoric as a result of taking oral progesterone. If this persists, they need to switch to using suppositories or the rectal fluid, or, in the most severe cases, to injections. Taking progesterone with food may help.

Oral capsules and tablets—In the past, natural progesterone was not taken orally because it was destroyed by the action of the stomach. Then a fairly effective oral progesterone capsule in oil was produced, and, more recently, a micronized oral tablet (some pharmacies also make a lozenge). One pharmacist says that the micronized oral tablet is longer acting, because the compression of the tablet affords more gradual absorption, and its smaller particles have a greater surface area, which makes for better absorption.

Another pharmacist says that the powder-only tablet is still largely destroyed by the stomach, and very large doses would be needed. When the capsule is in oil, the progesterone is absorbed through the lymphatic system, and doses are lower.

Suppositories may be made with more than one base; for example, glycerinated gelatin, cocoa butter, or polyethylene glycol. Progesterone absorption has been found to be significantly higher from the polyethylene glycol. If a woman uses suppositories vaginally, she will need to wear a pad, as the melted wax leaks. In the rectum, the sphincter muscle holds the suppository in place so it does not leak. However, it can stimulate a bowel movement, and should be used only after a bowel movement, if possible. Some women find that the rectal suppositories cause gas or diarrhea. Women seem to tolerate the cocoa butter/fatty acid based suppositories better rectally.

Rectal fluid—The rectal fluid often absorbs better than suppositories and is almost half the price. Rectal fluid can also be made with a variety of bases, and absorption can vary. For best results, do not insert the syringe higher than an inch into the rectum. Past a certain point, the fluid is absorbed into the colon, passes into the portal system, and is destroyed.

Sublingual powder capsules work well on their own for women who don't need a lot of progesterone. They are also often used as a booster with either suppositories or the rectal fluid for women who tend to have sudden attacks of anger or depression. Taking progesterone under the tongue works quickly, but it may cause blood levels of progesterone to rise and fall suddenly. That's why some women need to use it with another form of progesterone which will last longer in the blood stream.

The powder tends to clump under the tongue but is eventually swallowed. Keep it at the back of the mouth under the tongue as long as you can, but don't expect it to dissolve. You will gradually swallow it, but try to keep it there as long as you can for maximum absorption. For the same reason, don't drink beverages for about an hour after taking these powder capsules. Once you swallow the progesterone, it is not as effective. As mentioned before, sublingual capsules may cause "progesterone drunkenness," especially if more than one capsule is used. If this effect occurs regularly, cut the dose in half or try another form of progesterone.

Powder capsule as a suppository—Women who are allergic to wax may use the powder capsule as a suppository, using KY Jelly to lubricate it first. If you use the powder capsules vaginally, be aware that they are gritty, and both men and women may find them abrasive during intercourse.

Injections—Women with severe PMS or postpartum depression may benefit from daily intramuscular injections of progesterone, or, in the case of PMS, a booster shot of progesterone around ovulation, followed by daily use of another form until menstruation. In the United States, the injectable progesterone is prepared by Rugby (50 mg. per ml.) in a peanut oil base which can be very irritating, possibly causing redness, swelling, and even abscesses. Women who receive these shots on a regular basis may develop scar tissue.

If a woman develops an abscess, she should check with her physician. But if the injection site is slightly red or swollen, I have found charcoal compresses are helpful. Crush two or three charcoal tablets, adding a little water and spread it on gauze, put it over the injection site, and tape it on overnight. Charcoal draws out any swelling or infection that might be present. It is very messy, but effective.

Don't Be Discouraged

The above information is not meant to confuse or discourage. It is meant to show the various ways of taking progesterone and the difficulties some may find with each method. You need to be versatile and understand that both dosage and absorption vary among individuals. Many women have no problems with absorption, but some do, and they need to be patient and willing to experiment, keeping in close contact with their counselor or physician.

6. When to Begin and End Therapy

Therapy is very individual. Your physician and counselor will give you instructions on the best regime for you. It is important to start progesterone early enough in the cycle to build up the blood levels of progesterone prior to the time when symptoms would begin. Women often ignore this advice, taking progesterone only when they feel symptoms. Treatment is never as successful if begun too late. If the pattern of symptoms regularly occurs in the last few days or week of the cycle (pattern A), a woman should start taking her progesterone **five days ahead** of the time she expects her symptoms. If her symptoms occur at ovulation (patterns B and C), she should begin **two** days ahead.

Progesterone should be taken at least once or twice daily and for as many days as a woman's PMS symptoms would usually persist. Some women's symptoms stop when menstruation begins. Others have symptoms two or three days into their period. Still others have them until the end of their period. In all these cases, women must take progesterone until their symptoms would normally stop, then taper off gradually by cutting the dose in half for a day or two more, and then stop the progesterone. (As an example of tapering off capsules, if your symptoms normally stop on day two, and you are taking three capsules a day, take two capsules on day two, one or two on day three, one on day four, and stop on day five.)

Women are frequently told to stop taking their progesterone a couple of days before menstruation in order to bring on their period. This is not advisable because the period often doesn't start within the two days, and there may be a return and worsening of symptoms during menstruation. To prevent this, stay on the progesterone until bleeding occurs, even if the period is delayed each cycle for the first two or three cycles. Generally, women should not take progesterone after menstruation ends because it may cause breakthrough bleeding or irregular periods. But there are exceptions to this rule. For instance, if a woman has very severe, long-standing problems, some physicians prescribe continual progesterone therapy for two or three months to settle down their symptoms and then cycle the progesterone. If you did well for the first week after ovulation, but not so well around menstruation, you probably took **too little** progesterone, **too late** to help. You should take a high enough dose of progesterone, early enough (around the time of ovulation), to help you feel better just before your period occurs.

Taking Progesterone—A Summary

While much of the instruction seems complex, in actual experience, taking progesterone is simple. Remember the following points:

- **Faithfully fill in your calendar.** Work out from your previous month when you expect to ovulate this month. Mark the calendar to start the therapy two days ahead of ovulation (if that is when you start symptoms) or five days ahead of symptoms (if you have

Pattern A PMS).

- **Start the treatment early enough.** If you get symptoms a few days before they are expected, start the treatment then.
- Once you work out your individual dosage, **take the progesterone consistently** through the second part of the cycle when you need it. Maintain the dose as needed at an even rate on a daily basis. Don't skip doses or days. Once you increase the dose, keep it at that same level until you stop it.
- **Reorder progesterone early enough** so that you always have at least one month's supply on hand.
- **Stop the progesterone at the right time, and don't stop it suddenly.** Taper off the dosage (by cutting it in half for one or two days, and then stop it) at the time you would normally cease having symptoms.
- Make appointments with your counselor or physician for follow-up treatment until you feel better. It's worth it.
- Seek to become **symptom-free,** not just a little better.

The Necessity of Keeping a Treatment Calendar and/or Journal

You are largely responsible for monitoring your own therapy, and your subsequent well-being depends to a great extent on doing it properly. When you begin progesterone therapy, keep a calendar so you can calculate ahead when you need to start your progesterone. Buy a small pocket calendar which you can carry around with you. Write an M on the date of each day you bleed. Write down I against the date of the first day of bleeding. Count forward from the first day until the day you expect to ovulate (this only works if you are fairly regular). Then mark two days earlier, and that is when you should begin your treatment.

If symptoms begin earlier than expected, you may start the progesterone then. You should do this every first day of your period, so your calendar is marked ahead. Having PMS often means you find it hard to be disciplined, but discipline is needed to begin the therapy early enough and to make sure it is taken regularly. If you can't do this, you need to enlist someone else, perhaps your husband or a close friend, to help you remember. It is also very helpful to keep a journal noting how you feel day by day, which will help gauge your progress.

How Long Will I Have to Take Progesterone?

Some young women with PMS may be able to stop using progesterone after being on it for about six to nine months. This is because taking progesterone for a while sometimes stimulates the pituitary into producing its own progesterone, and the PMS condition corrects itself. This ability of the pituitary gland to start functioning properly on its own seems to decrease as women age, and the symptoms may return later in life. Women over thirty who have had PMS from puberty usually have to take progesterone at least until menopause.

When you have taken progesterone successfully for some months, you may try to lower the dosage or shorten the time during which you take it. Both should be done gradually; your symptoms will indicate whether you can manage with less progesterone since your symptoms will probably return. Some women can go off of it for a few cycles and then use it when necessary. But remember, women over thirty-five with severe symptoms should expect to stay on progesterone for a portion of every month until they begin menopause. Many can then discontinue treatment; but if a woman still has her uterus and starts taking estrogen at menopause, she will need to keep taking progesterone to counteract the effect of estrogen. A few women taking progesterone only will need to stay on progesterone into their sixties, because they still experience recurring PMS-like symptoms, despite the fact that menstruation has ceased.

Other Treatments for PMS

Not Every Woman Is the Same

While we have listed guidelines for treatment that will help the majority of women with PMS, not everyone responds to the same therapy. In fact, women whose symptoms and histories appear similar may respond to quite different therapies. Following are some suggestions for alternate treatments:

Treating Coexisting Conditions

Women with PMS caused by infections, or coexisting with other conditions such as endometriosis and polycystic ovaries, will require treatment for the other conditions, and this will sometimes stop their

PMS symptoms. This is also true when a woman has endocrine problems such as a swollen pituitary, a hypothalamic or pituitary tumor, or thyroid problems. The specific problem causing PMS or worsening PMS needs to be dealt with.

Estrogen for PMS

Dr. John Studd of St. Thomas' Hospital in London has used the surgical implantation of estrogen pellets as a treatment for PMS, and he has performed thousands of these minor surgeries with great success. Dr. Studd believes that women who do not ovulate do not get PMS, and the estrogen pellet with its continuous output of estrogen into the bloodstream prevents ovulation. However, I have worked with physicians who have seen many women who don't ovulate, who also have PMS-like symptoms (though not in a definite pattern). One of these doctors says that once he can produce ovulation in these women, he can treat their PMS. Despite the questions about Dr. Studd's theory, some women with PMS do respond to estrogen therapy, and should read the menopause chapters.

It is now known that taking estrogen increases the number of progesterone receptors and primes them. Also progesterone can switch off estrogen receptors, possibly a reason why some women who have been on progesterone for a while find it "no longer works." I believe these facts make the case for taking both hormones for PMS.

Young women with PMS may only need a very small dose of estrogen, such as 1/2 mg of Estrace taken daily.

The Thyroid Connection

Since the stimulating hormones for estrogen and progesterone are produced in the pituitary gland, it is not surprising that PMS may involve other pituitary hormones.

Thyroid disorders cause menstrual irregularities (heavy bleeding, cramps, infertility, or irregular periods) and in some cases may be the direct cause of PMS. Conversely, the ovary produces a thyroid hormone, and so PMS may enhance a thyroid condition.

It is not uncommon for women with hormonal problems to have a history of thyroid disorders among the female members of their families. Nearly half the women seeking help for PMS or menopause may have a subnormal functioning thyroid and need testing and medication. Thyroid blood tests may appear normal or low-normal in PMS women, yet the history discloses typical symptoms. The basal temperature is typically low (below 97.8°F). [See separate chapter on thyroid problems. We also suggest you read *Hypothyroidism, the Unsuspected Illness*, by Broda O. Barnes, M.D. and Lawrence Galton.]

The Adrenals May Be Involved

Very little has been written about the possibility of adrenal involvement in PMS, despite the fact that many women with PMS have severe allergic problems, terrible chronic fatigue, and recurrent infections—all symptoms of adrenal deficiency. Prednisone, the usual form of cortisone used for treating adrenal deficiency diseases, has understandably come into disfavor because of the very serious side effects of high doses. Some physicians I know will give women small physiologic doses of hydrocortisone, a much weaker type of cortisone which is several times weaker than prednisone.

As with thyroid, perhaps even more so, women should not try to medicate themselves or adjust dosage with adrenal medication because the side effects are much more serious than with progesterone or estrogen, and overmedication can be fatal.

Treating Yeast and Allergies

Many women with hormonal problems suffer from systemic yeast and/or allergy problems. In fact, some researchers believe candida (yeast) is the primary cause of PMS. However, when the immune system is not functioning properly, adrenal function is low, and PMS, infections, and allergies often occur together. Sometimes hormonal therapy alleviates candida and allergies because it helps the immune system. This is particularly true if allergies only appear premenstrually. Sometimes candida worsens with progesterone therapy because progesterone increases the metabolism of sugar.

Treatment for candida ranges from dietary changes to medical treatment for either local yeast manifestations or systemic yeast problems. A blood test is available to test systemic yeast.

Changes in life-style include eliminating all types of sugars, grains, foods that mold easily, and anything else in the diet that encourages the growth of the yeast. Some researchers think fruit should be largely eliminated, at least for a while. Others think grains are more of a problem. Health food stores sell different types of antifungal agents such as pau d'arco, a South American herb, and Caprystatin, caprylic acid.

Vaginal infections can be treated locally—for instance, with Monistatt or Gynelotramin or other, stronger medications. Yeast in the digestive tract may respond to oral tablets of Nystatin. Systemic treatment includes Nizoral, which is potent and expensive. Women on Nizoral need frequent tests of their liver enzyme levels. There is also a newer drug out, called Diflucan (generic, fluconazole), that is even stronger, and it is very expensive. [We suggest you read *The Yeast Syndrome*, by John Parks Trowbridge, M.D.]

Chronic Fatigue Syndrome

Having a son with CFS, I know how debilitating this disease can be. Every so often, I see women who are unfortunate enough to have CFS together with hormonal problems, and I feel terribly sorry for them. It's enough to have either problem; terrible to have both.

CFS is an immune system disease in which, it is believed, a person's killer cells multiply and start attacking the immune system. At present researchers think it is the hyperactivity of these killer cells that is responsible for the miserable symptoms this disease produces.

In the past, CFS has been blamed on various viruses—such as Epstein-Barr, Herpes VI, or Cytomegalovirus—but now these are seen as opportunistic diseases which occur because the immune system is damaged.

Those with CFS have extraordinarily incapacitating fatigue, which strikes them in varying degrees. Some sufferers are fairly functional, but others cannot even lift their heads off the pillow.

There is presently no known cure for CFS. The body must mend itself. But certain remedies have been helpful for a few, such as Acyclovir and Zovirex, which have been helpful in treating the herpes virus. A combination of gamma globulin and sex hormones may help others. As with PMS, there are all sorts of supplements toted to cure CFS. They probably all help some people, and there is nothing to lose by trying them. Rest and nutrition are extremely important, and counseling for behavior modification may help, since those with CFS usually have very driven personalities.

Treatment for Chronic Depression

Women with severe hormonal depression are often sent to psychiatrists for treatment with antidepressants. I have talked to women who have tremendous benefits from taking antidepressants and tranquilizers, and others who take the whole gamut of available treatment and are treatment failures. Sometimes women with these problems are even given shock therapy, which is coming back into favor as a treatment choice. (The ones I have talked to had no benefit from it.)

Women who are taking antidepressants or contemplating taking them would benefit from reading Harvard psychiatrist Peter Breggins' book *Toxic Psychiatry*. He is very much opposed to antidepressants and shock therapy and, while some may think his view is too narrow, his book is very thorough. It is a viewpoint that must be heard, and I feel the emphasis is correct; though I still acknowledge the fact that some women have miraculous results from this type of medication.

Women with PMS are often put on Prozac; and it does seem to help some women dramatically, while others don't respond at all, even to higher doses. A female psychiatrist friend says that a quarter dose of liquid Prozac may be all that is needed to treat PMS.

Dr. Breggins says that people will feel better on Prozac because it is an upper. He worries that its basic action—making seratonin more available in the brain—will backfire one day because women will eventually need more and more seratonin and will end up worse off than when they began the therapy. He also worries that Prozac is similar in chemical make-up to the neuroleptics, such as Stelazine, and may eventually produce similar side effects—a 30 to 40 percent chance of tardive dyskinesia (where the patient may shoot the tongue out, and have involuntary muscle jerking) and other similar problems which can be permanent. He says there is already some evidence in the literature that this is so. Also, the serious side effects of Prozac prompting some people to violence and suicide has already been well publicized.

Among my case histories, you will read of Sandra who had the worst hormonal problems I have seen to date, who was not stabilized emotionally until she went on lithium. You will also read of Jeannie who had the opposite result and was made worse by Parnate. The reader needs to read about these medications, their possible benefits and side effects, and make an informed choice.

As mentioned earlier in the book, there have been studies on both estrogen and natural progesterone showing that there is positive action by both on the CNS and neurotransmitters in the brain. These hormones, particularly estrogen, have an antidepressant action, and a catalyst action which enhances the use of antidepressants. What this means is that some women with hormonal depression may respond to hormone therapy alone and others may need a combination of hormones and an antidepressant. There are also a few women who appear to have a hormonal depression but do not respond to hormone therapy.

Information on how to obtain natural progesterone and other natural hormones can be found overleaf on page 244. The nonprescription creams tend to be weaker than the prescription progesterone, but they work well for some women with less severe problems.

Footnotes
1. *Depression After Childbirth*, p. 117-118.

Sources of Natural Progesterone
& Other Natural Hormones

CHAPTER 24

Treatment for Postpartum Depression

T erie is a friend of mine who has never really known what it is to have mood swings, even though she had a hysterectomy and oophorectomy in her thirties. However, she was subsequently put on estrogen because she had developed osteoporosis, partly due to having a benign tumor on her parathyroid gland.

Shortly after she first met her husband, he asked her if she ever had periods, because she was the only woman he knew who didn't have mood swings. She laughed and told him that of course she had periods, but she has never had PMS. In her twenties, she delivered her only children—twin boys. The delivery was very difficult, and afterwards for about two years, she had a terrible problem with insomnia. Even with medication, she would not sleep for more than three hours a night.

At a party one day, Terrie overheard a psychiatrist talking about someone who sounded as though she had a similar problem to hers. She made an appointment for the whole family to see this counselor, and he told her that the rest of the family was fine, but she was depressed. In her case, it had nothing to do with mood swings—it was a sleep disorder. He gave her Elavil at a fairly low dose and told her that if this was her problem, she would sleep for a long time. After taking the first dose, she slept continuously for three days. She continued taking the Elavil for six months and then went off of it and had no more problems Despite having her ovaries removed in her thirties, she does not get depressed whether she takes estrogen or not, but, as mentioned, she does have osteoporosis and takes estrogen for that problem.

Terrie's problem was not specifically hormonal though it occurred after a pregnancy. I have related it to illustrate the fact that PPD manifests itself in different ways. For some women, it will go away of itself in a few days or in a week or two. Others may have it for a few months and then it will lift. Some have it for a year, and then it fades away. A few have it forever after.

There are also different levels of severity. One woman will feel sad for a short time. Another woman might become psychotic and hallucinate. Treatment depends on severity. Most women can take comfort from the fact that most PPD will go away of itself when it has run its course, and may not occur with another pregnancy.

When women feel alienated, depressed, and anxious, they need the reassurance of knowing they are not alone in having this problem. They are not going insane, and the depression in most cases will not last forever. For some women, that reassurance is enough to get them through.

However, if PPD is interfering seriously with a woman's life, there are options for treatment. As with Terrie, a short course of the right antidepressant may deal well with the problem. Other women will need one or more hormones, and may even need an added antidepressant as well.

It is obviously extremely important for all women with PPD to get as much emotional and practical support as possible while having these problems. They need lots of rest and plenty of opportunity for sleep, and, obviously, lots of sympathy.

Dr. Dalton's Treatment

The treatment recommended by Dr. Katherina Dalton, for women who have delivered their babies but have not yet resumed menstruation, is daily administration of 100 mg. intramuscular shots of natural progesterone (in alternate hips to prevent scarring). Dr. Dalton favors injections into the outer lower buttock where fat and muscle combine.

For women with mild problems, instead of injections, she recommends 400 mg. vaginal or anal suppositories of natural progesterone one to three times a day, depending on symptoms. This regimen varies according to the response of the individual woman.

Dr. Dalton has written a book called *Depression After Childbirth* on

PPD. It is available from PMS Access, in Madison, Wisconsin, phone 1-800-222-4PMS. Dr. Dalton has also written a brochure called *Guide to Progesterone for Postnatal Depression*. It is available from PMS Help, P.O. Box 100, St. Albans, Herts., AL1 4UQ, England.

Other Suggestions

Physicians in the U.S. frequently use natural progesterone (not synthetic progestins) in oral form, that is, micronized powder made into capsules or tablets. Tablets and capsules in oil may be swallowed. Powder capsules are frequently used under the tongue. (See progesterone treatment section in the chapter on PMS for details.)

According to Dr. Dalton, **you may keep breast-feeding while taking progesterone,** because progesterone is quickly metabolized and does not migrate to the milk. Dr. Dalton says using progesterone may actually help increase milk flow.

Once menstruation resumes, progesterone is usually given during the last half of the cycle, as with PMS.

Some women may need a little estrogen, but should not breast-feed their babies if they decide to take it. Other women may need a little thyroid temporarily, or sometimes permanently. Sometimes, it is the onset of hypothyroidism or the appearance of a goiter that directly causes PPD. Some women treated with thyroid will lose their depression.

Some women do not respond to hormones and need treatment with an antidepressant. Dr. Dalton particularly recommends Nardil, an MAO inhibitor. As mentioned, research recently found that progesterone functions similarly to this type of antidepressant. Nardil has some food restrictions—those foods containing tyrosine (including cheese, bananas, alcohol, etc.) and the side effects if you happen to eat those foods can be dangerous. Nardil is the same class of drug as Parnate which I have mentioned elsewhere. Overdose is dangerous.

Other women seem to benefit from other antidepressants.

Women with severe PPD may be better off to stop breast-feeding to see if it helps the hormones return to normal. While prolactin is high, the ovarian hormones may remain subnormal. Other women are fine while they breast-feed, and have problems when they stop. So this is not a hard and fast rule.

Most women will come out of PPD within a year of their delivery.

Preventive Treatment

Having low levels of progesterone causes many premature births and also causes repeated miscarriages in some women. Women with a history of repeated miscarriages or toxemia may be given natural progesterone during pregnancy. So may women who are presently experiencing psychosis or depression during pregnancy.

Women who have PPD after each pregnancy can be given injections of progesterone immediately after delivery for prevention.

Dr. Hamilton's Treatment

Dr. Alexander Hamilton of San Francisco sees PPD as a polyendocrine disorder caused by the sudden drop of estrogen and progesterone immediately after delivery, which can cause pituitary shock, which affects the levels of cortisol, and thyroxine. I have not spelled out the details of the treatment he suggests to avoid misquoting him, but the details can be found in his article *The Picture Puzzle of Psychiatric Illness After Childbirth*, written for The York Hospital Conference, in York, Pennsylvania, April 6, 1988.

He suggests women receive preventive treatment when they have had previous bouts of severe PPD. He gives a shot of estrogen at delivery, oral estrogen days one to fourteen, injections of intramuscular natural progesterone at delivery and for the following seven days, followed by progesterone suppositories twice a day for two months or until onset of menstruation. He also mentions giving 50 mg. of vitamin B6 for days one to thirty after delivery, because he believes this substance possibly prevents a drop in the neurotransmitter, seratonin.

He theorizes that, for extreme cases, taking a little cortisone twice a day for three weeks may help postpartum psychosis (experienced from day three or four); and a low dose of thyroid, starting three weeks after delivery, may help late depressive syndrome. The thyroid should be closely monitored.

CHAPTER 25

Treatment for Thyroid

*I*n his book, *Nutrition and Vitamin Therapy,* Dr. Michael Lesser says that he prescribes organic iodine with vitamin BI (thiamine), B complex and vitamin E for people who have sluggish thyroids. He recommends kelp, seafood, and iodized salt as sources of iodine. There are some problems with the iodization of salt, but it is pretty difficult to buy plain common salt which is not iodized these days.

Dr. Lesser also mentions foods that contain goitrin, an antithyroid factor—beans, beets, cabbage, carrots, lettuce, peaches, spinach, and strawberries.

When Thyroid Is Needed

When there is obvious thyroid deficiency, determined by blood tests, family and personal history, symptoms, and basal temperature, thyroid supplementation may be needed. **The following recommendations are only general and can only be given under the supervision of a physician.**

Women with symptoms of subclinical thyroid function may be started on .05 mg. or .I mg. of Synthroid daily, and 5 mcg. of Cytomel may be added if the afternoon fatigue does not go away.

Different Types of Thyroid

Just as there is more than one estrogen in the female body, there is also more than one form of thyroid, and finding the type of thyroid that is most suitable can be important for some individuals.

Some physicians prefer to use animal thyroid for the same reason that they like to use conjugated animal estrogens—they consider them more "natural" than other forms of synthesized thyroid, because they contain all the different types of thyroid a human produces, plus the hormone calcitonin. Synthetic thyroid is usually only one type of thyroxine, such as T3 or T4. Still, animal thyroid is only "natural" for cattle, and humans may have side effects from animal thyroid, just as they have sometimes using Premarin, which comes from pregnant mares' urine. The hormone cell receptors probably detect the differences.

Dr. Broda Barnes, who helped develop Armor thyroid, felt his patients did much better on it than on Synthroid But, generally, pharmacists and physicians prefer synthetic forms of thyroid because the dose is more reliable. They say animal thyroid tablets vary in strength, depending on which animal they are taken from. They also believe that synthetic thyroid, such as Synthroid, is a good copy of human thyroid. Animal thyroid works immediately, but human thyroid takes five to six weeks to reach its optimal effect. In this respect, synthetic thyroid more closely resembles human thyroid. When women take Synthroid, T4, their bodies usually break it down to T3. In some women, this does not happen, and they may need to also take Cytomel, synthetic T3.

In practice, some women will do better on synthetic thyroid, while others will feel better on animal thyroid.

Caution with Thyroid

Many physicians are understandably cautious about treating with thyroid. Taking thyroid above certain doses can cause the pituitary gland to cease production of thyroxine and create the need to take thyroid indefinitely—and what this "certain dose" is varies with the individual. Moreover, overmedication with thyroid can affect the heart and bones adversely. And, if a woman who is manic-depressive is given thyroid, it may send her into a serious manic state.

The ideal amount to give is that which normalizes the TSH levels, not causing them to drop to zero. Experimenting with different doses and types of thyroid may be necessary, but all dose changes should be done with the full knowledge and consent of your physician. While physicians who use progesterone for PMS encourage women to experiment with their dose, they don't encourage women to change their thyroid dose at will. The potential side effects of thyroid are much more serious than those with progesterone.

Nevertheless, some women with PMS will benefit immensely from thyroid treatment; but it is critical for women on thyroid medication to regularly check their pulse and temperature, which both tend to rise if the medication is too high. Occasional blood tests to monitor thyroid levels are also wise.

Be Careful of Side Effects

Because the doctors I work with only use small doses, we rarely see serious side effects. But we caution women to watch for signs and symptoms.

When beginning thyroid medication, patients may experience more rapid heartrate as the thyroid stimulates the heart. They may feel nervous and have trouble with insomnia. They may get severe headaches. Their temperature may rise (temperature and pulse rate tend to go together). They may get reddening of the hands and feet as the blood rushes to the extremities. These symptoms may just be a temporary problem because of the sudden stimulation of the heart by the extra thyroid, or they can be a continual problem and really indicate overdose.

If a patient experiences initial, increased fatigue, increasing the dose is done slowly. Sometimes the thyroid gland becomes sore and tender, and this is treated symptomatically. If heart palpitations, nervousness, and irritability occur, the patient is advised to stop the medication for three days, then try again. If the symptoms recur, the patient should again stop the medication for three days and then begin again on the miminal dose. Again, don't use this information as a manual. Consult with your physician.

Beware of Overdose

People should be aware that overmedication with thyroid can be dangerous. It can lead to "thyroid storm" with rapid heartrate and, potentially, to a heart attack, and too much thyroid long-term can cause osteoporosis. **This is why adjustment in thyroid doses should never be treated casually and should be monitored by a physician.**

Treatment for the APICH Syndrome

The APICH syndrome is essentially thyroiditis, oophoritis, and associated immune system problems (see chapter on thyroid in the problem section of the book). In Dr. Nathan Becker and Phyllis Saifer's article about it, women with symptoms of the APICH Syndrome are treated as follows: L-Thyroxine (Synthroid, T4) is given in small doses to start, with the dose gradually increased over four to six weeks to .15 mg. or .2 mg. daily (approximately 80 percent of the body weight). That is, if you are 150 lbs., you would take approximately 1.25 mg. of Synthroid.

For people who build up excess levels of T4 (the main thyroid your body produces) and do not convert T4 to T3, a low dose of T3 (Cytomel) may be added to give instant energy and help with afternoon fatigue. Rarely, a patient with the APICH syndrome may develop Grave's disease. There are rare patients with the APICH Syndrome whose thyroiditis and high antibody levels are not controlled by L-Thyroxine, and who require a total thyroidectomy with subsequent thyroid replacement.

Other Treatments for Women with the APICH Syndrome

For those women with severe allergies, immunization therapy has sometimes been helpful.

A physician I know gives injections of Depo-Medrol, a distant cousin to cortisone with fewer side effects, to women with evidence of antibodies. After six to eight weeks, he starts women on hormones. This, of course, is not a commonly-accepted practice, but it will be helpful information for some women.

Women with cyclical, PMS-type symptoms may need treatment with natural progesterone or a combination of estrogen and natural progesterone. (See the respective chapters for treatment with these hormones.)

Because of the history of allergy, infection, and menstrual problems, many women with APICH syndrome have been on the birth control pill or on repeated antibiotics. This may have allowed yeast overgrowth (candidiasis), causing all sorts of problems, including repeated vaginal infections. Where there is evidence of yeast-related problems, a trial of oral Nystatin has been used for three weeks, with success. There are many natural antifungal agents available without prescription from health food stores.

Effect of Estrogen on the Thyroid

Estrogen therapy is known to increase the uptake and release of iodide. It also affects plasma thyroglobulin concentration, and helps the metabolism of T4. What this means is that taking estrogen may help raise your thyroid levels. Women who are hypothyroid may need readjustment of their thyroid medication if they begin estrogen therapy.

CHAPTER 26

Treatment for
Premenopause and Menopause

Many women with estrogen-deficiency symptoms may be able to control them with simple life-style changes and natural remedies, at least for a while. The recommendations for life-style changes for PMS are also appropriate for women with estrogen-deficiency symptoms. (Read the two chapters on diet and treatment for PMS.)

Treatment for Hot Flashes

During menopause, if the only symptom you experience is hot flashes, treatments other than hormonal therapy can be effective. Using the herb vitex agnus castus helps balance the hormones, and taking Korean ginseng capsules, vitamin E, and hormones such as black cohosh can be helpful. Women are advised to avoid caffeine and alcohol which tend to worsen hot flashes, and also to avoid large doses of niacin (vitamin B3) as it also affects vasomotor stability.

Herbal Preparations

Hormones were only isolated in the early decades of this century. By contrast, women have used herbs for thousands of years to help balance the endocrine system and the menstrual cycle. Many herbs contain estrogen, and others help produce progesterone; but, since it may be dangerous to take herbs haphazardly, try to find a well-informed herbologist who uses only fresh organic herbs.

Some helpful herb preparations for menopause include black and blue cohosh, licorice, wild yam, sassafras, sarsaparilla, vitex, kelp, valerian root, ginger, motherwort, licorice, yellow dock, dong quai, false unicorn, sage, dandelion, gingko, gota kola, and ginseng. Bee pollen and spirulina are also helpful.

Herbs that produce high-calcium levels include comfrey, oatstraw, horsetail, borage, and nettle. Some herbs that alleviate hot flashes are sage, blue vervain, motherwort, blessed thistle, and rosemary. Rosemary Gladstar Slick's *Herbs for Menopause* gives very practical and helpful guidance. See the book list at the end of this book for information on how to obtain her book.

A Caution Against Herbs

Dr. Lila Nachtigall points out that ginseng is a natural plant estrogen and has the same effects on the body as taking prescribed estrogen. She warns against using it excessively because of the risk of hyperplasia (excessive buildup of the lining of the uterus), and because ginseng is usually taken alone and not countered with progesterone.

She also warns against overdosing on herbs because, while many are used as the basis of our modern pharmacology, they have not been subjected to controlled studies. If you find someone who is well-informed, taking herbs should not be a problem.

Calcium Supplements

Medical opinion on taking calcium for bone-protection differs. Some physicians strongly recommend calcium, along with estrogen. Others believe calcium has little effect on restoring bone, particularly during the two or three years following menopause when the highest proportion of bone loss occurs.

If you decide to take calcium, remember that milk has a high-calcium content, but is a poor source because of its high-protein content. Better sources of calcium are green vegetables, oranges, almonds, and other calcium-rich foods found listed on a food chart. The recommended daily dose for calcium is 1,000 mg. per day.

Estrogen Therapy

Hormonal treatment should begin only after a physician
examines the patient to discount any physical problems.
The patient should remain under a physician's
supervision while taking hormones.

Estrogen Is Back in Favor

Research in the 1970s seemed to show that estrogen was linked with an increase in endometrial cancer, because estrogen promotes the growth of the endometrium. This led physicians to stop prescribing it, and women became afraid to use it.

However, estrogen doses have been substantially lowered, and progestins have been added to the estrogen therapy. Progestins inhibit the endometrial growth by reducing the number of cell receptors for estrogen and increasing an enzyme that converts estradiol to estrone sulphate which is easily excreted. Studies have found that among women who take ten or more days of progestin, hyperplasia does not develop. Actually, **correct use of lower doses of estrogen with progesterone is more likely to protect against cancer than cause it.** While there is less certainty about breast cancer, reliable studies have been done showing there is no increased risk for breast cancer associated with the postmenopausal doses of estrogen.[1]

Medical concern is now focused on osteoporosis and heart disease in postmenopausal women, which are more prevalent than breast cancer and are among the leading causes of death in older women. The benefits of estrogen therapy in treating these diseases far outweighs any danger from cancer; and for this reason, estrogen-replacement therapy has come back into favor.

Do You Need Estrogen?

A doctor may decide you need estrogen when you have a high-follicle stimulating (FSH) hormone blood level (over 40 MIU/ml is a definite sign that you are postmenopausal, but some doctors feel these levels are far too high), or low estradiol blood levels, a premenopausal or menopausal Pap smear, or on the basis of the obvious symptoms you are experiencing.

Do You Want Estrogen?

Many women do not want to take estrogen, and, of course, this is their prerogative. Some of them do not need it; others of them would be better off taking it.

There are several reasons why women stop taking estrogen—they do not want to continue having periods; they have side effects from taking Premarin, or, especially, Provera; they don't like taking medication; they put on weight on hormones.

Most women will stop having periods if they take their hormones continually, though it may take six months. Changing the medication to other types of estrogen and natural progesterone may dissipate the side effects. Women tend to put on weight at menopause—approximately ten to twelve pounds, according to a recent study; this is not always directly related to taking estrogen, but reflects a general change in metabolism at mid-life.

Estrogen's Benefits on the Heart

According to Dr. Leon Speroff, a review of the current literature shows overwhelming support for a reduced risk of cardiovascular disease in estrogen users, especially among nonsmokers.[2] Unfortunately in 1978 and 1985, the Framingham Study suggested there was a 50 percent increase for cardiovascular disease among estrogen users. While this study was highly respected, it is now believed the conclusion about estrogen increasing heart disease was wrong. In fact, the study was reevaluated in 1991, and the conclusion was reversed.

The Nurse's Health Study, following 121,964 nurses on estrogen-replacement therapy, has been running for about twenty years. It concludes that there is a 50 percent reduction in heart disease in women who have been on estrogen at some time. Current users showed a 70 percent reduction.

The reason estrogen is so helpful in preventing heart disease is that it elevates the levels of HDL-cholesterol, by retarding its metabolism by the liver. This mainly occurs when estrogen is taken orally. Dr. Speroff says that while the patch, the implant, and the topical cream may have profound impact on hot flashes, vaginal dryness, and moods, estrogen taken by these routes has only a limited impact on HDLs (though estrogen does make a second pass to the liver).

Dr. Speroff comments that the public health importance of the impact of estrogen on cardiovascular disease is even more significant than estrogen's effect on osteoporosis.

Estrogen's Effect on Osteoporosis

Dr. Speroff mentions that three-quarters of the bone loss which occurs in women during the first twenty years after menopause can be attributed to estrogen loss, rather than the process of aging itself. Vertebral bone is particularly vulnerable, and can begin to decline from the age of twenty onwards.

There are two important factors controlling the risk of fracture:
1. Bone mass achieved at maturity
2. Subsequent rate of bone loss

Exercise and both early and continuing diet are very important in preventing osteoporosis, but neither will stop bone loss if estrogen levels are below normal.

Taking estrogen will lead to a 50 to 60 percent decrease in arm and hip fractures. When calcium is added to the estrogen, an 80 percent reduction in fractures of the vertebrae is seen. Natural progesterone is also helpful, adding bone formation in the matrix.

The beneficial effect of estrogen on the bones is only seen in current users. Present recommendations are to take estrogen close to menopause, and to take it long-term or lifelong.

Estrogen for Migraines

When estrogen levels drop suddenly before and during menstruation, this causes spasms in the blood vessels in the base of the neck, and can be responsible for severe headaches. Estrogen (and natural progesterone) frequently help relieve severe hormonal headaches. Sometimes, taking estrogen causes headaches. When this happens, women should try lowering the dose or take an alternate form of estrogen that bypasses the liver, before giving it up.

Estrogen for Depression and Panic Attacks

In the past, when women have complained about the emotional symptoms connected with menopause, many physicians have not taken them seriously. Even now, books on menopause say that depression at menopause is a side effect of poor sleep patterns or hot flashes or low self-esteem. However, many women know that the depression and anxiety they experience at menopause are valid symptoms in their own right and find that their emotional health improves when they are treated with estrogen for physical symptoms.

We have already mentioned several times the impact of estrogen on the mind and the mood. Estrogen functions somewhat like an antidepressant and has MAO inhibitory and antidopaminergic properties. It increases seratonin and seratonin receptors; it increases norepinephrine in the hypothalamus; and it raises the endorphins. A lot of work is being done experimentally with older women taking estrogen.

Studies show that estrogen increases the ability to do abstract reasoning. It improves short-term verbal memory; it increases paragraph recall; it improves patients with dementia, for instance, in Alzheimer's disease. It helps intelligence, performance of tasks, psychosocial function, interpersonal relations, care of the self, and memory.[3]

Many women with hormonal problems, particularly premenopause, experience onset of severe panic-attacks in their thirties and forties. These panic attacks, often with heart palpitations and prestroke symptoms, are usually attributed to stress and treated with Xanax. Rarely is the connection made with hormones.

Summary of Benefits from Estrogen
There are many physical and emotional benefits from estrogen therapy. Estrogen can help **relieve hot flashes**. It can keep **the skin toned and moist**. It can **restore the vagina to a more youthful state**—thicker, more moist, more flexible, and with added lubrication.

Estrogen can **help prevent vaginal and bladder infections** caused by estrogen deficiency. It can **prevent further bone loss**, and accompanying symptoms. By **improving the cardiovascular system,** and **lowering cholesterol,** estrogen **can protect women from heart disease.** Because estrogen dilates the blood vessels, it **reduces headaches and migraines.**

A recent study has shown that estrogen may also help some women **avoid rheumatoid arthritis** later in life. But for many women, the **emotional benefits** of taking estrogen are most important.

Who Should Take Estrogen?

- Women who have severe menopausal symptoms—severe hot flashes, vaginal atrophy, recurrent bladder infections from thinning of the vaginal tissues
- Women with severe hormonal depression and anxiety
- Women at high risk for osteoporosis
- Possibly, women with high risk of heart disease (though this is not used as a medical reason yet)
- Possibly, women with a history of rheumatoid arthritis (though this is not used as a medical reason yet)
- Women who wish to enjoy sex past the age of sixty

Who Shouldn't Take Estrogen?

A woman with any of the following should not use estrogen:

- Known or suspected cancer of the breast, particularly those breast cancers with estrogen receptors in them
- Known or suspected cancer of the endometrium
- Known or suspected estrogen-dependent cancers
- Undiagnosed vaginal bleeding
- Active clotting disorders
- Past history of clotting disorders caused by estrogen (but make sure it was)
- Women with fibroids that enlarge with estrogen
- Some women with epilepsy, asthma, migraine, heart, or kidney disease, in which fluid retention might worsen the disease
- Severe liver disease or jaundice associated with the contraceptive pill (but see next section)

Treating Women for Heavy Bleeding

Irregular bleeding can occur because of too much estrogen, too little estrogen, or too little progesterone.

Dr. Lila Nachtigall feels that women who have very heavy bleeding during premenopause should not be on estrogen therapy. She says that, at this time when the ovaries are running out of eggs, the pituitary tries to compensate by putting out large doses of follicle stimulating hormone. This can produce high levels of estrogen; hence the heavy bleeding. These women, she believes, need more progesterone to slough off the excess endometrial lining, rather than estrogen which adds to it.

But if a woman has continual spotting, taking estrogen can sometimes stop the bleeding immediately, because it helps stabilize the endometrial lining of the uterus.

Sometimes, women have symptoms of estrogen deficiency for only part of the month. They may produce excessive estrogen in the first half of the cycle, which leads to heavy periods, but still have very low levels in the second half of the cycle. Dr. Winnifred Cutler mentions that some women may need a little estrogen only in the second half of the cycle.

Sometimes, the bleeding problem is because the woman is not ovulating or because progesterone levels are low. These women benefit from treatment with progesterone for several cycles.

Changes in Thought Concerning Estrogen Use

In the past, FDA warnings about estrogens listed many medical conditions which were either caused or aggravated by the estrogen therapy then in current use. Because of this, certain groups of women, predisposed to these medical conditions, were advised against taking estrogens. For instance, if a women had a personal or family history of hormonal cancer, high blood pressure, thrombosis, stroke, heart disease, or diabetes, estrogen was contraindicated in her case.

Recommendations against the use of estrogens were made because of the high incidence of side effects, which occurred for several reasons, including:

1. The type of estrogen then used (synthetic ethinyl estradiol which is also found in the birth control pill), incurred more side effects than forms currently used.
2. Much higher doses were then commonly prescribed.
3. Estrogen was taken continually, without the countering effect of progesterone.

These warnings were given, even though these issues had not been widely studied at the time. Today, research has found that natural forms of estrogens are generally benign when taken in smaller doses along with progesterone. Therefore, many women who previously were advised against using estrogen are now free to use it.

- **Endometrial cancer** is no longer a concern because prescribed doses are now smaller, and progesterone or progestin is added to counter the effects of estrogen on the uterus. Women are actually less likely to get endometrial cancer on the correct hormonal protocol.

  Although estrogen does not cause endometrial cancer, those women who already have endometrial cancer should not use it. Women should know that three-quarters of the cases of endometrial cancer occur in those who have never been on estrogen. Also, compared to the large numbers of women who die from osteoporosis and heart disease, endometrial cancer is less of a life threat (2,900 a year die of endometrial cancer and only a quarter of them have been on estrogen therapy).

- **Breast cancer**—Since estrogen influences breast tissue, there has always been concern about its causing or acting as a catalyst to breast cancer. Many studies show no link between estrogen therapy and breast cancer. Other studies indicate estrogen therapy helps prevent breast cancer. Currently, it is believed that estrogen does not cause breast cancer and low levels of estrogen combined with progesterone or progestogen decrease one's chances of developing this cancer. Estrogen is often not given to someone who has had breast cancer or has a strong history of estrogen-dependent breast cancer, but medical opinion in favor of giving estrogen is changing. As mentioned earlier, some experts on breast cancer are now giving estrogen and progestin therapy within a year of a simple lumpectomy; others are waiting two or three years. This advice is totally different from that given even a few years ago.

  Another favorable advantage of hormone replacement therapy for the breasts is that correcting hormonal balance may improve fibrocystic breast disease.

- **Fibroids**—In the past, it was thought that estrogen therapy would cause these benign uterine growths to increase in size. Generally, the estrogen doses given postmenopausally are too small to affect fibroids but, occasionally, even low doses of estrogen will cause the growth of fibroids.

- **High blood pressure**—In the past, estrogen elevated levels of the enzymes renin and angiotensin in the kidneys and caused high blood pressure in some predisposed women. Taking estrogen by a method that bypasses the liver counters this problem.

- **Gallbladder disease** and **liver disease**—women with these problems should take estrogen in cream or patch form, which bypasses the liver.

- **Diabetes**—If you have diabetes or if it is a part of your family history, it is usually acceptable to take estrogen, but it should be taken under a physician's scrutiny.

- **Bloodclotting**—Women on the high-estrogen contraceptive pill were once considered at risk for thrombosis. But the low, post-menopausal doses of estrogen are not considered dangerous. Some women are at higher risk for thrombosis than others, but this is relatively rare, and can be detected by testing a woman's blood levels of antithrombin, which will show high if the woman is in the high risk group. She can have regular blood tests to screen these levels.

Side Effects from Taking Estrogen

Most women respond favorably to estrogen therapy, but some experience various difficulties with it. A woman who doesn't receive immediate results from HRT (hormone-replacement therapy) should not be discouraged since there is a wide range of options. HRT is very individual, and every woman needs to find, through experimentation, the HRT that suits her best.

Some of the side effects experienced when first taking estrogen may include depression, nausea, vomiting, bloating, increased weight, cramps, swollen or tender breasts, headaches, vertigo, an increased susceptibility to vaginal yeast infections, and breakthrough vaginal bleeding.

The body may take a couple of months to adjust to estrogen, in which case these symptoms often quickly disappear. If they don't disappear spontaneously, you may need to adjust your dose, try a different type of estrogen, or vary the method of taking it. About 25 percent of women may have some abnormal uterine bleeding and may need an occasional endometrial biopsy. This should not be required more than once a year. But, if progesterone is taken properly, a biopsy should not be necessary.

There Are Different Types of Estrogen

There are three main types of estrogen produced in the female body—estradiol, estrone, and estriol, given in order of potency. Conjugated (mixed) estrogens contain them all. Other brands of estrogen may only contain one. Here is a list of natural and synthetic forms of estrogen available on prescription (brand name in brackets):

Natural Estrogens

- (Premarin)—Animal conjugated estrogens, made from pregnant mare's urine. The predominant estrogen is estrone sulphate.
- (Ogen)—Estropipate.
- (Estrace)—Micronized estradiol, in tablets, capsules, shots, the patch, and surgically-implanted pellets.
  Note, there are a couple of brands of estrogen—Menrium and PMB—that contain estrogen and a tranquilizer.

Synthetic Estrogens

- (Estinyl)—Ethinyl estradiol, the estrogen in the contraceptive pill.
- (Estrovis)—Quinestrol, broken down by the body into ethinyl estradiol.

Natural Hormones versus Synthetic

We all like to hear the word "natural." However, we know from food labels that "natural" doesn't necessarily mean "good." Rather than ask, "Is it natural?" it is better to ask, "Does this hormone (whether it be estrogen, progesterone, or thyroid) match my body chemistry?" If the hormone matches the substance you normally produce, your body is programmed to accept it. As an illustration, consider the difference between progesterone, progestins, and progestogens. Progesterone matches your body chemistry, and the body is programmed to break it down into pregnanediol which can then be excreted. Progestins and progestogens are made in the laboratory and are "in-between hormones," whose chemical makeup is different from the hormones produced in the human body. The body is not programmed to handle them, and they cause side effects because they remain circulating in the bloodstream and are difficult to excrete.

Hormonal Therapy Is an Art and a Science

Hormonal therapy can be complicated. It can't be done in a rush. When women seek hormonal therapy, it is typical for their physicians to prescribe a standard regimen for all women. The problem is that women aren't all the same, and their needs and responses vary tremendously.

A standard procedure is for a physician to give all his patients with PMS fourteen doses of progesterone to be taken once a day and then stopped to allow bleeding. And he might give every woman with menopausal problems the standard regimen of conjugated estrogens from day one to twenty-five in the calendar month and a progestogen from day sixteen to twenty-five, and then a break.

Because women vary in the extent and severity of their hormonal problems and their sensitivity and reaction to medication, these treatments don't always work effectively, and women may experience side effects. Treatment needs individual tailoring and fine-tuning, which is sometimes called IHRT (individual hormone-replacement therapy).

The Correct Estrogen for You

Different types of estrogen are prepared in several forms—oral tablets, injections, patches, pellets, and creams. Oral estrogens are more beneficial because they pass through the liver, causing an increase in high density lipids, (HDLs, the good cholesterol), and this effect is not as pronounced when women use other methods of taking estrogen. However, some doctors say there is a second pass to the liver, and the pellet and higher dose patch do increase the HDLs.

Not everyone responds equally well on all forms of estrogen. Some women find certain forms of estrogen give them cramps or sore breasts, while other forms do not. Some estrogens take away hot flashes and others don't. Some estrogens leave them depressed, while others won't. Some cause headaches for some women; others don't. So, women may need to try various types and doses of estrogen therapy before their menopausal symptoms successfully disappear.

Conjugated Oral Estrogens

Conjugated oral estrogens, such as Premarin, are the most commonly prescribed, having been on the market since 1941. They are the most tested, the most advertized, and are considered reliable and trustworthy. Some physicians promote the use of these estrogens (made from pregnant mare's urine) because they are "natural" and contain all the estrogens. Others disagree, saying that the quantities and proportions that are natural for horses are not natural for humans. There are approximately seventy different estrogenic chemicals in conjugated estrogens, including equine equilin sulphate, an estrogen specific to horses. The human body finds this horse estrogen difficult to metabolize or excrete, and it can remain for long periods of time in the human system. The so-called "horse factor" is believed to be a major reason for increased side effects with conjugated estrogens. Some women may also be allergic to the coloring in the tablets.

Some women with a tendency towards PMS find that conjugated estrogens cause depression or headaches. Also, conjugated estrogens can have a slightly adverse effect on the liver function. Nevertheless, many women feel better on conjugated estrogens than on other forms. That's why you should be prepared to try more than one estrogen to find the best for you.

Other Oral Estrogens

If a woman experiences side effects from conjugated estrogens, she may feel better on either Estrace or Ogen. Estrace matches estradiol, the most potent estrogen in the female body. Ogen matches estrone, a weaker human estrogen. These hormones are chemically different, and women may do better on one or the other. My experience has been that many women feel better and significantly less depressed on Estrace. Others agree.[4]

Oral tablets work perfectly well for some women, and, as mentioned before, help increase the beneficial HDLs. But tablets may not be effective for others, because the liver screens incoming chemicals from the stomach via the blood stream. In its action to prevent "foreign invasion," the liver may destroy incoming oral estrogen and also cause side effects.

Possible side effects from taking oral estrogen include:
- **May increase fatty deposits** on the inside of the arteries.
- **May increase antithrombin III** which adversely affects clotting.

Women at risk should have their antithrombin levels tested.

- **May increase production of the enzymes, renin and angiotensin** in the kidneys (in approximately one out of twenty women). This causes an increase in blood pressure.
- **May thicken and concentrate the bile** produced by the liver which can aggravate gallstones. When estrogen is taken by another route, this problem can be avoided.
- Estrogen should not be taken orally by women with **damaged livers**, but can be taken by other methods.
- About one in twenty women may experience **an increase in blood pressure** when taking estrogen
- Another problem with taking either oral tablets or injectable estrogen may be the subsequent **peaking and dipping of hormone levels, which may cause mood swings.**

Women who are troubled by some of these side effects may wish to use the estrogen transdermal patch or soon-to-be marketed Band-Aid patch, have an estrogen implant, or use vaginal cream or a gel that can be rubbed on the arm. These methods bypass the liver.

More Than One Route

Some women don't fully lose their symptoms on oral estrogens, but want to continue receiving the beneficial effects on the lipids provided by tablets. If their physician is willing, they may need to take estrogen by both the oral and another route. For instance, some may opt to take a low dose of the patch and a low oral dose.

Injections

Monthly injections of long-lasting estrogen are a very reliable source of estrogen, but for some women, with a rapid rate of metabolism, the same shot may only last a week. This may be especially apparent in women who exercise vigorously.

There are several advantages to injectable estrogen. Some women prefer the convenience of having an injection once a month instead of taking tablets every day. Others find injections work more consistently than tablets or the patch. The dose of estrogen can be adjusted, at will, by varying how much is taken up in the syringe.

Some physicians give women with extreme symptoms more frequent injections at a lower dose, (even as many as two or three a week), adding progesterone and testosterone to the shot. They decrease the number of shots as the woman improves.

But many women find it a disadvantage to make regular visits to the doctor's office for an injection. Another disadvantage is that some women who have shots may develop abscesses or, over a period of years, develop scar tissue in the hip at the injection site, and absorption of estrogen is consequently poor.

Surgeons often choose to use injections directly after an oophorectomy, because women often don't respond well to the oral tablets or the patch at that time. After about three months, the physician will switch the patient from injections to another form of estrogen.

Peak-and-Valley Experience

One problem some women encounter with tablets and, to a lesser extent, monthly injections, is that they have a peak-and-valley type of effect. Women feel good a short time after taking the pill, but the effect runs out as the hormone levels drop. Their experience is not consistent.

Sometimes, hormonal levels are more stable when the patch or implant is used.

Wearing the Patch

Because it bypasses the liver, the transdermal patch was hailed for its benefits when it first came out. It promised better absorption, a more consistent dose of estrogen, and diminished side effects.

A large percentage of women have been pleased with the overall effect of the patch, but some are disappointed for two reasons:

1. It comes off easily, although it can be reattached by gently blowing warm air on the estrogen paste with a blow-dryer.

2. Many women develop a skin allergy either to the alcohol in the patch or the patch adhesive, which produces red, hive-like swellings under and around the patch. Some women find that applying the patch to the hip, rather than the abdomen, alleviates this problem. Others find this doesn't help. Another suggestion is to apply a little I percent hydrocortisone cream on the place where the patch will be applied. Then place the patch where the cream was rubbed in. This

will help some women, but there will be some who still can't tolerate the patch. There is a new Band-Aid patch soon to be marketed which will do away with the skin problems created by the old patch.

Estrogen Gel

A new estrogen gel is available in the U.S., a virtually identical product to the one that has been available and widely used in Europe for over a decade. This gel is rubbed on the arm, the inner thighs, or the abdomen daily or twice daily and apparently provides stable levels of estradiol.

Implanting Estrogen Pellets

The implantation of one or more estradiol pellets, by a minor surgical procedure, into the fatty subcutaneous tissue of the abdomen or hip, works very well for women with severe estrogen deficiency. Sometimes testosterone pellets are used with the estrogen. Like the patch, the implant gives continuous and constant estrogen levels, and bypasses the liver. The estrogen in this form goes directly to the estrogen receptors in the brain and has a wonderful effect on the emotions. For some women, taking estrogen by implant is far superior to taking it any other way.

The beneficial effects of the implant last three to six months, and, for some women, up to a year. The disadvantage of implants is that once they are in, they are not easy to remove if a woman experiences any side effects.

The pellet was, I believe, FDA-approved at one time, but is not at the present time. However, approval of a pellet in gel-form is imminent. The studies necessary for its approval have been submitted, but it will take a few years for approval to come through. A few researchers presently have permission to do estrogen-implant surgery.

How Much Estrogen?

The degree of symptoms strongly influences the amount of estrogen a woman should take, and individual rate absorption and metabolism are also important variables. A physician might, for example, suggest a woman take a low dose on alternate days if she seems to be getting overdose symptoms like nausea. Or he might increase the dose if the lower one does not alleviate her hot flashes. If a higher dose still does not help the symptoms, the doctor might switch to another brand or method of taking it. Height and weight also make a difference. Generally, women who need estrogen before menopause need a higher dose than those who take it after menopause. **General practice, then, is to give premenopausal women about twice the amount given to postmenopausal women.**

The following is a list of the more common forms of estrogen with dosages.

Oral tablets—Premarin (conjugated estrogens). The standard dose is 1.25 mg. (a yellow football-shaped tablet) per day. A smaller dose, given to postmenopausal women, who don't need as much estrogen, is .625 mg. (a red-brown football-shaped tablet). Other doses are available for women who need more or less estrogen—2.5 mg. (a purple tablet), 0.9 mg. (a white tablet), and 0.3 mg. (a dark green tablet).

Estrace (estradiol)—comes in 2 mg. (green tablet) and 1 mg. (violet-blue tablet).

Ogen (estropipate)—available in 1.25 mg. (orange tablet), and a .625 mg. (yellow tablet). A 2.5 mg. (blue tablet), and a 5 mg. (pale-green tablet) dose are also available.

Injections—more than one brand of injectable estrogen is available. Delestrogen, Depo-Estradiol, and Depo-Testadiol (with a little testosterone) are various brands of long-lasting estrogen injections, usually given about once a month. For instance, half a cc. of Delestrogen (40 mg. per cc.) can be given intramuscularly in the hip. Dose can be adjusted up or down, depending on the need.

Estraderm Transdermal Patch—there are two strengths—.1 mg. and .05 mg.

Pellets—Typically, five 25 mg. estrogen pellets and one 75 mg. testosterone pellet are implanted separately, (i.e., north, south, west, and east of a specific point), using a trocar deep in the lateral thigh or buttocks, and beneath the fascia of the muscle. If they are inserted too close to the skin's surface, the site may swell and the pellets be expelled. Also scar tissue may form when the site is too close to the surface, and absorption will be hindered.

Using several pellets is better than using one large one as there is more surface area. For example, a woman will get .25 mg. of Estradiol daily from one 100 mg. implant, but .40 mg. Estradiol from four 25 mg. implants. Depending on metabolism, the implant's effectiveness lasts from about three months to a year, after which symptoms will abruptly or slowly return. Taking oral estrogen concurrently with the pellet, after the pellets have been inserted for a month or so, will help lengthen the potency of the implant.

Different Ways of Taking Oral Tablets

Women on estrogen who have not had a hysterectomy are always given enough progestogen to avoid too great a buildup of the lining of the uterus. While this is common practice, the FDA has never officially approved Provera for this purpose, and the long-term effects of progestogens are still unknown.

The standard way to take hormone-replacement therapy has been to use estrogen from day one to twenty-five of the calendar month, and a progestogen for ten days, from day sixteen to twenty-five of the calendar month, which corresponds with a woman's cycle. She then goes off of her hormones the rest of the month. This protocol is now considered outdated. Many women experience a "kickback" from going off estrogen for five or six days a month. Because of this, some physicians suggest they only go off of it for two or three days a month, or **stay on the estrogen all the time.** Taking estrogen all the time is probably best to maintain emotional stability. As long as the woman also takes adequate progesterone, taking estrogen continually is not a problem.

Some women take both estrogen and progesterone daily for five days each week and go off of their hormones at the weekend. This suggestion was made for women with breast problems to avoid over-stimulation with estrogen, but simply lowering the daily dose without stopping estrogen also overcomes these problems. So this method, too, is probably outdated.

As mentioned before, other women have been put on a daily dose of both estrogen and a progestogen or progesterone. This method works well for women who have completed menopause because, generally, it stops the annoyance of having periods after menopause (a major reason many women dislike estrogen therapy). After the first three or four months, menstrual-type bleeding often stops.

Women Who Still Have Periods

There is some difference of opinion here. Some doctors will not put women who still have periods on hormones at all, because they say that if they have periods, they have enough estrogen. Others believe that women can produce enough estrogen to have periods, but still be functionally low in estrogen.

Some doctors will put women with estrogen-deficiency symptoms on estrogen only while their periods continue to be normal and regular. They will watch them carefully, and maybe even do occasional endometrial sampling, but they say that if they continue to ovulate, they probably are producing adequate progesterone themselves and don't need it. These doctors believe that estrogen has more impact on elevating mood and that progesterone (even sometimes the natural type) tends to lower the mood. When these women begin having bleeding irregularities and irregular periods, these physicians will add progesterone to the protocol.

Other doctors choose to treat women who still have periods with daily estrogen and cyclical progesterone. Taking estrogen and progesterone continually doesn't work as well for them because this tends to cause breakthrough bleeding.

Hormone-Replacement Therapy—A Typical Protocol

Estrogen: If a woman is premenopausal, doctors might prescribe from 1/2 mg. to 2 mg. per day of Estrace to be **taken daily.** On the lowest dose, she would cut the 1 mg. Estrace tablet in half and take 1/2 mg. once a day. On a subsequent month, she might try taking 1/2 mg. in the morning, and 1/2 mg. at night (or 1 mg. once a day). The upper average dose would be 1 mg. twice a day. It is probably preferable to divide the dose to avoid the peak-and-valley effect. Some women who exercise hard find they metabolize the estrogen they take in the morning, and have none left by night. If a woman has nausea on even the lowest dose of estrogen, she might take it once at night to see if she can sleep off the symptoms.

If the Estrace is not effective, she might try Ogen or Premarin in equivalent doses. Another alternative would be to use the estrogen patch—first trying the low dose (.05 mg), then the higher dose (.1

mg.). Some women may feel better on the low-dose patch along with a low dose of oral estrogen—that is, taking it by two routes.

Progesterone: If a woman does not have a history of PMS, she will be taking progesterone only to make the necessary changes in the uterine lining, not for symptoms. (If a woman has PMS and her symptoms do not go away on estrogen, she should look at the protocol on taking progesterone in the PMS chapter of this book.)

While a woman is still menstruating, and if her doctor decides she should take progesterone along with the estrogen, she will probably want to take the progesterone from ovulation till menstruation. That is, she would take the estrogen every day, adding progesterone during the second half of the cycle. To determine when she should start the progesterone, she would first work out how long her cycles are (say twenty-eight days), and subtract thirteen (the number of days she needs to take progesterone). In a twenty-eight-day cycle, that would be day fifteen. She would take 150 mg. of natural progesterone twice a day (i.e., 100 mg. in the morning and 200 mg. at night), or 5-10 mg. of Provera once a day for thirteen days, and then stop to have a period.

If a woman is postmenopausal—this can be difficult to determine if she is already on hormone-replacement therapy, but she could have an FSH test—she could take the progesterone every day. She would halve the dose of natural progesterone (100 to 150 mg. per day), and take it every night. Or she could take 2.5 mg. of Provera each day.

Women with side effects from using Provera or Norlutate, or those who wish to use a progesterone that better matches the body's chemistry, may prefer to use natural progesterone. Dr. Don Gambrell suggests using either 25 mg. suppositories twice a day for ten to thirteen days a cycle (this seem too low a dose) or oral capsules of micronized progesterone in capsules—100 mg. in the morning and 200 mg. at night.[5] The major side effect of natural progesterone is sedation, and usually this can be controlled by lowering the dose or taking it with food.

Brittle menopause

Some women have what I call "brittle" PMS or menopause, and they are similar to brittle diabetics whose blood sugars levels are extremely hard to control. These women have severe hormonal deficiencies which are extremely difficult to control, caused by poorly understood factors—possibly fluctuating blood sugar levels, altered rate of metabolism, or allergic reaction.

I know this is true because of my own problems. After ten years of contact with numerous women with severe problems, I consider myself very fortunate to have found a hormonal protocol that works very well for me, though I find fine-tuning my hormones is a process which requires continual adjustment.

I have estrogen pellets implanted—I get them from Australia, every three months. The implant is supposed to last from six months to a year, but, for me, it only lasts two and a half months. If I go to aerobics three times a week, it only lasts six weeks. After I have had the pellets implanted for about a month, I begin supplementing it with oral estrogen (Estrace), which makes the implant last longer. But after about two and a half months, three at the most, I suddenly feel the implant wear off. The symptoms slowly return, and gradually worsen, even while taking a full dose of estrogen orally. I get headaches, joint pains, midbone pains, sciatica, become irritable, terribly exhausted, and slide towards depression.

I never return to the physical state I was in prior to going on hormones, because I know what to do. I call my physician who gives me another implant and, within a couple of hours, my symptoms disappear and I feel normal again.

I always marvel at the profound effect estrogen has on me—not only physically but emotionally. I am humbled and grateful that I am able to have this help, because life without it is a real struggle for me. If I am careless about taking estrogen, I go through a death-and-resurrection experience; and this keeps me sympathetic towards the women I work with. I genuinely know how they feel.

Estrogen is responsible for a sense of joy and well-being in women. Earlier in the book, I mentioned that studies show that women universally feel better just before they ovulate, whether they have hormonal problems or not. That is the time of the month when estrogen is high. I know from repeated experience over the years, the amazing effect estrogen has on my mind. Estrogen increases the blood flow to the brain and raises endorphin levels in the brain, and there is no doubt that estrogen alters the brain chemistry in some marvelous way for me. Still, fine-tuning my hormones is a process which requires continual adjustment.

I have included this section because I know there are other women like me who have real difficulties balancing their hormones. I should mention that some other women have the opposite effect and become irritable on estrogen—which shows the necessity of looking at the individual response during treatment. Treatment with natural progesterone is similar. Some women respond dramatically to progesterone as I do to estrogen. But progesterone doesn't help me, even though I have adjusted the dose and taken all forms of it, including injections and suppositories made in England. I take it for the physical benefits, because I still have my uterus, but it doesn't help my depression.

Taking Estrogen—A Summary

- Find a **type of estrogen** that controls your symptoms and doesn't create new ones. **You may need to experiment** with different brands.
- Find a **method of taking estrogen**—oral, injectable, cream, patch, gel, or implant—that suits you and does the job adequately. You may even need to take it by two routes, if your physician agrees.
- Take **the lowest dose** that will cover your symptoms and still protect your bones and heart.
- **Be consistent** in taking your medication. Don't stop and start it sporadically.
- **If you are taking estrogen for twenty-five days each cycle and experience a return of symptoms whenever you stop it at the end of each month, try taking it every day without a break.** Women commonly experience a "kickback" during the time they are off estrogen until a few days after taking it again.
- Take **adequate progesterone** or a progestogen, if you still have your uterus (but see next section, "The Necessity of Taking Progesterone"). Even if you have had a hysterectomy, you may still wish to take the progesterone to protect your breasts against estrogen stimulation.
- If you find you are depressed or have other adverse symptoms from taking progestogens, ask your physician if you can **try natu-**

ral progesterone instead of, or with the progestogen.

- See your physician if you have abnormal bleeding, and return for an annual checkup.

The Necessity of Taking Progesterone

Women on estrogen therapy must also go on progesterone therapy to avoid hyperplasia or endometrial cancer. An exception to this is when women are still ovulating and having normal bleeding—some doctors will just given them estrogen until the bleeding becomes erratic. They watch them carefully for hyperplasia.

Progesterone therapy is particularly important for postmenopausal women who still have their uterus. But it's a good idea for women who have had a hysterectomy to take progesterone or a progestogen as a protection against estrogen's breast-stimulating properties, even though evidence, to date, does not link estrogen as a direct cause of breast cancer.

How Much Progestogen Is Needed?

Women who have never had PMS may do perfectly well taking a progestogen along with estrogen. General recommendations in the United States are to give women Provera or Norlutate for thirteen days at the end of each cycle. Dr. Lila Nachtigall suggests 5 mg. of Provera (a progestogen) for ten days each month, or 10 mg. for seven days. Some women who bleed heavily or have hyperplasia need to take 5 to 10 mg. for thirteen days.

If women wish to take estrogen and a progestogen each day to avoid menstrual bleeding, the usual dose of the progestogen is 2.5 mg. to 5 mg. daily. After three or four months on **daily** estrogen and progestogen, menstrual bleeding usually stops if a woman is well past menopause.

Some Women Can't Tolerate Progestogens

Some women have problems taking the progestogen part of their therapy.[6] Provera and other progestins may cause mood alterations, particularly in women who have a genetic tendency towards PMS. The combination of Premarin and Provera, though the latter is not FDA-approved, is the most common regimen of hormone replacement therapy, and it is considered "tried-and-true."

If it works for you, and you don't have side effects on it, you should probably stick with it. If you have completed menopause, you may take your Premarin and Provera on a daily basis. When the dose of Provera is halved and taken daily (usually 2.5 mg.), the irritability is not such a problem. And after a few months, bleeding will cease, except for occasional breakthrough bleeding. (It doesn't always work, however!)

But, if you just can't tolerate Provera, natural progesterone may suit you better. And, personally, I think natural progesterone should be the first choice, not the last. If you can't take natural progesterone either, you may do better adding a little testosterone, which will act as a progestin, but recognize that this is not well studied.

Doses for Natural Progesterone

Doctors resist giving progesterone as a part of hormonal-replacement therapy, because they feel uncomfortable with the lack of studies done on natural progesterone. But some studies have been done. Some physicians give 100 mg. of natural progesterone twice daily, for thirteen days (100 mg. oral capsules of micronized progesterone in oil). Others say this is not enough, and give 100 mg. in the morning and 200 mg. at night. The dose in suppositories suggested by Dr. Don Gambrell is 25 mg., used twice a day (this seems rather low).

Recent studies have shown that daily capsules containing both micronized estradiol and natural progesterone prevented hyperplasia in postmenopausal women, and, after six months, no more periods occurred.[7] The dosage is .5 mg. of estradiol and 100 mg. of oral micronized progesterone, taken two or three times a day.

When a Progestogen May Be Better Than Natural Progesterone

Progestogens can be mass produced and marketed much cheaper than natural progesterone. Their effectiveness in protecting the lining of the uterus has been widely studied, and doses are well established. Progestogens are much more potent and effective in preventing endometrial cancer. Drug companies have a strong financial interest to protect in promoting progestogens, and they are much more widely available.

While some physicians believe an annual endometrial biopsy should be done as a matter of course for all women on estrogen therapy, even if they are taking Provera; other physicians have had so much experience with Provera and have so much confidence in it that they feel an annual endometrial biopsy is unnecessary.

Doctors generally do not have this confidence in natural progesterone because doses that will make the necessary changes in the uterus have not been established. But, as we have mentioned, Provera is not FDA-approved either; and, while much less research has been compiled on natural progesterone's effectiveness in changing the endometrium, some has been done.

Because natural progesterone has a poor absorption rate and is rapidly metabolized, it is necessary to take higher, more frequent doses than with a progestogen to effect similar changes. Natural progesterone is also much more expensive than progestogens like Provera, costing from about 45 cents to a dollar per dose at present.

When Natural Progesterone May Be Better Than a Progestogen

Nevertheless, despite Provera's advantages, if a woman has had a long-term battle with PMS, she will probably find that the progestogen component of her estrogen-replacement therapy gives her side effects.

Many susceptible women, who react adversely to progestogens, may wish to try natural progesterone because they tend to be less depressed and irritable on natural progesterone. For those women who find that progestogens, like Provera, aggravated their emotional symptomse, using progesterone, instead, may be an absolute necessity.

Another advantage of taking natural progesterone is that it does not reverse estrogen's beneficial effect in reducing high-density lipoproteins. Progestogens do, to some extent, thereby reversing the beneficial effect of estrogen on the heart. Dr. Winnifred Cutler in her book *Hysterectomy: Before and After* mentions a study from Sweden showing that the adverse changes in lipids produced by 250 mg. of levonorgestrel or 10 mg. of Provera per day, did not occur when 100 mg. of natural progesterone was taken twice a day.[8]

Progesterone often helps women with fibrocystic breasts, and it is also good for the bones.[9] A study on marathon runners and osteoporosis found that the "normal" women (average age thirty-five) who acted as controls were losing bone too. Each month, the researchers checked the hormone levels and the bone density of both groups—the controls and the marathoners. They found that when the "normal" women didn't ovulate (that is, did not produce progesterone), they lost up to 4 percent of their bone mass.

Since it is normal not to ovulate every month from your thirties on, because the egg supply lessens as the years progress, it means that all women begin the process of osteoporosis earlier than has been expected. Another interesting conclusion of the study highlights the importance of progesterone for osteoporosis, not just estrogen.

While estrogen helps reduce calcium loss, studies are showing that natural progesterone actually increases bone mass. Partly because of this positive effect on the bones, I believe natural progesterone, as an alternative to Provera and Norlutate at menopause, will soon be accepted as a superior treatment.

Having a Period Is Not the Issue

Don't think that if you are having regular periods and the lining of the uterus is being sloughed off, that you can't have problems with the cells in your uterine wall. Endometrial cancer can occur where there is no nontypical bleeding.

Some women are severely emotionally affected by having a period, no matter which progesterone is used. These women, understandably, are often tempted to lower the dose of progesterone they take and shorten the number of days they are on it.

Women who are ultrasensitive to having periods, yet who need to induce them to ensure protection for the uterus, might talk to their doctors about inducing a period every second or third month, and taking the progesterone thoroughly then, or taking testosterone. Your doctor may wish to give an annual endometrial biopsy or an ultrasound to determine the thickness of the lining. The lining should ideally be less than 5 mm. and no more than 8-10 mm. thick, and the X-Ray technician has to be well-trained to know what to look for.

According to Dr. Winnifred Cutler, women who take testosterone with estrogen do not need to take progesterone. This may be an answer for women who have trouble on all types of progesterone and progestins. They might take Estratest HS, a combination of estrogen and testosterone, or have a testosterone shot once a month. This is not well-studied.

Do You Need Testosterone?
When a woman's ovaries are removed, she loses the major source of her female hormones and the male hormone, testosterone. Sometimes the addition of a little testosterone to an estrogen shot, or use of both testosterone and estrogen pellets together, makes the estrogen work better and longer. It also helps those women with sore muscles and a flagging libido.

The physician has to decide whether adding testosterone will be beneficial. If a woman has a stressful job—for instance, as a trial attorney or a business owner—she will not be as successful in situations that cause confrontational stress after having her ovaries removed. On the other hand, while testosterone treatment itself won't elevate her risk of heart disease, the increased aggression and stress may shorten a woman's life. Treatment with testosterone makes some women aggressive, sexually excited, and may give them violent dreams.

Footnotes
1. Speroff, L., "Hormone Replacement Therapy and the Risk of Breast Cancer."
2. "Update on Estrogen-Progestin Replacement Therapy," by Dr. Leon Speroff quoting Kaufman, D.W., Miller, D.R., Rosenberg, L., Helmrich, S.P., Stolley, P., Schootenfeld, D., Shapiro, S., "Noncontraceptive Estrogen Use and the Risk of Breast Cancer," *JAMA*, 252:63, 1984.
3. Vliet, E.L., M.D., "New Perspectives on the Relationship of Hormone Changes to Depression and Anxiety in the Menopause," presentation at the North American Menopause Society meeting, September 1992. Dr. Vliet is a clinical assistant professor at Eastern Virginia Medical School, Norfolk, VA. "Estrogen and Memory in Postmenopausal Women," Sherwin, Barbara, B., Ph.D., McGill University, Montreal, Canada. "Estrogens Regulate Brain Structure and Chemistry," Bruce S. McEwen, Ph.D., Laboratory of Neuroendocrinology, New York.
4. Dr. Katherine O'Hanalan, professor of medicine and associate

director of the Gynecologic Cancer Service at Stanford University in Palo Alto, California, says she prescribes Estrace for most of her patients because "it is pure estradiol." *M-News,* Vol. 2, Issue 2. Dr. Antonio Scommegna, a reproductive endocrinologist at the Menopause Clinic at the University of Illinois Hospital, prefers Estrace because it's more physiologic and it's estradiol. When women become sick on Estrace, he puts women on Premarin, then Ogen. *M-News,* Vol. 2, Issue 5, September/October, 1992. Telephone 1-800-241-MENO for subscription information.

5. Gambrell, Don, "Progestogens and Postmenopausal Women," *The Female Patient,* Vol. 17, April 1992, p. 52.

6. Dr. Winnifred Cutler mentions Drs. Lorraine Dennerstein and Graham Burrows, Australian researchers, who have found that natural progesterone has a hypnotic effect, more pleasant than the tension and irritability incurred by some women on progestins. *Hysterectomy: Before and After,* p. 166. "Dennerstein, L., Burrows, G., (1986), "Psychological Effects of Progestogens in the Post-Meno-pausal Years," *Maturitas,* 8: 101-106.

7. Gambrell, D., (see footnote 2). See also "Menopausal Hormone Replacement Therapy With Continuous Daily Oral Micronized Estradiol and Progesterone," Hargrove, J.T., Maxson, W.S., Colston Wentz, A., and Burnett, L., *Obstetrics & Gynecology,* April, 1989, p. 606, ff. See also Whitehead, M.I., Townsend, P.T., Pryse-Davies, J., Ryder, T.A., King R.J.B. (1981), "Absorption and Metabolism of Oral Progesterone," *Br. Med. J.,* 289:825-827.

8. According to Dr. Winnifred Cutler, *(Hysterectomy: Before and After,* pp. 168-69), Dr. Malcolm Whitehead and his colleagues con-cluded that natural progesterone does not harmfully alter blood lipids and might be useful with estrogen for menopause. See ar-ticle listed under footnote 4. See also Fahraeus, L., Larsson-Cohn, U., Wallentin, L. (1983), "L-norgestrol and progesterone have different influences on plasma lipoproteins," *Eur. J. Clin. Invest.,* 13:447. See also, Ottoson, U.B., Johansson, B.G., von Schoultz, B. (1985), "Subfractions of high density lipoprotein cholesterol during estrogen replacement therapy: comparison between progesto-gens and natural progesterone." *Am. J. Obstet. Gynecol.* 1151:746.

9. Dalton, K, *Progesterone and Bone Mineral Density.*

Further Recommended Reading

* Sandra Cabot's books are available from Women's Health Advisory Service, P. O. Box 217, Paddingon, NSW 2021, Australia Phone 011612331-5014.

** Dr. Winnifred Cutler's books are available from her at: The Athena Institute, 30 Coopertown Road, Haverford, PS, 19041. Buying them direct from her helps finance her research.

† Dr. Dalton's books and other PMS books can be obtained from PMS Access in Madison, Wisconsin (1-800-222-4PMS).

†† Susan Lark's books are available from Celestial Arts, P. O. Box 7327, Berkeley, CA 94707, 1984. You can write or call for the book at Self Help Options for Women, 675 Fairview Drive, Suite 207B, Carson City, NV 89701 (1-800-835-2246, ext. 78).

• Rosemary Gladstar's booklets are available from Sage, P. O. Box 42, E. Barre, VT 05649.

Premenstrual Syndrome

† *Once a Month*, Katherina Dalton, M.D., Hunter House, 1990 ed.

† *Premenstrual Syndrome and Progesterone Therapy*, Katherina Dalton, M.D., Year-Book Publications, 1984.

†† *PMS Self-Help Book*, Susan Lark, M.D.

PMS Premenstrual Syndrome and You, Nils Lauersen, M.D., and Eileen Stukane, Simon & Schuster, 1983.

PMS Premenstrual Syndrome, Ronald Norris, M.D., with Colleen Sullivan, Rawson Associates, Berkeley Edition, 1984.

Self-Help for Premenstrual Syndrome, Michelle Harrison, M.D., Random House, N.Y., 1982.

Curing PMT the Drug-Free Way, Moira Carpenter, Arrow Books, 1986. The British address is Arrow Books Limited, 62-65 Chandos Place, London WC2N 4NW, England. It offers herbal and homeopathic remedies and information about diet and acupressure, etc.

Menopause and Hysterectomy

A Friend Indeed is a newsletter for women going through menopause, published by Janine O'Leary Cobb. It is available from P.O. Box 1710, Champlain, New York 12919-1710. Price $30.00; ten issues a year.

** *Hysterectomy, Before and After*, Winnifred B. Cutler, Ph.D., Harper & Row, N.Y., 1988.

** *Menopause: A Guide for Women and the Men Who Love Them*, Winnifred B. Cutler, Ph.D., and Celso-Ramón Garcia, (Revised Edition), W. W. Norton & Co., Inc., NY and London, 1992.

Estrogen, Lila Nachtigall, M.D. and Joan Rattner Heilman, The Body Press, 1986.

Positive Approaches to Menopause—The Pause, Lonnie Barbach, Ph.D., Dutton, published by the Penguin group, 1993.

The Silent Passage—Menopause, Gail Sheehy, Random House, 1991,92.

* *Menopause—You Can Give It a Miss*, Dr. Sandra Cabot.

†† *Menopause Self-Help Book*, Susan Lark, M.D.

Menopause Naturally, Dr. Sadja Greenwood, Volcano Press, 1989.

No More Hot Flashes and Other Good News, Penny Wise Budoff, M.D., Warner Books, 1983, 84.

• *Herbs for Menopause*, Rosemary Gladstar Slick

Postpartum Depression

Postpartum Psychiatric Illness: A Picture Puzzle, ed. James Alexander Hamilton, M.D., University of Pennsylvania Press, Philadelphia, 1992.

† *Depression After Childbirth*, Katherina Dalton, M.D., Oxford University Press, 1988.

† *Guide to Progesterone for Postnatal Depression*. It is available from PMS Help, P.O. Box 100, St. Albans, Herts., AL1 4UQ, England.

A great deal of helpful information about postpartum depression is available from:

Depression After Delivery, P.O. Box 1282, Morrisville, Pennsylvania 19067, U.S.A.

Hypothyroidism

Hypothyroidism: The Unsuspected Disease, by Dr. Broda Barnes and Lawrence Galton, Harper & Row, 1976.

General Reading

Natural Progesterone: The multiple roles of a remarkable hormone, John Lee, M.D., available from BLL Publishing, P.O. Box 2068, Sebastopol, CA 95473, ($9.95, plus $2.00 postage).

The Pill on Trial, Paul Vaughan, Penguin Books, U.K., 1970.

* *Women's Health*, Dr. Sandra Cabot, Pan Books, 1987.

* *Don't Let Your Hormones Ruin Your Life*, Dr. Sandra Cabot.

• *Herbs for Women's Health*, Rosemary Gladstar Slick.

** *Love Cycles: The Science of Intimacy*, Dr. Winnifred Cutler, Villard Books, 1992. This is a book on the connection between hormones, sexuality, fertility, and influences in nature.